Easy Reference Table o

MW00675750

CONTENTS AT A GLANCE
Winter 2007/Spring 2008

This guide is about making gluten-free grocery shopping safe, easy, and full of choices. It's packed with the information you need to find gluten-free items in thousands of regular grocery stores across the country. I hope you find this guide as useful a tool as I have.

I've been gluten-free since 2001. For me, trying to shop for gluten-free groceries was initially overwhelming. A large grocery store can carry over 10,000 products; who has time to read all those labels? Where do you even start?

Utterly frustrated, I spent the first few weeks of my new gluten-free diet subsisting on canned tuna fish and potato chips, while I furiously researched additional foods and brands to add to my shopping list.

It took several months for me to upgrade that initial list from pitiful to passable, but even then, it was nothing close to what I was accustomed to buying before going gluten-free.

The quest to fill my pantry took me to three different stores weekly, I was still missing a ton of the things I wanted, and it felt like I spent nearly all my free time either trying to figure out what I could eat, or sourcing it.

While that was over five years ago, my early gluten-free experience has stuck with me ever since – and it has become the inspiration for compiling this guide.

In the five plus years since I first went gluten-free, a lot has changed. There are over three times as many specialty gluten-free products on the market now – and those products have far better distribution than I ever would have imagined. Even mainstream manufacturers have started to understand gluten-free and have drastically improved their labeling practices (largely thanks to new labeling laws).

But, as much as things have improved, gluten-free grocery shopping is still a challenge. Very few gluten-free items are clearly labeled "gluten-free." And, as individual consumers searching for gluten-free products, we're often left guessing in grocery store aisles, or calling dozens of manufacturers on a regular basis. We need a better way to identify products that are likely gluten-free, so that we can focus our efforts on reading labels and contacting the manufacturers of the products most likely to be gluten-free.

This guide is designed to address these needs. We've pulled together information about thousands of gluten-free products from hundreds of

manufacturers, and compiled it all into one convenient, easy-to-use grocery guide. Our goal is for you to use this guide as a starting point to find the right products, so that you can hone in on items that are likely to suit your needs, quickly and easily, with less frustration and time wasted.

With the increasingly widespread availability of gluten-free foods and improved labeling practices of manufacturers, it's our belief that gluten-free consumers can now meet a lot of their food needs in traditional grocery stores. This is the tool to help you do exactly that.

Please enjoy this first edition of The Essential Gluten-Free Grocery Guide and, as always, I would love to hear your questions and comments.

Here's to Happy Shopping!

Ross Cohen
President
Triumph Dining
ross@triumphdining.com

iStockphoto.com/Sean Locke

GENERAL TIPS FOR GROCERY SHOPPING

CHAPTER 1

Everyone knows how to grocery shop – we've all been doing it most of our adult lives. The interesting thing is that each person approaches shopping slightly differently. Some people spend hours methodically comparing prices in search of the best deal, others race through the store as quickly as possible so they can move on to other things. There's no right or wrong way to shop, but what follows are a few basic tips and ideas to help make your gluten-free shopping trips a little more successful – no matter what your personal shopping style is.

Choosing a Grocery Store

Some grocery stores are simply better for the gluten-free shopper than others. Generally, I prefer to do my shopping in stores that cater to gluten-free clientele in some way – it makes my shopping easier, and I prefer to support the businesses that focus on my needs.

A store's focus on gluten-free customers can manifest itself in several ways:

1. Stocking separate gluten-free aisles, like Ukrop's in Virginia;

2. Stocking an extensive selection of gluten-free products – many smaller, specialty stores like Martindale's in Springfield, PA, The Natural Way in Naperville, IL, and The Gluten Free Trading Company in Milwaukee, IL pride themselves on carrying hundreds or thousands of specialty, gluten-free items;

3. Labeling gluten-free foods – either in the grocery aisle, or on packaging itself; Wegman's in New York marks their gluten-free, private label foods with a little "G";

4. Publishing a list of gluten-free items that can be found in their stores, like the Whole Foods Market and Trader Joe's chains.

Stores that fit into these categories will tend to have more options for gluten-free customers, resulting in a better shopping experience. Try to frequent these types of stores when you can.

But, we understand that not everyone lives near a Trader Joe's, or can afford to buy all their groceries from premium and specialty stores. That's why this guide is designed to help you find gluten-free options in any grocery store – whether it specifically caters to gluten-free customers or not.

5

Common Pitfalls to Avoid

One ongoing concern for people on the gluten-free diet is cross-contamination. It can happen anywhere, there's no way to know whether it's happened to a product, and it's rarely ever flagged for us. Also, the Food Allergen Labeling and Consumer Protection Act does not set specific standards for using cross-contamination advisory statements or require manufacturers to identify the possibility of inadvertent cross-contamination. (See the next chapter for a more in-depth discussion of the FALCPA.)

And, concerns about cross-contamination extend beyond grocery store shelves, to bulk bins, deli/meat counters, and the prepared foods sections.

Bulk Bins

Bulk bins are largely left unattended by grocery store personnel. There's often no way to tell that other customers haven't inadvertently shared serving scoops across products, potentially contaminating anything that otherwise would have been gluten-free. And, there's no indication whether products rotate through the bins or, if they do, whether the bins are thoroughly cleaned before transitions. In other words, the bin that holds a seemingly gluten-free product today could have been full of wheat flour last week. For these reasons, we recommend avoiding bulk bins and buying packaged items, instead.

The Deli Counter

Deli counters and prepared food sections present a different challenge. Here, store personnel directly handle food products meant for your consumption. The easiest way to navigate these challenges is to think of the deli counter and prepared food section like "mini restaurants." (For more information about issues to consider in gluten-free restaurant dining, please refer to *The Essential Gluten-Free Restaurant Guide*, also available from Triumph Dining.)

Before you make a purchase, you need to understand both the ingredients in the food and the preparation methods used to create it. There are many issues to consider in making a decision about these foods. Some examples include: Do gluten-containing meats go in the deli slicer? What, if any, precautions are taken in the prep area to avoid cross-contamination? Are there ingredient labels on the prepared foods? How accurate are those labels?

Often times, however, it's challenging to interface with the employees who prepared these foods. At some grocery stores we've seen, the prepared foods are made offsite or by an early morning crew that's long since cleared out by the time the typical person shops, making it hard to get questions answered about dish contents and preparation methods. For these reasons, we recommend frequenting deli counters and prepared food sections only when you've done sufficient due diligence to confirm the products you're purchasing truly are gluten-free.

Selecting Your Groceries

Despite a restricted diet, there are still many wonderful foods for gluten-free shoppers to choose from. When given a choice, I prefer to support the

©iStockphoto.com/Simon Smith

companies that cater to the needs of gluten-free customers. Some of these companies produce specialty products for the gluten-free market. Others have dedicated manufacturing lines and/or clearly label gluten-free status on packaging. Please consider buying their products and calling or writing in to let them know you appreciate their efforts. The more we support these businesses, the more products we'll have to choose from in the future.

Consider Your Information Source

When thinking about which products to purchase and evaluating information available to you, please keep in mind that primary source information, like ingredient statements on packages and manufacturer statements, is always better and more reliable than secondary source information, like postings on message boards and compilation lists (this guide included). Think of it like a game of telephone – the more people who handle information before you receive it, or the older that information gets, the greater chance there is of it having inaccuracies or other problems.

Always Read Labels

Product formulations can change without notice, companies can make mistakes on their gluten-free list, and people compiling information can make mistakes, as well. That's why you need to read labels every time you make a purchase, and regularly contact the company to confirm the gluten-free status of the products you consume. Section 3 of this guide contains the contact information for over a thousand companies. Please take advantage of this resource.

Never Make Assumptions

When contacting companies, please keep in mind that the FDA has yet to issue a rule defining the term "gluten-free." Meanwhile, there's a lot of conflicting information on the gluten-free diet, even among dieticians, support groups and the many other experts in the field. Some believe that blue cheese is gluten-free, others do not. Some say distilled vinegar is safe, others choose to steer clear. And, the emerging question about the suitability of oats in the gluten-free diet adds even more confusion. So, don't expect a company to guess what your definition of gluten-free is. Always ask questions to make sure you understand what their particular definition of gluten-free is.

Where to Find More Information

This guide pre-supposes that you are already familiar with the gluten-free diet. But for those just starting out, there are some excellent resources available to help you understand the gluten-free diet and to make informed choices. For example, there are a host of helpful resources available from local and national support groups, widely available books, and online materials. Doctors and nutritionists are also an excellent source of information. In short, please be proactive about educating yourself. When it comes to the gluten-free diet, an educated shopper is really a healthy shopper!

CHAPTER 2

Effective January 1, 2006, the Food Allergen Labeling and Consumer Protection Act of 2004 (FALCPA), sets requirements for the labeling of eight major allergens on packaged foods. This is a quick overview of the elements of the FALCPA that are likely to be relevant to consumers on a gluten-free diet.[1]

Allergens Covered

The FALCPA covers eight major allergens that are credited with causing 90% of all food allergies. Those allergens include: milk, eggs, fish, shellfish, tree nuts, peanuts, soybeans, and, most importantly, wheat. The FDA notes that, for the purposes of the FALCPA, wheat includes common wheat, durum wheat, club wheat, spelt, semolina, einkorn, emmer, kamut, and triticale.

Allergens Not Covered

It's important to note that the FALCPA does **not** cover barley or rye. Nor does it cover oats, which is likely to be cross-contaminated with wheat.

Labeling: What's Required

The FALCPA requires food manufacturers to identify allergens in ingredient lists in one of two ways:

1. In the ingredient listing, the common or usual name of the major food allergen must be followed in parenthesis by the name of the food source from which the major allergen is derived. For example: "Enriched flour (wheat flour…)," or

2. Immediately following the ingredient listing, a "Contains" statement must indicate the name of the food source from which the major food allergen is derived. For example: "Contains: milk, wheat, and eggs."

Allergens present in flavorings, coloring, and additives must also be identified in one of the two ways listed above.

Labeling: What's Not Required

It is important to note that the FALCPA does not apply to major food allergens that are unintentionally added to food as a result of cross-contamination. Cross-contamination can result during the growing and harvesting of crops, or from the use of shared storage, transportation, or production equipment.

---

[1]Please note this brief overview is not meant to be comprehensive, nor is it intended as medical or legal advice. If you have questions about food labeling laws or their impact on your dietary choices and decision making, please consult a legal professional, dietician or doctor, as appropriate.

The FALCPA also does not address the use of advisory labeling, including statements designed to identify the possibility of cross-contamination. The FALCPA does not require the use of such statements, nor does it specifically articulate standards of use for advisory statements.

Application

The FALCPA applies to all packaged foods sold in the United States that are regulated by the FDA, whether produced domestically or imported, that are required to have ingredient statements.

It's important to note that the FALCPA does not apply to meat products, poultry products, and egg products that fall under the authority of the USDA.

The Big Picture

What does this all mean for people following the gluten-free diet? There are three important limitations of the FALCPA to keep in mind:

1. As far as gluten is concerned, the FALCPA does not cover it. The FALCPA covers wheat, but not rye, barley, or other potentially troublesome grains.

2. The FALCPA covers only products regulated by the FDA that require ingredient lists. For any product that does not require an ingredient list (such as raw fruits and vegetables), or that falls outside the FDA's jurisdiction (such as meat, poultry, and egg products that fall under the authority of the USDA), the FALCPA does not require manufacturers to identify major allergens.

3. The FALCPA does not require manufacturers to identify the possibility of inadvertent cross-contamination, nor does it set specific standards for using advisory statements warning of potential cross-contamination.

The important thing to remember is that, despite improved labeling laws, hidden gluten in grocery items is still a very real possibility. Gluten can come from non-wheat sources, result from cross-contamination, or can occur in products not covered by the FALCPA. For those reasons, it's important to remain vigilant and carefully scrutinize the products you buy. It's not enough to just read labels; contacting manufacturers directly is often necessary.

What is Gluten-Free Anyway?

One final note on the FALCPA: The FALCPA requires the FDA to issue a rule to define and permit the use of the term "gluten-free" on food labels by August 2008. This law does not require food companies to label gluten-free products as such. Rather, the law requires the FDA to establish a uniform standard definition of the term "gluten-free" to be used voluntarily by food manufacturers. The FDA published its proposed rule on the definition of "gluten-free" in January 2007. For more information, please visit the FDA at www.fda.gov.

CHAPTER 3

Our goal is for this guide to make your shopping trips easier, safer, and full of choices. There are a few things you need to know about this guide's content and organization to help us fulfill on that goal.

Products Listed

Our guide covers over 20,000 products from hundreds of different brands. The products listed are groceries likely to be found in typical American grocery stores like Safeway, Kroger, Albertson's, etc. They include brand names, as well as private label brands from some of the larger grocery chains. In cases where the grocery chain's name is different from their private label brand, we've also put the chain's name in parentheses next to the private label brand name.

Some brands publish a list enumerating each gluten-free item, while others chose to simply say all foods in a particular category are gluten-free. In the latter case, we list the brand name in the appropriate category and sub-category, followed by a description of the products covered and the word "All," where applicable. For example, if a company's cheeses are all gluten-free, it will be listed under "Brand X," followed by "Cheeses, All." Alternatively, sometimes the brand communicated that all of their products were gluten-free, in which case, they will be noted in the guide as "Brand X, All."

Products Not Listed

You will not find "boutique" gluten-free brands in this guide, unless those brands are likely to be found in typical grocery stores. This list is also far from comprehensive; there are smaller brands and new items popping up all the time. Just because a product isn't listed in these pages, doesn't mean it's not gluten-free. If there's something you're interested in that's not listed in this guide, call the company directly or let us know, and we'll look into adding it for the next edition.

There are some obvious, large brands missing from the product listings. In many cases, these brands are not included in the product listing section because they do not provide lists of their products that are gluten-free. Instead, they have "full disclosure" policies where the presence of wheat, rye, barley, or oats in any product would be clearly stated in the ingredients list. If you don't see your favorite product among the products listed in Section 2, please flip to the Company Contact Information in Section 3 to see if the brand in question has a "full disclosure" policy for their labels.

We haven't listed some items that are generally accepted and widely known to be gluten-free. For example, plain dairy milk is not listed. However, we have listed flavored milk, sour cream and other items that contain ingredients (e.g., thickeners or other additives) that may be a concern to some shoppers. Of course, what is "generally accepted" and "widely known" to be gluten-free is subjective. So while one person may find an entire genre of items we cover in the guide to be obviously gluten-free, some will not. We try to be as inclusive as possible for the sake of the latter audience.

Finally, for the sake of simplicity, this guide only lists items on a company's gluten-free list. We have excluded items that were reported to contain gluten.

General Overview of Organization

The product list is organized into a three tier system: first by category, then by subcategory, then by product name.

Organization by Category

The products listed in this guide are arranged like a typical grocery store. The list is organized first by master categories that align with aisles in a typical grocery store, like those for Dairy and Eggs, Snacks, and Frozen Foods. The objective is that organizing the guide by grocery aisle will make your trip through the store quicker – you can follow along in the guide as your shop through the store.

There are a few exceptions to the link between master category and grocery aisle: in some cases our consumer research found it more helpful to organize items by general category as opposed to aisle. For example, while refrigerated orange juice is typically found in the Dairy and Eggs aisle, you'll find it listed here in the Beverages category.

Organization by Sub-Category

Each master category is further sub-divided by sub-categories that align with the particular types of food products found in the master category aisle. For example, subcategories within the master category Snacks include: Chips, Cookies, Crackers, etc. Sub-categories are organized alphabetically within the master category. The Easy Reference Table of Contents on the inside front cover is a quick visual reference for the different categories and sub-categories.

Organization by Brand & Product

Within these subcategories, you'll find individual products listed alphabetically by brand name (in bold), then product name (not in bold). While we've done our best to organize the products into the "correct" category and sub-category, we hope you'll understand it was a subjective process and there will be some variances.

Differing Store Layouts

With our master and sub-category choices, we've attempted to stay as true as possible to the general layout of a grocery store, with the understanding that all grocery stores are not identical. Different chain stores have very different

layouts (for example, just compare a Trader Joe's to a Safeway), and even the same chain will demonstrate some regional and store-specific differences in layout, depending on store location and facility size/resources. For these reasons, it may take you a little time to build familiarity with this guide's layout, depending on where you choose to shop and how much that store's layout deviates from the template we're following.

Icons and Disclaimers

Where applicable, in the Product List, Section 2, we've noted with icons common disclaimer types that companies provided with their gluten-free lists. Definitions of the icons' meanings can be found at the beginning of that section.

If a disclaimer applies to a brand as a whole, we placed it next to the brand name. If it only applies to a particular product, the disclaimer icon will only appear next to the specific product. For example, if Brand X's entire line of ice cream comes with a cross-contamination warning, the disclaimer icon will appear next to the Brand X name. If the warning only applies to its Chocolate Chip flavor, we place the disclaimer icon next to the Chocolate Chip flavor listing only.

We have also elaborated on each disclaimer in the notes contained in Section 3, the Company Contact Information Section. Since we've only noted the common disclaimers companies make in Section 2, we always recommend flipping to the company's notes in Section 3 for more complete information.

Another thing to keep in mind is that any information, including disclaimers like cross-contamination warnings, are provided by companies at their discretion. Companies are not required by law to warn shoppers of cross-contamination, so just because a company does not have a cross-contamination warning does not mean it's not an issue! We sincerely hope that the FDA will resolve this issue in the near future.

GF

"GF" is shorthand for "gluten-free," as commonly used in Sections 2 and 3.

More on Contact Information in Section 3

While the contact information for the brands/companies whose gluten-free lists are published in this guide is listed in Section 3, we've also provided contact information for companies that do not have gluten-free lists and some companies that did not reply to our inquiries. After all, just because a company did not reply to us, does not mean that you will never have a need to contact them!

Where applicable, we've noted the date we received correspondence from the company, or the date that we contacted the company. And, whenever possible, we list the company's web address, phone number and any pertinent notes they may have written in the correspondence. Please use this information to contact companies directly.

©iStockphoto.com/van Mateev

While we hope that this guide makes gluten-free shopping easier, we do recognize that there are some limitations, which we would like to call out so that you can make informed shopping decisions.

Gluten-Free Lists

As mentioned in previous chapters, there is currently no FDA rule defining gluten-free and generally no consensus in the community as to an exact definition. (Consider the controversies surrounding blue cheese, vinegar and oats, just to name a few.) So when a company reports that its products are gluten-free, there is the possibility that their definition of gluten-free may differ from yours. We provide the contact information for over a thousand companies in Section 3 to make it easier to contact companies.

In addition, the information published in this guide for each food item has been obtained directly from that item's manufacturer, the entity that licensed the manufacturing, or an affiliate. We have made no attempt to verify the accuracy of the information provided by these sources.

Always Read Labels

It's important to keep in mind that product formulations and ingredient sourcing can and do change without notice, companies can make mistakes on their gluten-free list, and people compiling and categorizing large volumes of information (like the content for this guide) can make mistakes, as well. For these reasons, Triumph Dining cannot assume any liability for the correctness or accuracy of any information presented in this guide. You should read labels every time you make a purchase, and regularly contact companies to confirm the gluten-free status of the products you consume.

Contact the Company with Questions

Section 3 contains the contact information for over a thousand companies, including those whose products are listed in this guide. Please contact them directly with any questions or for updates. Any information provided in this guide was obtained from the company, and they will always be your best source of information on their products.

A Question of Semantics

Since there is still no FDA regulation defining the term "gluten-free" and no requirement that companies report the possibility of cross-contamination, as consumers, we're very much still on our own. A company may claim its products are "gluten-free" and free of "cross-contamination," but since there's no universally accepted definition of either term, you may still not be getting the whole story. Therefore, a product's appearance in this guide does not mean that the product is entirely free of gluten (that would likely be an impossible standard, as the most sensitive, sophisticated commercially-available tests for gluten do not measure to 0 ppm).

What an appearance here indicates is that the product's company believes the product is "gluten-free" based on that company's own standards and thresholds for the term. For the foregoing reasons, Triumph Dining cannot assume any liability for any losses or damages resulting from your use of this product listing. It's up to you to determine whether a product is appropriate based on your individual dietary needs. For more information about a particular company's testing practices, standards and thresholds, please contact that company directly.

Common Sense is Your Best Guide

A guide like this should never be a replacement for your own knowledge, common sense, and diligence. This guide is intended as a starting point only, and not a final determination that a listed product is gluten-free, suitable for the gluten-free diet, or safe for you personally to consume. It is not a substitute for reading labels and contacting companies. Rather, this guide is designed to help you hone in on the products most likely to be suitable for the gluten-free diet, so that you can focus your label-reading and company-contacting efforts on the most promising products, without wasting dozens and dozens of hours chasing dead ends. Always exercise caution when using a list like this one – if something doesn't feel right, it probably isn't.

Some Final Notes

The information published in this guide is intended for use in the United States and with products manufactured with the intent to be sold in the United States, only. Products sold or intended to be sold outside the United States may have completely different ingredients than their U.S. counterparts, and may not be gluten-free.

This guide is for limited educational purposes only and is not medical advice. If you have questions about the gluten-free diet, what ingredients are appropriate to consume, whether or not particular items are appropriate for your consumption, etc. please consult with your physician.

Use of this guide indicates your acknowledgement of and agreement to these terms.

Section 2:
Gluten-Free Product List

Symbols Defined

The following symbols are used to indicate the presence of common disclaimers and other information you need to know about a company's gluten-free list:

Good news! This could be one of several possibilities:
a) *Dedicated gluten-free* manufacturing lines or facilities are used;
b) *Gluten testing* is done on products or their ingredients;
c) *A gluten-free symbol* is present on the package.

Cross-contamination is a possibility.

Missing information is an issue, such as the following:
a) The company states only that the *ingredients* of its products are gluten-free, but makes no such statement – positive or negative – about the products themselves;
b) The gluten-free list defined gluten, but that definition was incomplete. For example, gluten may have been defined as wheat and rye, but barley was not mentioned.

To the best of their knowledge, or a similar qualifier, is attached to the gluten-free list.

Read labels. (We use this icon where the company reminded consumers to do so in their communications, but regardless, please always read labels.)

Miscellaneous. A common miscellaneous disclaimer is for a company to recommend consulting a physician before consuming their products.

Continued on Next Page >>>

Whenever a symbol appears in Section 2, please reference the company notes in Section 3 for a full explanation of why that symbol is used. Section 3 also includes each company's contact information, should you have more questions about the company's gluten-free list.

The disclaimers above were present in the gluten-free list provided by the brand, manufacturer or company representative. But, the absence of such a disclaimer is not an indication that the issue in question is not a concern. For example, a company's failure to mention cross-contamination does not guarantee that cross-contamination is not a potential issue with their products. (Remember: companies are not necessarily required by law to disclose all possibilities or instances of cross-contamination. For more information on the new food labeling law, please see Chapter 2.)

Don't forget to read Section 1, particularly Chapters 3 and 4 for more information on the information presented in this guide and how to use it. And remember to keep safe and always read labels.

Happy shopping!

DAIRY & EGGS

BUTTER

Hy-Vee ⁄ ◉
    Sweet Cream Butter (Solid), 16 oz
    Sweet Cream Butter Quarters, 16 oz
    Unsalted Sweet Cream Butter Quarters, 16 oz
    Whipped Sweet Cream Butter, 8 oz

Laura Lynn (Ingle's) ◉
    Butter

Lucerne (Safeway) ⁄ ◉
    Butter

Meyenberg
    Goat Milk Products, All

Nature's Promise (Stop & Shop) ⁄ ◉
    Organic Butter

Skyr.is
    Icelandic Butter

Stop & Shop ⁄ ◉
    Salted Butter Quarters
    Unsalted Butter Quarters

Tillamook
    Butter, All

Wegman's ⁄ ◉ ()
    Butter - Salted & Whipped (Tub), 8 oz
    Butter - Unsalted & Whipped (Tub), 8 oz
    Club Pack Sweet Cream Butter Sticks - Salted
    Solid Butter, 16 oz
    Sweet Cream Butter Sticks - Salted, 16 oz
    Sweet Cream Butter Sticks - Unsalted, 16 oz

Winn-Dixie ◉
    Butter
    Salted Sweet Cream Butter
    Taste Like Butter
    Unsalted Sweet Cream Butter
    Whipped Butter

BUTTERMILK

Hood
    Buttermilk

Winn-Dixie ◉
    Cultured, Nonfat Buttermilk

CHEESE & CHEESE SPREADS

A & E Cheese
    Pre-Sliced American Cheese, Item# 02260 - 7 oz
    Pre-Sliced Colby Jack Cheese, Item# 02420 - 7 oz
    Pre-Sliced Havarti Cheese, Item# 02340 - 7 oz
    Pre-Sliced Mild Cheddar Cheese, Item# 02300 - 7 oz
    Pre-Sliced Mozzarella Cheese, Item# 02460 - 7 oz
    Pre-Sliced Muenster Cheese, Item# 02180 - 7 oz
    Pre-Sliced Pepper Jack Cheese, Item# 02140 - 7 oz
    Pre-Sliced Provolone Cheese, Item# 02100 - 7 oz
    Pre-Sliced Swiss Cheese, Item# 02220 - 7 oz
    Shredded Colby Jack Cheese, Item# 02440
    Shredded Mexican Mix Cheese, Item# 02560
    Shredded Mild Cheddar Cheese, Item# 02320
    Shredded Mozzarella Cheese, Item# 02480
    Shredded Sharp Cheddar, Item# 02520

Alouette
    Alouette, All

Applegate Farms ◉ ⁄
    Applegate Farms, All BUT Chicken Nuggets &
      Chicken Pot Pie

BelGioioso Cheese
    American Grana
    Asiago
    Auribella
    Blue Cheese
    Burrata
    CreamyGorg
    Crèma Di Mascarpone
    Crescenza-Stracchino
    Crumbly Gorgonzola
    Fontina

DON'T SEE YOUR FAVORITE BRAND? LOOK IT UP IN SECTION 3!

Fresh Mozzarella - Water-Packed, Curd & Thermoform
Italico
Kasseri
Manteche
Mascarpone
Parmesan
Parmesan for Vegetarians
Pepato
Peperoncino
Provolone - Medium
Provolone - Mild
Provolone - Sharp
Ricotta Con Latte 73
Ricotta Con Latte 75
Ricotta Con Latte 75 Smooth
Romano
Tiramisu Mascarpone
Toscanello

Boar's Head 👁 ⓘ
Cheeses, All

Cabot Creamery
Cabot Creamery, All

Cantaré Foods
Cantaré Foods, All BUT Baked Brie & Brie hors d'Oeuvres

Finlandia Cheese
Cheeses, All

Friendship Dairies
Friendship Dairies, All BUT Toasted Onion Flavored Sour Cream

Heini's
All-Natural Amish Farm Milk Cheeses, All

Heluva Good Cheese
Solid Block Style Cheese

Hy-Vee ✔ 👁
American Cheese Food, 3 lb
American Party Cheese, 8 oz
American Singles, 8 oz
American Singles, 16 oz
American Singles 2% Milk, 12 oz
Cheddar Party Cheese, 8 oz
Cheeze-eze, 12 oz
Colby 1/2 Moon Longhorn Cheese, 10 oz
Colby Cheese, 16 oz
Colby Hunk Cheese, 24 oz
Colby Jack 1/2 Moon Longhorn Cheese, 10 oz
Colby Jack Cheese, 8 oz
Colby Jack Cheese, 16 oz
Colby Jack Cheese Cubes, 8 oz
Colby Jack Hunk Cheese, 24 oz

Colby Jack Slices, 8 oz
Colby Longhorn Cheese, 16 oz
Deluxe Sliced American Singles, 12 oz
Extra Sharp Cheddar Cheese, 16 oz
Fancy Shredded 4 Italian Cheese, 8 oz
Fancy Shredded Cheddar Jack Cheese, 8 oz
Fancy Shredded Colby Jack Cheese, 8 oz
Fancy Shredded Mild Cheddar 2% Cheese, 8 oz
Fancy Shredded Mild Cheddar Cheese, 12 oz
Fancy Shredded Mozzarella 2% Milk, 8 oz
Fancy Shredded Mozzarella Cheese, 8 oz
Fat Free Singles, 12 oz
Fat Free Swiss Cheese Slices, 12 oz
Finely Shredded Colby Jack Cheese, 12 oz
Finely Shredded Mild Cheddar Cheese, 8 oz
Grated Parmesan Cheese, 8 oz
Hot Pepper Cheese, 8 oz
Low Fat Ricotta Cheese, 15 oz
Medium Cheddar Cheese, 8 oz
Medium Cheddar Cheese, 16 oz
Medium Cheddar Longhorn Cheese, 10 oz
Mild Cheddar Cheese, 8 oz
Mild Cheddar Cheese, 16 oz
Mild Cheddar Cheese Cubes, 8 oz
Mild Cheddar Hunk Cheese, 24 oz
Mild Cheddar Slices, 8 oz
Monterey Jack Cheese, 8 oz
Monterey Jack Cheese, 16 oz
Monterey Jack Hunk Cheese, 24 oz
Mozzarella Cheese, 8 oz
Mozzarella Cheese, 16 oz
Mozzarella Hunk Cheese, 24 oz
Muenster Cheese Slices, 8 oz
Part Skim Ricotta Cheese, 15 oz
Pepper Jack Cheese, 16 oz
Pepper Jack Cheese Cubes, 8 oz
Pepper Jack Hunk Cheese, 24 oz
Pepper Jack Singles, 12 oz
Pepper Jack Slices, 8 oz
Provolone Cheese, 16 oz
Provolone Cheese Slices, 8 oz
Sharp Cheddar Cheese, 8 oz
Sharp Cheddar Cheese, 16 oz
Sharp Cheddar Hunk Cheese, 24 oz
Sharp Cheddar Longhorn Cheese, 10 oz
Sharp Cheddar Party Cheese, 8 oz
Shredded Colby Jack Cheese, 8 oz
Shredded Mexican Blend Cheese, 8 oz
Shredded Mild Cheddar Cheese, 4, 8 & 16 oz
Shredded Mild Cheddar Cheese, 12 oz
Shredded Mozzarella Cheese, 4, 8 & 16 oz
Shredded Mozzarella Cheese, 12 oz

Shredded Parmesan Cheese, 6 oz
Shredded Pizza Cheese, 8 oz
Shredded Sharp Cheddar Cheese, 4, 8 & 16 oz
Shredded Sharp Cheddar Cheese, 12 oz
Shredded Taco Cheese, 8 oz
Sliced Low-Moisture Part-Skim Mozzarella, 8 oz
Swiss Cheese, 16 oz
Swiss Singles, 12 oz
Swiss Slices, 8 oz

Laura Lynn (Ingle's) 👁
Cheese Chunks, All Sizes
Parmesan & Romano Cheese
Parmesan Cheese
Ricotta Cheese, 15 oz

Lucerne (Safeway) 〳 👁
Cheese, All Varieties
Ricotta Cheese
String Cheese

Maggio
Ricotta Cheese
Solid Block Style Mozzarella

Meyenberg
Goat Milk Products, All

Midwest Country Fare (Hy-Vee) 〳 👁
American Sandwich Slices, 10 oz
Shredded Cheddar Cheese, 8 oz
Shredded Mozzarella Cheese, 8 oz

Primo Taglio (Safeway) 〳 👁
American Cheddar
Caesar Jack Cheese
Crumbled Danish Blue
Danish Havarti
Hot Pepper Jack
Lacy Swiss Cheese
Muenster
Provolone
Regular Jack Cheese
Shredded Asiago
Smoked Fontina Cheese

Redwood Hill Farm & Creamery
Cheese

Ricos
Cheese

Safeway 〳 👁
Grated Parmesan Cheese, 3, 8 & 16 oz

Select Brand (Safeway) 〳 👁
Cheese Fondue

Skyr.is
Höfðingi (Mould Cheese)
Stóri Dímon (Mould Cheese)

Stop & Shop 〳 👁
Colby & Monterey Blend, All
Colby Half Moon Single Slices
Fat Free White Cheese Singles
Feta, All
Havarti, All
Horseradish Cheddar Cheese
Mexican Cheese Blend
Mild Cheddar, All
Mild Longhorn Style Cheddar, All
Monterey Jack, All
Mozzarella, All
Muenster, All
NY Extra Sharp Cheddar, All
NY Sharp Cheddar, All
Parmesan Cheese, All
Port Wine Cheddar Cheese
Provolone, All
Ricotta, All
Sharp Cheddar, All
Sharp Cheddar Cold Pack Cheese Food
String Cheese
Swiss Cheese, All
Taco Cheese Blend
Vermont Sharp Cheddar, All
Vermont White Cheddar Cheese
Wisconsin Sharp, All

Tillamook
Cheese, All

Vermont Butter & Cheese Company
Vermont Butter & Cheese Company, All

Wegman's 〳 👁 ()
Colby - Sliced, 1 lb
Colby Jack Cheese, 8 oz
Colby Jack Cheese - Shredded, 8 oz
Extra Sharp White Cheddar Cheese, 8 & 16 oz
Extra Sharp Yellow Cheddar Cheese, 8 & 16 oz
Heart O' Swiss Cheese - Sliced, 1 lb
Longhorn Style Colby Cheese, 16 oz
Mexican Cheese - Fancy Shredded, 8 & 16 oz
Mild Cheddar Cheese - Fancy Shredded, 8 oz
Mild Cheddar Cheese - Shredded, 32 oz
Mild White Cheddar Cheese, 8 & 16 oz
Mild White Cheddar Cheese - Shredded, 8 oz
Mild Yellow Cheddar Cheese, 8 & 16 oz
Monterey Jack Cheese, 8 & 16 oz
Mozzarella Cheese - Low Moisture, Part Skim & Shredded, 8, 16 & 32 oz
Mozzarella Cheese - Whole Milk & Shredded, 8 oz
Muenster Cheese, 8 & 16 oz
Parmesan & Romano Cheese - Grated, 8 oz
Parmesan Cheese - Finely Shredded, 6 oz

Parmesan Cheese - Grated, 8 oz
Pepper Jack Cheese, 8 oz
Romano Cheese - Grated, 8 oz
Romano Wedge, 1 lb
Sharp Cheddar Cheese - Shredded, 8 & 16 oz
Sharp Vermont Cheddar Cheese, 8 oz
Sharp White Cheddar Cheese, 8 & 16 oz
Sharp Yellow Cheddar Cheese, 8 & 16 oz
Swiss Cheese - Chunk, 8 & 16 oz
Taco Cheese - Fancy Shredded, 8 oz

Winn-Dixie 👁

American Singles
Cheese Spread
Colby Cheese
Colby Jack Cheese
Deluxe American Cheese
Edam Cheese Ball
Extra Sharp Cheddar Cheese
Fancy Shredded Cheddar Cheese
Fancy Shredded Parmesan Cheese
Fancy Shredded Romano Cheese
Gouda Cheese
Grated Parmesan & Romano Cheese
Grated Parmesan Cheese
Medium Cheddar Cheese
Mild Cheddar Cheese
Monterey Jack Cheese
Mozzarella Cheese
Mozzarella String Cheese
Muenster Cheese
New York Extra Sharp Cheddar Cheese
New York Sharp Cheddar Cheese
Pepper Jack Cheese
Ricotta Cheese
Sharp Cheddar Cheese
Shredded Cheese
Smooth & Cheesy
Swiss Cheese
Swiss Singles
Twist String Cheese
White American Singles

CHEESE, VEGAN

Rice
Rice, All
Soy Feta
Soy Feta Cheese Alternatives
Vegan
Vegan, All
Vegan Gourmet
Cheddar

Monterey Jack
Mozzarella Cheese Alternative
Nacho
Veggie
Veggie, All
Veggy
Veggy, All
Wholesome Valley Organic
Wholesome Valley Organic, All

COTTAGE CHEESE

Axelrod
Cottage Cheese
Crowley Foods
Cottage Cheese
Friendship Dairies
Friendship Dairies, All BUT Toasted Onion Flavored Sour Cream
Hood
Cottage Cheese, All
Hy-Vee 〰 👁
4% Large Curd Cottage Cheese, 24 oz
4% Large Curd Cottage Cheese, 12 oz
4% Small Curd Cottage Cheese, 24 oz
4% Small Curd Cottage Cheese, 12 oz
Low Fat 1% Small Curd Cottage Cheese, 24 oz
Low Fat 1% Small Curd Cottage Cheese, 12 oz
Laura Lynn (Ingle's) 👁
Cottage Cheese, All Sizes
Lucerne (Safeway) 〰 👁
Cottage Cheese, All BUT Fruit Added
Midwest Country Fare (Hy-Vee) 〰 👁
1% Small Curd Cottage Cheese, 24 oz
4% Small Curd Cottage Cheese, 24 oz
Penn Maid
Cottage Cheese
Stop & Shop 〰 👁
Cottage Cheese - Calcium Added
Cottage Cheese - Lowfat
Cottage Cheese - Nonfat with Pineapple
Wegman's 〰 👁 ()
1% Large Curd Cottage Cheese, 16 oz
1% Small Curd Cottage Cheese, 16 & 24 oz
4% Small Curd Cottage Cheese, 16 & 24 oz
Non Fat Cottage Cheese, 16 oz
Pineapple FF, 16 oz
Winn-Dixie 👁
Cottage Cheese

CREAM

Hood
Creams, All

Lucerne (Safeway) ⁄ ◉
Whipping Cream - Regular, Light & Heavy

Stop & Shop ⁄ ◉
Heavy Whipping Cream
Light Cream
Whipping Cream

Wegman's ⁄ ◉ ()
Ultra Heavy Cream, 1/2 pt

Winn-Dixie ◉
Whipping Cream

CREAM CHEESE

Hy-Vee ⁄ ◉
1/3 Less Fat Cream Cheese, 8 oz
Blueberry Cream Cheese, 8 oz
Cream Cheese, 8 oz
Fat Free Cream Cheese, 8 oz
Fat Free Soft Cream Cheese, 8 oz
Fat Free Strawberry Cream Cheese, 8 oz
Garden Vegetable Cream Cheese, 8 oz
Onion/Chive Cream Cheese, 8 oz
Soft Cream Cheese, 8 oz
Soft Cream Cheese, 12 oz
Soft Light Cream Cheese, 8 oz
Strawberry Cream Cheese, 8 oz
Whipped Cream Cheese, 8 oz

Laura Lynn (Ingle's) ◉
Cream Cheese Bar, 8 oz
Fat Free Cream Cheese Bar, 8 oz
Neufchatel Bar, 8 oz
Onion & Chive Cream Cheese, 8 oz
Soft Cream Cheese (Cup), 8 oz
Strawberry Cream Cheese, 8 oz
Whipped Cream Cheese, 8 oz

Lucerne (Safeway) ⁄ ◉
Cream Cheese - Fat Free
Cream Cheese - Garden Vegetable
Cream Cheese - Light
Cream Cheese - Neufchatel
Cream Cheese - Onion/Chive
Cream Cheese - Soft Bars
Cream Cheese - Strawberry
Cream Cheese - Whipped Spread

Nature's Promise (Stop & Shop) ⁄ ◉
Organic Cream Cheese

Stop & Shop ⁄ ◉
Cream Cheese - Chive & Onion (Lite, Regula.
 Whipped)
Fat Free Cream Cheese
Garden Vegetable Cream Cheese (Lite, Regular &
 Whipped)
Honey Walnut Cream Cheese (Lite, Regular &
 Whipped)
Neufchatel Cheese
Plain Cream Cheese (Lite, Regular & Whipped)
Strawberry Cream Cheese (Lite, Regular & Whipped)

Wegman's ⁄ ◉ ()
Chive & Onion Cream Cheese, 8 oz
Cream Cheese with Honey Nut Flavor, 8 oz
Fat Free Tub Cream Cheese, 8 oz
Light Cream Cheese (Tub), 8 & 12 oz
Soft Cream Cheese, 8 & 12 oz
Soft Cream Cheese - Pineapple, 8 oz
Soft Cream Cheese - Strawberry, 8 oz

Winn-Dixie ◉
Block Cream Cheese
Cream Cheese, All
Neufchatel Cheese

EGG SUBSTITUTES

All Whites
Retail Items, All

Better'n Eggs
Better'n Eggs, All

Ener-G
Ener-G, All BUT Low Protein Products

Food You Feel Good About (Wegman's) ⁄ ◉ ()
Egg Busters, 32 oz

Hy-Vee ⁄ ◉
Refrigerated Egg Substitute, 12 & 16 oz

Laura Lynn (Ingle's) ◉
Egg Starts, All

Lucerne (Safeway) ⁄ ◉
Best of the Egg

Nulaid
Nulaid, All

Wegman's ⁄ ◉ ()
Egg Busters, 16 oz

EGGNOG & OTHER NOGS

Hood
Cinnamon EggNog
Golden EggNog
Light EggNog

Dairy & Eggs

Pumpkin EggNog
Lucerne (Safeway) ✗ 👁
Egg Nog
Stop & Shop ✗ 👁
Egg Nog - Regular & Light
Vitasoy
Holly Nog, UPC# 6195400109
Peppermint Chocolate, UPC# 6195400110

Half & Half

Hood
Simply Smart Fat Free Half & Half
Lucerne (Safeway) ✗ 👁
Half & Half
Stop & Shop ✗ 👁
Half & Half - Regular & Fat Free
Wegman's ✗ 👁 ()
Fresh Half & Half
Half & Half, 16 oz
Ultra Half & Half, 1 pt
Winn-Dixie 👁
Fat Free Half & Half

Margarine & Spreads

Benecol
Benecol Spreads
Brummel & Brown 👁
Margarine & Spread Products, All
Hy-Vee ✗ 👁
100% Corn Oil Margarine, 16 oz
Best Thing Since Butter, 16 oz (2 pack) & 48 oz
Best Thing Since Butter, 16 oz
Rich & Creamy Soft Margarine, 16 oz
Soft Margarine, 16 oz
Soft Spread, 32 oz
Soft Spread, 48 oz
Vegetable Margarine Quarters, 16 oz
Laura Lynn (Ingle's) 👁
Lite Spread Margarine (Tub), 3 lb
Margarine Quarters
Margarine Spread, 16 oz
Margarine Spread (Tub), 3 lb
Squeezable Margarine Spread, 12 oz
Taste Like Butter Spread, 16 oz
Parkay
Parkay, All
Safeway ✗ 👁
Margarine

Vegetable Oil Spreads - 70%, 37% Light & 70% 1/4 lb sticks (Homestyle)
Wegman's ✗ 👁 ()
48% Vegetable Oil Spread (Tub), 16 oz
48% Vegetable Oil Spread, 3 lb
52% Vegetable Oil Spread (Club Pack), 5lb.
52% Vegetable Oil Spread (Tubs), 2 - 8oz
80% Vegetable Oil Quarters, 16 oz
Winn-Dixie 👁
40% Lite Spread
48% Vegetable Oil Spread
Reduced Fat Spread
Soft Margarine
Spread

Milk, Chocolate & Flavored

Hood
Calorie Countdown Dairy Beverages, All Flavors & Fat Levels
Chocolate Milk - Full & Low Fat, All Sizes
Lucerne (Safeway) ✗ 👁
Chocolate Milk
Nesquik 👁 ✗ ☕
Ready-To-Drink Milk, All Flavors
Safeway ✗ 👁
Milk Drinks - Chillin Chocolate
Milk Drinks - Marvelous
Milk Drinks - Mocha Cappuccino
Milk Drinks - Vanilla Shake
Milk Drinks - Very Berry Strawberry
Turkey Hill 👁
Drink Products, All
Wegman's ✗ 👁 ()
Low Fat Chocolate Milk, 1/2 gal & 1 gal
Winn-Dixie 👁
Chocolate Milk

Milk, Lactose-Free

Laura Lynn (Ingle's) 👁
Lactose Reduced Milk, 64 oz
Stop & Shop ✗ 👁
Lactose Free Milk - Calcium Fortified Fat Free
Lactose Free Milk - Whole

Sour Cream

Axelrod
Sour Cream

Dairy & Eggs

Cascade Fresh
Sour Cream

Crowley Foods
Sour Cream

Food You Feel Good About (Wegman's) ⁄ ☉ ()
Sour Cream - Light, 8 &16 oz

Friendship Dairies
Friendship Dairies, All BUT Toasted Onion Flavored
Sour Cream

Hood
Sour Cream, All

Hy-Vee ⁄ ☉
Sour Cream, 8, 16 & 24 oz

Laura Lynn (Ingle's) ☉
Sour Cream, All Sizes

Lucerne (Safeway) ⁄ ☉
Sour Cream - Regular, Low Fat & Non Fat

Penn Maid
Sour Cream

Stop & Shop ⁄ ☉
Sour Cream - Light
Sour Cream - Nonfat

Tillamook
Sour Cream, All

Wegman's ⁄ ☉ ()
Sour Cream, 8, 16 & 32 oz
Sour Cream - Fat Free, 16 oz

Winn-Dixie ☉
Sour Cream, All

SOYMILK & MILK ALTERNATIVES

Blue Diamond Growers () ☸
Almond Breeze Non-Dairy Almond Milk

Eden Foods
EdenBlend, UPC# 024182009019
EdenSoy Unsweetened, UPC# 024182005066

Ener-G
Ener-G, All BUT Low Protein Products

Health Market (Hy-Vee) ⁄ ☉
Organic Chocolate Soy Milk, 32 fl oz
Organic Original Soy Milk, 32 fl oz
Organic Vanilla Soy Milk, 32 fl oz

Hy-Vee ⁄ ☉
Chocolate Soy Milk, 32 fl oz
Original Soy Milk, 32 fl oz
Refrigerated Chocolate Soymilk, 64 fl oz
Refrigerated Original Soy Milk, 64 fl oz
Refrigerated Vanilla Soy Milk, 64 fl oz
Strawberry Soy Milk, 32 fl oz

Vanilla Soy Milk, 32 fl oz

Laura Lynn (Ingle's) ☉
Harvest Farms Soy Milk

Living Harvest
Hempmilk, All

Lundberg Family Farms
Drink Rice - Original
Drink Rice - Vanilla

Nature's Promise (Stop & Shop) ⁄ ☉
Chocolate Soymilk
Organic Soymilk - Chocolate
Organic Soymilk - Plain
Organic Soymilk - Vanilla
Ricemilk - Plain
Ricemilk - Vanilla

Select Brand (Safeway) ⁄ ☉
Organic Soy Beverage

Silk ⁄
Silk, All

Vitasoy
Fiber Fortified Original, UPC# 6195400094
Fiber Fortified Sweet, UPC# 6195400095
Fortified Original Soymilk, UPC# 6195400048
Fortified Sweet Soymilk, UPC# 6195400043
Original Soymilk, UPC# 6195400041
Sweetened Soymilk, UPC# 6195400042

Winn-Dixie ☉
Soy Milk, All

ZenSoy
Zensoy, All

WHIPPED TOPPINGS

Axelrod
Aerosol Topping

Crowley Foods
Aerosol Topping

Hood
Instant Whipped Cream
Sugar Free Light Whipped Cream

Hy-Vee ⁄ ☉
Frozen Extra Creamy Whipped Topping, 8 oz
Frozen Fat Free Whipped Topping, 8 oz
Frozen Lite Whipped Topping, 8 oz
Frozen Lite Whipped Topping, 12 oz
Frozen Whipped Topping, 8 & 16 oz
Frozen Whipped Topping, 12 oz
Real Whipped Cream, 7 oz
Real Whipped Lite Cream, 7 oz

Dairy & Eggs

Ingles Markets 👁
Frozen Whipped Toppings

Lucerne (Safeway) 〰 👁
Aerosol Whipping Cream - Light & Non Dairy
Whipped Topping - Regular, Light & Lactose Free

Penn Maid
Aerosol Topping

Stop & Shop 〰 👁
Frozen Whipped Topping - Fat Free
Frozen Whipped Topping - French Vanilla
Frozen Whipped Topping - Lite
Frozen Whipped Topping - Non Dairy
Frozen Whipped Topping - Regular
Sweetened Whipped Light Cream

Wegman's 〰 👁 ()
Fat Free Whipped Topping (Frozen), 8 oz
Lite Whipped Topping (Frozen), 8 oz
Lite Whipped Topping (Frozen), 16 oz
Whipped Light Cream, 7 & 14 oz
Whipped Topping - Extra Creamy, 7 oz
Whipped Topping - Fat Free, 7 oz
Whipped Topping - Lactose Free, 7 oz
Whipped Topping (Frozen), 8 & 16 oz
Whipped Topping (Frozen), 12 oz

Winn-Dixie 👁
Non Dairy Whip Topping
Super Fat Free Super Whip
Super Whip
Super Whip Lite
Whipped Light Cream

YOGURT

Axelrod
Yogurt

Brown Cow
Plain Yogurts - Nonfat, Low Fat & Whole Milk

Cascade Fresh
Yogurts, All

Crowley Foods
Yogurt

Dannon
Plain DanActive
Plain Lowfat
Plain Natural
Plain Nonfat

Friendship Dairies
Friendship Dairies, All BUT Toasted Onion Flavored
Sour Cream

Hy-Vee 〰 👁
Banana Cream Non Fat Yogurt, 6 oz
Black Cherry Low Fat Yogurt, 8 oz
Blueberry Low Fat Yogurt, 8 oz
Blueberry Non Fat Yogurt, 6 oz
Cherry Non Fat Yogurt, 6 oz
Cherry-Vanilla Low Fat Yogurt, 8 oz
Fat Free Plain Yogurt, 32 oz
Key Lime Pie Fat Free Yogurt, 6 oz
Lemon Chiffon Non Fat Yogurt, 6 oz
Lemon Low Fat Yogurt, 8 oz
Mixed Berry Low Fat Yogurt, 8 oz
Peach Non Fat Yogurt, 6 oz
Peach Yogurt, 8 oz
Plain Low Fat Yogurt, 8 oz
Raspberry Low Fat Yogurt, 8 oz
Raspberry Low Fat Yogurt, 32 oz
Raspberry Non Fat Yogurt, 6 oz
Strawberry Banana Low Fat Yogurt, 8 oz
Strawberry Banana Low Fat Yogurt, 32 oz
Strawberry Banana Non Fat Yogurt, 6 oz
Strawberry Low Fat Yogurt, 8 oz
Strawberry Low Fat Yogurt, 32 oz
Strawberry Non Fat Yogurt, 6 oz
Vanilla Non Fat Yogurt, 32 oz
Whipped Low Fat Cherry Yogurt, 4 oz
Whipped Low Fat Key Lime Pie Yogurt, 4 oz
Whipped Low Fat Orange Cream Yogurt, 4 oz
Whipped Low Fat Peaches N Cream Yogurt, 4 oz
Whipped Low Fat Raspberry Yogurt, 4 oz
Whipped Low Fat Strawberry Yogurt, 4 oz
Yogurt to Go Strawberry, 8 - 2.25 oz
Yogurt to Go Strawberry & Blueberry, 8 - 2.25 oz
Yogurt to Go Strawberry/Banana & Cherry, 8 - 2.25 oz

Laura Lynn (Ingle's) 👁
Low Fat Yogurt, 8 oz
Non Fat Yogurt, 8 oz
Non Fat Yogurt, 32 oz

Lucerne (Safeway) 〰 👁
Yogurt - All Varieties: Pre-Stirred Low Fat, Fat Free, Yo on the Go & Yo Cups

Old Chatham Sheepherding Company
Yogurts, All

Penn Maid
Yogurt

Redwood Hill Farm & Creamery
Yogurt

Seven Stars Farm
Yogurt, All Flavors

Silk ✎

    Silk, All

Skyr.is

    Blueberry

    Natural

    Vanilla

Stop & Shop ✎ 👁

    Grab'Ums Yogurt to Go - Cotton Candy/Melon

    Grab'Ums Yogurt to Go - Strawberry/Blueberry

    Grab'Ums Yogurt to Go - Tropical Punch/Raspberry

    Lowfat Blended Blueberry

    Lowfat Blended Peach

    Lowfat Blended Raspberry

    Lowfat Blended Strawberry

    Lowfat Blended Vanilla

    Lowfat Fruit on the Bottom - Blueberry

    Lowfat Fruit on the Bottom - Peach

    Lowfat Fruit on the Bottom - Raspberry

    Lowfat Fruit on the Bottom - Strawberry

    Lowfat Fruit on the Bottom - Strawberry/Banana

    Nonfat Light Banana

    Nonfat Light Blueberry

    Nonfat Light Cherry

    Nonfat Light Cherry Vanilla

    Nonfat Light Coffee

    Nonfat Light Peach

    Nonfat Light Raspberry

    Nonfat Light Strawberry

    Nonfat Light Strawberry/Banana

    Nonfat Light Vanilla

    Nonfat Plain

Tillamook

    Yogurt, All

Wallaby Yogurt Company

    Plain Yogurt

Wegman's ✎ 👁 ()

    Blended Blueberry Lowfat Yogurt, 6 oz

    Blended Cherry Lowfat Yogurt, 6 oz

    Blended Coffee Lowfat Yogurt, 6 oz

    Blended Key Lime Lowfat Yogurt, 6 oz

    Blended Lemon Lowfat Yogurt, 6 oz

    Blended Mixed Berry Lowfat Yogurt, 6 oz

    Blended Orange Cream Lowfat Yogurt, 6 oz

    Blended Peach Lowfat Yogurt, 6 oz

    Blended Raspberry Lowfat Yogurt, 6 oz

    Blended Strawberry Banana Yogurt, 6 oz

    Blended Strawberry Lowfat Yogurt, 6 oz

    Blended Vanilla Lowfat Yogurt, 6 oz

    Fruit on the Bottom Fat Free - Black Cherry Yogurt, 6 oz

    Fruit on the Bottom Fat Free - Blueberry, 6 oz

    Fruit on the Bottom Fat Free - Lemon Yogurt, 6 oz

    Fruit on the Bottom Fat Free - Mixed Berry Yogurt, 6 oz

    Fruit on the Bottom Fat Free - Peach, 6 oz

    Fruit on the Bottom Fat Free - Raspberry Yogurt, 6 oz

    Fruit on the Bottom Fat Free - Strawberry, 6 oz

    Fruit on the Bottom Fat Free - Strawberry/Banana, 6 oz

    Fruit on the Bottom Lowfat - Apricot Mango Yogurt, 6 oz

    Fruit on the Bottom Lowfat - Blueberry Yogurt, 6 oz

    Fruit on the Bottom Lowfat - Cherry Vanilla Yogurt, 6 oz

    Fruit on the Bottom Lowfat - Cherry Yogurt, 6 oz

    Fruit on the Bottom Lowfat - Lemon Yogurt, 6 oz

    Fruit on the Bottom Lowfat - Mixed Berry Yogurt, 6 oz

    Fruit on the Bottom Lowfat - Peach Yogurt, 6 oz

    Fruit on the Bottom Lowfat - Pina Colada Yogurt, 6 oz

    Fruit on the Bottom Lowfat - Pineapple Yogurt, 6 oz

    Fruit on the Bottom Lowfat - Raspberry Yogurt, 6 oz

    Fruit on the Bottom Lowfat - Strawberry Banana Yogurt, 6 oz

    Fruit on the Bottom Lowfat - Strawberry Kiwi Yogurt, 6 oz

    Fruit on the Bottom Lowfat - Strawberry Yogurt, 6 oz

    Light Blended Blueberry Nonfat Yogurt, 6 oz

    Light Blended Keylime Nonfat Yogurt, 6 oz

    Light Blended Mixed Berry Nonfat Yogurt, 6 oz

    Light Blended Orange Cream Nonfat Yogurt, 6 oz

    Light Blended Peach Nonfat Yogurt, 6 oz

    Light Blended Raspberry Nonfat Yogurt, 6 oz

    Light Blended Strawberry Banana Nonfat Yogurt, 6 oz

    Light Blended Strawberry Nonfat Yogurt, 6 oz

    Light Blended Vanilla Nonfat Yogurt, 6 oz

    Plain Lowfat Yogurt, 6 oz

    Plain Lowfat Yogurt, 32 oz

    Plain Nonfat Yogurt, 32 oz

    Vanilla Lowfat Yogurt, 6 oz

    Vanilla Lowfat Yogurt, 32 oz

WholeSoy & Co.

    Yogurt, All

Winn-Dixie 👁

    Nonfat Yogurt, All

    Yogurt, All

MISCELLANEOUS

Kozy Shack

    Gel Treats, All

Safeway ✔ 👁

    Classic Potato Salad (Deli Counter) ◊

    Deviled Egg Potato Salad (Deli Counter) ◊

    Kreme Koolers

    Mustard Potato Salad (Deli Counter) ◊

    Old Fashioned Potato Salad (Deli Counter) ◊

Simply Potatoes

    Simply Potatoes, All

BEVERAGES

CARBONATED

7Up
7Up, All

A & W
A & W, All

Adirondack Beverages
Beverages, All

Airforce Nutrisoda
Airforce Nutrisoda, All

Alta Springs (Winn-Dixie) 👁
Carbonated Drinks

Aqua (Wegman's) ⁄ 👁 ()
Italian Sparkling Mineral Water, 25.4 fl oz

Barq's
Barq's Root Beer
Caffeine Free Barq's Root Beer
Diet Barq's Red Creme Soda
Diet Barq's Root Beer

Boylan Bottling Co.
Boylan Bottling Co., All

Canada Dry
Canada Dry, All

Chek (Winn-Dixie) 👁
Soda, All

China Cola
China Cola

Clearly Prestige (Winn-Dixie) 👁
Carbonated Drinks

Coca-Cola Company, The
Caffeine Free Coca-Cola Classic
Coca-Cola Black Cherry Vanilla
Coca-Cola Blak
Coca-Cola C2
Coca-Cola Classic
Coca-Cola with Lime
Coca-Cola Zero

Coke
Caffeine Free Diet Coke
Cherry Coke
Cherry Coke Zero
Diet Cherry Coke
Diet Coke
Diet Coke Black Cherry Vanilla
Diet Coke Sweetened with Splenda
Diet Coke with Lime
Diet Vanilla Coke
Vanilla Coke

Crush
Crush, All

Diet Rite
Diet Rite, All

Dr. Pepper
Dr. Pepper, All

Food You Feel Good About (Wegman's) ⁄ 👁 ()
Lemon Sparkling Water, 4 pack - 20 fl oz
Lemon Sparkling Water, 33 fl oz
Lime Sparkling Water, 4 pack - 20 fl oz
Lime Sparkling Water, 33 fl oz
Mandarin Orange Sparkling Water, 33.8 fl oz
Mixed Berry Sparkling Water, 4 pack - 20 fl oz
Mixed Berry Sparkling Water, 33 fl oz

Fresca
Fresca

Frizzante (Wegman's) ⁄ 👁 ()
Blood Orange, 33.8 fl oz
Blueberry Lemon, 33.8 fl oz
Sicilian Lemon, 33.8 fl oz
Sour Cherry Lemon, 33.8 fl oz

Hansen's
Hansen's, All

Hires
Hires

Hy-Vee ⁄ 👁
Cherry Cola, 2 L
Club Soda, 2 L

Club Soda, 1 L
Cola, 2 L
Cola, 12 pack
Cream Soda, 12 pack
Diet Cola, 12 pack
Diet Heee Haw, 12 pack
Diet Root Beer, 12 pack
Diet Tonic, 2 L
Dr. Hy-Vee, 2 L
Dr. Hy-Vee, 12 pack - 144 fl oz
Gingerale, 2 L
Grape, 2 L
Grape, 12 pack
Heee Haw, 2 L
Heee Haw, 12 pack
Lemon Lime, 2 L
Orange, 2 L
Orange, 12 pack
Root Beer, 2 L
Root Beer, 12 pack
Seltzer Water, 2 L
Sour, 2 L
Strawberry, 2 L
Strawberry, 12 pack
Tonic Water, 1 L

IBC
IBC, All

Izze Beverage Company
Izze Beverage Company, All

Martinelli's
Martinelli's, All

Mirinda
Soft Drinks, All

Mountain Dew
Soft Drinks, All

Mug
Soft Drinks, All

Pepsi
Soft Drinks, All

Prestige (Winn-Dixie) 👁
Carbonated Soft Drinks

RC
RC, All

Reed's
Reed's, All

Schweppes
Schweppes, All

Select Brand (Safeway) 🖊 👁
Clear Sparkling Water Beverage, All
Soda, All

Sierra Mist
Sodas, All

Sprite
Diet Sprite Zero
Sprite

Squirt
Squirt, All

Steaz Green Tea Soda
Drinks, All

Stewart's Beverages
Stewart's, All

Stop & Shop 🖊 👁
100% Natural Sparkling Apple Juice (Shelf Stable & Ready-to-Drink)

Sundrop
Sundrop, All

Sunkist (Cadbury Schweppes/Soda)
Sunkist, All

Tropicana Twister Soda
Soft Drinks, All

Vernors
Vernors, All

Virgil's
Virgil's, All

Wedge (Wegman's) 🖊 👁 ()
Diet Cherry-Grapefruit Flavored Soda, 12 pack - 144 fl oz
Diet Cherry-Grapefruit Flavored Soda, 2 L
Diet Grapefruit Soda, 20 fl oz & 2 L
Diet Grapefruit Soda, 12 pack - 144 fl oz
Diet Peach Grapefruit Flavored Soda, 2 L
Diet Peach-Grapefruit Flavored Soda, 12 pack

Wegman's 🖊 👁 ()
Berry Sparkling Water, 6 pack - 72 fl oz
Black Cherry Soda, 2 L
Black Cherry Soda, 12 pack - 144 fl oz
Black Cherry Sparkling Beverage, 4 pack - 20 fl oz
Black Cherry Sparkling Beverage, 33.8 fl oz
Club Soda, 33.8 fl oz
Club Soda (Cans), 12 pack
Cola, 24 pack
Cola, 20 oz
Cola - Diet, 20 fl oz
Cola Caffeine Free, 2 L
Cola CF Diet, 2 L
Cola CF Diet, 12 pack - 144 fl oz
Cola Diet, 2 L
Cola Diet, 12 pack - 144 fl oz
Cola Regular, 2 L
Cola Regular, 12 pack - 144 fl oz

Cranberry Raspberry Sparkling Beverage, 33.8 fl oz
Cranberry Sparkling Juice Blend, 25.4 fl oz
Cream Soda, 12 pack - 144 fl oz
Diet Tonic, 1 L
Dr. W, 2 L
Dr. W - Diet, 2 L
Dr. W Soda, 12 pack - 144 fl oz
Fountain Root Beer, 2 L
Fountain Root Beer, 12 pack - 144 fl oz
Fountain Root Beer - Diet, 2 L
Fountain Root Beer - Diet, 12 pack
Ginger Ale, 2 L
Ginger Ale, 12 pack - 144 fl oz
Ginger Ale - Diet, 2 L
Ginger Ale - Diet, 12 pack - 144 fl oz
Grape, 2 L
Grape Soda, 12 pack
Green Apple Sparkling Soda, 2 L
Green Apple Sparkling Soda - Diet, 20 fl oz
Green Apple Sparkling Soda - Diet, 2 L
Key Lime Sparkling Beverage, 4 - 20 fl oz
Key Lime Sparkling Beverage, 33.8 fl oz
Kiwi Strawberry Sparkling Beverage, 33.8 fl oz
Lemon Diet Cola, 2 L
Lemon Sparkling Water, 6 pack - 72 fl oz
Lime Cola - Diet, 20 fl oz
Lime Cola - Diet, 2 L
Lime Diet Cola, 12 pack
Lime Sparkling Water, 6 pack
Merge Cola (Cans), 6 pack
Mixed Berry Sparkling Beverage, 4 pack - 20 fl oz
Mixed Berry Sparkling Beverage, 33.8 fl oz
Mt. W, 2 L
Mt. W, 12 pack - 144 fl oz
Orange Diet Soda, 2 L
Orange Flavored - Diet, 12 pack
Orange Soda, 2 L
Orange Soda, 12 pack - 144 fl oz
Orange Sparkling Water, 6 pack
Peach Grapefruit Sparkling Beverage, 33.8 fl oz
Peach Sparkling Beverage, 4 pack - 20 fl oz
Peach Sparkling Beverage, 33.8 fl oz
Pink Sparkling Grape Juice, 25.4 fl oz
Raspberry Sparkling Water, 1 L
Red Raspberry Sparkling Beverage, 33.8 fl oz
Red Sparkling Grape Juice, 25.4 fl oz
Sparkling Cranberry Soda, 2 L
Sparkling Lemonade, 20 fl oz & 2 L
Sparkling Lemonade, 12 pack - 144 fl oz
Strawberry Sparkling Beverage, 33.8 fl oz
Strawberry with Sweeteners Sparkling Beverage, 33.8 fl oz

Tangerine Lime Sparkling Water, 33.8 fl oz
Tangerine Lime with Sweeteners Sparkling Beverage, 33.8 fl oz
Tonic, 1 L
Vanilla Cola, 20 fl oz & 2 L
Vanilla Cola, 12 pack
Vanilla Cola - Diet, 20 fl oz & 2 L
Vanilla Cola - Diet, 12 pack
W Red Naturally Flavored Citrus Cherry Soda, 20 fl oz & 2 L
W Red Naturally Flavored Citrus Cherry Soda, 12 pack
W Up, 2 L
W Up - Diet, 2 L
White Grape with Sweeteners Sparkling Beverage, 33.8 fl oz
White Sparkling Grape Juice, 25.4 fl oz
W-Up, 12 pack - 144 fl oz
W-Up Diet, 12 pack

Welch's ⓘ
Welch's, All

CHOCOLATE DRINKS & MIXES

Astor (Winn-Dixie) 👁
Astor Hot Cocoa
Hot Cocoa Mix

DariFree
Chocolate

Equal Exchange ()
Hot Cocoa

Hy-Vee 〆 👁
Chocolate Syrup, 48 oz
Chocolate Syrup, 24 oz
Instant Chocolate Flavored Drink Mix, 30 oz
Instant Hot Cocoa Mix, 20 oz
Instant Hot Cocoa Mix, 10 oz
No Sugar Added Instant Hot Cocoa Mix, 4.24 oz

Manischewitz
Chocolate Syrup

McNess
Hot Cocoa Drink Mix
Hot Cocoa with Mint Drink Mix

Midwest Country Fare (Hy-Vee) 〆 👁
Chocolate Flavored Syrup, 24 oz
Hot Cocoa Mix, 10 oz
Instant Chocolate Flavored Drink Mix, 2 lb

Nesquik 👁 〆 ⛄
Syrup, All

Nestlé Hot Cocoa Mix 👁 ✎ ☀
  Hot Cocoa Mix, All BUT Double Chocolate Meltdown (47 & 60 oz), Rich Chocolate Flavor (60 oz), Fat Free & Fat Free with Marshmallows

Safeway ✎ 👁
  Chocolate Syrup
  Hot Cocoa Mix - Fat Free, Sugar Free & With Marshmallows
  Instant Chocolate Drink Mix

Select Brand (Safeway) ✎ 👁
  Cocoa Mix - European

Stop & Shop ✎ 👁
  Chocolate Syrup
  Hot Cocoa - Fat Free No Sugar Added, Mini Marshmallows, Light & Regular

Winn-Dixie 👁
  Chocolate Drink Mix
  Chocolate Syrup
  Instant Chocolate Drink Mix

Yoo-hoo
  Yoo-hoo, All

COFFEE

Alter Eco Fair Trade
  Coffee, All

El Cafetal (Winn-Dixie) 👁
  Coffee

Equal Exchange ()
  Coffee, All

Folgers 👁
  Coffees, All

Green Mountain Coffee
  Coffees, All

Hy-Vee ✎ 👁
  100% Colombian Coffee, 34.5 oz
  Breakfast Blend Coffee, 34.5 oz
  Coffee, 26 & 39 oz
  Coffee, 13 oz
  Decaffeinated Coffee, 26 oz
  Decaffeinated Instant Coffee, 4 oz
  French Roast Coffee, 34.5 oz
  Instant Coffee, 8 oz
  Instant Coffee, 4 oz

Illy Caffé
  Coffee, All

Laura Lynn (Ingle's) 👁
  Coffees, All

Melitta
  Melitta, All

Millstone Coffee Company 👁
  Millstone Coffees, All

Nescafé 👁 ✎ ☀
  Classic Instant Coffee

Safeway ✎ 👁
  Espresso Coffee Beans

Select Brand (Safeway) ✎ 👁
  Coffee Beverage - Instant Flavored
  Whole Bean Flavored Coffees - Flavored

Soyfee
  Soyfee, All

Taster's Choice Instant Coffee (Nescafé) 👁 ✎ ☀
  Flavored & Unflavored

Wegman's ✎ 👁 ()
  100% Colombian - Decaf & Whole Bean Coffee Medium Roast, 12 oz
  100% Colombian - Medium Roast & Ground Coffee, 12 oz
  100% Colombian Ground Coffee, 11.5 fl oz
  100% Colombian Ground Coffee (Club Pack), 34.5 oz
  Caffeine Lite - Ground Coffee, 11.5 oz
  Caffeine Lite - Ground Coffee (Club Pack), 34.5 oz
  Dark Espresso Roast - Decaffeinated & Whole Bean Coffee, 11 oz
  Dark Espresso Roast - Whole Bean Coffee, 11 oz
  Decaffeinated Ground Coffee, 13 oz
  Decaffeinated Ground Coffee (Club Pack), 34.5 oz
  Espresso Dark Roast - Ground Coffee, 11 oz
  French Roast Coffee, 12 oz
  French Roast Ground Coffee (Club Pack), 34.5 oz
  Instant Coffee, 8 oz
  Traditional Coffee Singles, 3 oz - 19 bags
  Traditional Ground Coffee, 13 oz
  Traditional Ground Coffee (Club Pack), 30 oz
  Traditional Light Roast - Ground Coffee, 13 oz

Winn-Dixie 👁
  100% Colombian Whole Bean Coffee
  All-Purpose 100% Colombian Coffee
  All-Purpose Coffee
  Creole Coffee with Chicory
  Decaffeinated Instant Coffee
  Decaffeinated Whole Bean Coffee
  Filter Pack Coffee
  Instant Coffee
  Rich Roast All-Purpose Coffee
  Rich Roast Decaffeinated All-Purpose Coffee

Beverages

COFFEE CREAMERS & FLAVORINGS

Coffee-mate 👁 🗡 ☀
Nestlé Coffee-Mate Liquid - Flavored & Non-Flavored
Nestlé Coffee-Mate Powder - Flavored & Non-Flavored

Hood
Country Creamer

Hy-Vee 🗡 👁
Fat Free Coffee Creamer, 16 oz
French Vanilla Coffee Creamer, 8 oz
Hazelnut Coffee Creamer, 8 oz
Original Coffee Creamer, 16, 22 & 35.3 oz
Original Coffee Creamer, 11 oz
Refrigerated Fat Free French Vanilla Coffee Creamer, 2 fl oz
Refrigerated Fat Free Hazelnut Coffee Creamer, 2 fl oz
Refrigerated French Vanilla Coffee Creamer, 2 fl oz
Refrigerated Hazelnut Coffee Creamer, 2 fl oz

International Delight
International Delight, All Flavors

Laura Lynn (Ingle's) 👁
Non Dairy Creamer (Refrigerated), 16 oz

Lucerne (Safeway) 🗡 👁
Coffee Creamer - French Vanilla, Original & Powdered
Light Non Dairy Creamer

Nescafé 👁 🗡 ☀
Ice Java Coffee Syrup, All Flavors

Nulaid
Nulaid, All

Silk 🗡
Silk, All

Stop & Shop 🗡 👁
Fat Free Nondairy Creamer

Wegman's 🗡 👁 ()
Non Dairy Coffee Creamer (Frozen), 16 oz

Winn-Dixie 👁
Coffee Creamers
Non Dairy Creamer

DIET & NUTRITIONAL

Ensure ☀
Liquid Products

Gatorade
Gatorade Nutrition Shakes, All

Glucerna ☀
Glucerna Shakes, All
Glucerna Snack Shakes, All
Glucerna Weight Loss Shakes, All

Hy-Vee 🗡 👁
Chocolate Nutritional Supplement, 6 - 8 oz cans
Chocolate Nutritional Supplement Plus, 6 - 8 oz
French Vanilla Diet Shake, 66 fl oz
Milk Chocolate Diet Shake, 66 fl oz
Strawberry Diet Shake, 66 fl oz
Strawberry Nutritional Supplement, 6 - 8 oz
Strawberry Nutritional Supplement Plus, 6 - 8 oz
Vanilla Nutritional Supplement, 6 oz
Vanilla Nutritional Supplement Plus, 6 - 8 oz

Kashi
Go Lean Shake Mix - Chocolate
Go Lean Shake Mix - Vanilla

Safeway 🗡 👁
Nutritional Shake/Drinks, All Flavors, including Plus
Weight Loss Shakes - Chocolate Royale, Milk Chocolate & Vanilla

Slim-Fast
Slim-Fast Easy to Digest Shakes - Vanilla, Chocolate & Coffee

ENERGY

Fuze ()
Fuze, All

Gatorade
Berry Gatorade Energy Drink
Grape Gatorade Energy Drinks
Orange Gatorade Energy Drink

Hansen's
Hansen's, All

Red Bull
Red Bull Energy Drink
Red Bull Sugarfree

FLAVORED OR ENHANCED WATER

Adirondack Beverages
Beverages, All

Aqua (Wegman's) 🗡 👁 ()
Lemon Flavored Italian Mineral Water, 25.4 fl oz
Lemongrass Flavored Mineral Water, 25.4 fl oz
Lime Flavored Mineral Water, 25.4 fl oz

Dasani
Dasani Lemon

Food You Feel Good About (Wegman's) 🗡 👁 ()
Spring Water with Fluoride, 20 fl oz

Fruitwater
Fruitwater, All

Hy-Vee ✔ ☙
    Black Cherry Water Cooler, 1 L
    Key Lime Water Cooler, 1 L
    Kiwi Strawberry Water Cooler, 1 L
    Mixed Berry Water Cooler, 1 L
    Peach Melba Water Cooler, 1 L
    Peach Water Cooler, 1 L
    Raspberry Water Cooler, 1 L
    Strawberry Water Cooler, 1 L
    White Grape Water Cooler, 1 L
Kellogg's
    Special K$_2$O Protein Water
Smartwater
    Smartwater, All
Tampico
    Tampico, All
Vitaminwater
    Vitaminwater, All

INSTANT BREAKFAST

Carnation Instant Breakfast ⓘ
    Carnation Instant Breakfast Powder, All BUT
        Chocolate Malt
Safeway ✔ ☙
    Instant Breakfast

JUICE DRINK MIXES

Crosby's Molasses
    Drink Crystals, All
Hy-Vee ✔ ☙
    Splash Cherry Drink Mix, 19 oz
    Splash Grape Drink Mix, 19 oz
    Splash Lemonade Drink Mix, 20 oz
    Splash Orange Drink Mix, 19 oz
    Splash Tropical Fruit Punch Drink Mix, 19 oz
Laura Lynn (Ingle's) ☙
    Orange Breakfast Drink
McNess
    Lemonade Drink Mix
Safeway ✔ ☙
    Spiced Cranberry Apple Cider Mix
    Sugar Free Lemonade Drink Mix
    Sugar Free Raspberry Drink Mix
Stop & Shop ✔ ☙
    Cherry Drink Mix
    Grape Drink Mix
    Lemonade Drink Mix
    Orange Drink Mix
    Pink Lemonade Drink Mix

Strawberry Drink Mix
Sugar Free Drink Mix - Fruit Punch, Iced Tea, Lemon
    Lime & Lemonade
Tropical Punch Drink Mix
Wegman's ✔ ☙ ()
    Lemonade Flavor Drink Mix, 19 fl oz
    Pink Lemonade Flavor Drink Mix, 19 fl oz

JUICES & FRUIT DRINKS

Apple & Eve
    100% Juices, All
AriZona
    Juice Products, All
Bolthouse Farms
    Bolthouse Farms, All
Bossa Nova
    Bossa Nova, All
Campbell's ☙
    Tomato Juice, All
Ceres
    Juices, All
Country Time (Cadbury Schweppes/Ready-to-Drink)
    Country Time Lemonades, All
Del Monte ✔ ☙
    100% Fruit Juices
    Tomatoes & Tomato Products, All BUT Del Monte
        Spaghetti Sauce Flavored with Meat
Eden Foods
    Apple Concentrate, UPC# 024182000726
    Apple Juice, UPC# 024182000672
    Apple Juice, UPC# 024182000641
    Cherry Concentrate, UPC# 024182000733
    Cherry Juice (Montmorency Tart Cherries), UPC#
        024182000702
Florida's Natural
    Premium Orange Juice
    Ruby Red Grapefruit Juice
Food You Feel Good About (Wegman's) ✔ ☙ ()
    100% Ruby Red Grapefruit Juice - Premium (Not
        from Concentrate), 2 qt
    Apple (Shelf Stable), 64 fl oz
    Apple Berry Flavor Juice Blend (Shelf Stable), 2 qt
    Apple Grape Flavor Juice Blend (Shelf Stable), 2 qt
    Apple Juice - Calcium Fortified (Shelf Stable Grip
        Bottle), 64 fl oz
    Apple Juice - Calcium Fortified (Shelf Stable), 96 fl oz
    Apple Juice (Shelf Stable), 96 fl oz
    Apple Juice (Shelf Stable), 16 fl oz

Beverages

Apple Raspberry Flavor Juice Blend (Shelf Stable), 2 qt

Blueberry Flavor Juice Blend (Shelf Stable), 64 fl oz

Cherry Flavor Juice Blend (Shelf Stable), 64 fl oz

Concord Grape Cranberry Flavor Juice Blend (Shelf Stable), 64 fl oz

Cranberry (Shelf Stable), 64 fl oz

Cranberry Apple Flavor Juice Blend (Shelf Stable), 64 fl oz

Cranberry Flavor Juice Blend (Shelf Stable), 16 fl oz

Cranberry Flavor Juice Blend (Shelf Stable), 12 -16 fl oz

Cranberry Juice Blend 100% Juice (Shelf Stable), 96 fl oz

Cranberry Peach (Shelf Stable), 64 fl oz

Cranberry Raspberry (Shelf Stable), 64 fl oz

Cranberry Raspberry Juice 100% Juice (Shelf Stable), 96 fl oz

Fruit Punch (Shelf Stable), 64 fl oz

Grape (Shelf Stable), 64 fl oz

Grape Juice (Shelf Stable), 16 fl oz & 3qt

Grape Juice (Shelf Stable), 12 case - 6 fl oz

Orange Juice - Calcium Enriched from Concentrate, 2 qt

Orange Juice (Shelf Stable), 16 fl oz

Orange Juice (Shelf Stable), 12 case -16 fl oz

Orange Juice from Concentrate, 2 qt

Orange Juice from Concentrate, 1 qt

Pomegranate Flavor Juice Blend (Shelf Stable), 64 fl oz

Premium 100% Orange Juice - Extra Pulp (Not from Concentrate), 3 qt

Premium 100% Orange Juice - Extra Pulp (Not from Concentrate), 2 qt

Premium 100% Orange Juice - No Pulp (Not from Concentrate), 8 pack - 6 fl oz

Premium 100% Orange Juice - Some Pulp (Not from Concentrate), 3 qt

Premium 100% Orange Juice with Calcium & Vitamins (Not from Concentrate), 2 qt

Premium 100% Orange Juice with Calcium (Not from Concentrate), 3 qt

Premium 100% Orange Juice with Calcium (Not from Concentrate), 2 qt

Premium Orange Juice - No Pulp (Not from Concentrate), 2 qt

Premium Orange Juice - No Pulp (Not from Concentrate), 1 gal

Premium Orange Juice - Some Pulp (Not from Concentrate), 2 qt

Prune Juice (Shelf Stable), 64 fl oz

Prune Juice (Shelf Stable), 48 fl oz

Ruby Red Grapefruit Juice - 100% Juice (Shelf Stable), 64 fl oz

Ruby Red Grapefruit Juice Blend (Shelf Stable), 16 fl oz

Ruby Red Grapefruit Juice Blend (Shelf Stable), 12 - 16 oz

Tomato Juice - 100% Juice (Shelf Stable Plastic Bottle), 46 fl oz

Vegetable Juice - 100% Juice (Shelf Stable), 46 fl oz

Vegetable Juice - No Salt Added, 100% Juice (Shelf Stable Plastic Bottle), 46 fl oz

White Grape Cranberry Juice Blend (Shelf Stable), 64 fl oz

White Grape Peach Blend (Shelf Stable), 64 fl oz

White Grape Raspberry Blend (Shelf Stable), 64 fl oz

Hansen's

Hansen's, All

Hawaiian Punch

Hawaiian Punch, All

Honest Tea

Beverages, All

Hood

Juices, All

Hy-Vee ✗ ◉

100% Apple Juice, 2 L

100% Apple Juice from Concentrate, 64 fl oz

100% Cranberry Juice Blend, 64 fl oz

100% Cranberry/Apple Juice Blend, 64 fl oz

100% Cranberry/Raspberry Juice Blend, 64 fl oz

100% Unsweetened Prune Juice from Concentrate, 46 fl oz

All Natural Tomato Juice, 64 fl oz

All Natural Tomato Juice, 46 fl oz

All Natural Vegetable Juice, 64 fl oz

Apple Juice from Concentrate, 128 fl oz

Concord Grape Juice, 64 fl oz

Cranberry Apple Juice Cocktail from Concentrate, 64 fl oz

Cranberry Grape Juice Cocktail from Concentrate, 64 fl oz

Cranberry Juice Cocktail from Concentrate, 64 fl oz

Cranberry Juice Cocktail from Concentrate, 128 fl oz

Cranberry Raspberry Juice Cocktail, 64 fl oz

Cranberry Strawberry Juice Cocktail, 64 fl oz

Fruit Punch, 2 L

Fruit Punch Coolers, 10 - 6.75 fl oz

Fruit Splash Fruit Punch, 64 oz

Fruit Splash Orange, 64 oz

Grapefruit Juice from Concentrate, 64 fl oz

Juice Splash Fruit Punch, 128 fl oz

Juice Splash Orange Drink, 128 fl oz

Beverages

Just Juice - Apple, 46 fl oz
Just Juice - Berry, 46 fl oz
Just Juice - Cherry, 46 fl oz
Just Juice - Grape, 46 fl oz
Just Juice - Punch, 46 fl oz
Just Juice - Strawberry, 46 fl oz
Lemon Juice, 32 fl oz
No Concentrate Country Style Orange Juice, 96 fl oz
No Concentrate Country Style Orange Juice, 64 fl oz
No Concentrate Orange Juice, 64 & 96 fl oz
No Concentrate Orange Juice, 128 fl oz
No Concentrate Orange Juice with Calcium, 64 & 96 fl oz
No Concentrate Orange Juice with Calcium, 128 fl oz
Not from Concentrate Ruby Red Grapefruit Juice, 64 fl oz
Ruby Red Grapefruit Juice Cocktail from Concentrate, 64 fl oz
Splash Cherry, 0.15 oz
Splash Grape, 0.15 oz
Splash Lemonade, 0.15 oz
Splash Orange, 0.15 oz
Splash Raspberry, 0.15 oz
Splash Strawberry, 0.15 oz
Splash Tropical Punch, 0.15 oz
Strawberry Kiwi Cooler, 10 - 6.75 fl oz
Tomato Juice from Concentrate, 6 oz
Tomato Juice from Concentrate, 46 fl oz
Tropical Punch Coolers, 10 - 6.75 fl oz
V-8 Juice, 46 fl oz
Vegetable Juice from Concentrate, 6 oz
Vegetable Juice from Concentrate, 46 fl oz
Wild Cherry Coolers, 10 - 6.75 fl oz

Ingles Markets 👁

Apple
Cocktail Juice
Cranberry
Cranberry Blend Juices
Grape
Grapefruit Juices
Lemon Juice
Light Cranberry Blends
Light Fruit Punch
Organic Juices
Peach Juice
Prune Juices
Vegetable Juice
White Cranberry & White Cranberry Blend Juices
White Grape

Knouse Foods (See Section 3 for Knouse Brands)

Apple Cider

Apple Juice
Apple Juice Drink
Fruit Punch
Grape Drink
Natural Apple Juice
Orange Pineapple Drink
Papaya Punch Drink
Premium Apple Juice
Sparkling Apple Cider

Manischewitz

Grape Juice

Martinelli's

Martinelli's, All

Midwest Country Fare (Hy-Vee) 🖊 👁

Apple Cider, 128 fl oz
Apple Cider from Concentrate, 64 fl oz
Apple Juice from Concentrate, 64 fl oz
Apple Juice from Concentrate, 128 fl oz
Cranberry Apple Juice Cocktail, 64 fl oz
Cranberry Juice Cocktail, 64 fl oz
Cranberry Juice Cocktail, 128 fl oz
Cranberry Raspberry Juice, 64 fl oz
Grape Juice from Concentrate, 46 fl oz
Ruby Red Grapefruit Juice Cocktail, 46 fl oz

Minute Maid

Light Lemonade

Mott's

Juice Products, All BUT Mr & Mrs T Pina Colada & Clamato

Naked Juice

Naked Juice, All BUT Green Machine

Nantucket Nectars

Nantucket Nectars, All Flavors

Nature's Promise (Stop & Shop) 🖊 👁

Organic Cranberry Juice from Concentrate (Shelf Stable & Ready-to-Drink)

Nestlé Juicy Juice 👁 🖊 ☁

Juicy Juice, All Flavors

Ocean Spray ⓘ

Beverages, All

Odwalla

Juices, All BUT Super Protein Vanilla Al Mondo & Superfood

POM Wonderful ⓘ ⚱

Pom Wonderful Juice, All

Red Gold ⓘ

Tomato Juice, All

Sacramento ⓘ

Tomato Juice

Safeway ✔ ◉
Apple Juice
Apple/Cranberry Juice
Berry Splash
Cranberry/Raspberry Juice
Grape/Cranberry Cocktail
Lemon Juice
Lemonade
Limeade
Orange Juice
Pink Grapefruit Juice
Prune Juice
Ruby Red Grapefruit Cocktail
Strawberry/Kiwi Splash
Tropical Splash
White Grape Juice
White Grapefruit Juice

Simply Lemonade
Simply Lemonade

Simply Limeade
Simply Limeade

Snapple
Snapple, All

Squeez-Eez
Lemon Juice, 2.5, 4.5 & 8 oz
Lime Juice, 2.5, 4.5 & 8 oz

Stop & Shop ✔ ◉
100% Apple Juice from Concentrate - Regular & Vitamin C Added (Shelf Stable & Ready-to-Drink)
100% Berry Juice (Shelf Stable & Ready-to-Drink)
100% Cherry Juice (Shelf Stable & Ready-to-Drink)
100% Cranberry Juice Blend (Shelf Stable & Ready-to-Drink)
100% Grape Cranberry Juice (Shelf Stable & Ready-to-Drink)
100% Grape Juice Blend (Shelf Stable & Ready-to-Drink)
100% Raspberry Cranberry Juice Blend (Shelf Stable & Ready-to-Drink)
100% Unsweetened Grapefruit Juice (Shelf Stable & Ready-to-Drink)
100% White Grape Juice (Shelf Stable & Ready-to-Drink)
100% White Grapefruit Juice (Shelf Stable & Ready-to-Drink)
Artificially Flavored Fruit Drink from Concentrate (Shelf Stable & Ready-to-Drink)
Berry Berry Cooler (Shelf Stable & Ready-to-Drink)
Big Apple Cooler (Shelf Stable & Ready-to-Drink)
Cosmic Orange Cooler (Shelf Stable & Ready-to-Drink)

Cran/Apple Juice Cocktail (Shelf Stable & Ready-to-Drink)
Cranberry Grape Juice Cocktail (Shelf Stable & Ready-to-Drink)
Cranberry Lime Juice Cocktail from Concentrate (Shelf Stable & Ready-to-Drink)
Cranberry Raspberry Juice Cocktail (Shelf Stable & Ready-to-Drink)
Fruit Punch/Juice Drink (Shelf Stable & Ready-to-Drink)
Fruity Punch Cooler (Shelf Stable & Ready-to-Drink)
Goofy Grape Cooler (Shelf Stable & Ready-to-Drink)
Grape Drink (Shelf Stable & Ready-to-Drink)
Grapefruit Juice (Chilled)
Lemon Juice Reconstituted (Chilled)
Lemon Lime Drink (Shelf Stable & Ready-to-Drink)
Light Cranberry Juice Cocktail from Concentrate (Shelf Stable & Ready-to-Drink)
Lite CranRaspberry Juice Cocktail (Shelf Stable & Ready-to-Drink)
Lite Grape Juice Cocktail (Shelf Stable & Ready-to-Drink)
Natural Apple Juice - Unsweetened & Added Calcium (Shelf Stable & Ready-to-Drink)
Orange Cranberry Juice (Chilled)
Orange Drink (Shelf Stable & Ready-to-Drink)
Orange Strawberry Juice (Chilled)
Pink Lemonade (Shelf Stable & Ready-to-Drink)
Prune Juice with Pulp (Shelf Stable & Ready-to-Drink)
Ruby Red Grapefruit Tangerine Juice (Shelf Stable & Ready-to-Drink)
Strawberry Kiwi Juice (Shelf Stable & Ready-to-Drink)
Tomato Juice (Shelf Stable & Ready-to-Drink)
Tropical Carrot/Strawberry/Kiwi Blend (Shelf Stable & Ready-to-Drink)
Tropical Juice Drink (Shelf Stable & Ready-to-Drink)
Unsweetened Apple Juice with Added Vitamin C (Shelf Stable & Ready-to-Drink)
Vegetable Juice from Concentrate (Shelf Stable & Ready-to-Drink)
White Cranberry Juice Cocktail (Shelf Stable & Ready-to-Drink)
White Cranberry Peach Juice Drink (Shelf Stable & Ready-to-Drink)
White Cranberry Strawberry Juice Drink (Shelf Stable & Ready-to-Drink)
Wild Cherry Juice Drink (Shelf Stable & Ready-to-Drink)
Wildberry Drink (Shelf Stable & Ready-to-Drink)

Beverages

Sunrise Valley (Stop & Shop) ✏ 👁
Orange Juice - Calcium Added (Chilled)
Orange Juice - Regular (Chilled)
Tampico
Tampico, All
Thrifty Maid 👁
Lemon Juice
Pineapple Juice
Tomato Juice
Vegetable Juice Cocktail
Tropicana Juices
100% Juice Products, All
Turkey Hill 👁
Drink Products, All
V8 👁
Diet Splash Juice Blends, All
Splash Juice Blends, All
Vegetable Juices, All
V-Fusion Blends, All
Wegman's ✏ 👁 ()
100% Orange Juice from Concentrate, 1 gal
Apple Natural (Shelf Stable), 64 fl oz
Berry Flavor Juice Blend (Shelf Stable), 64 fl oz
Berry Punch, 64 fl oz
Cranberry Juice Cocktail (Shelf Stable), 64 fl oz
Cranberry Raspberry Juice Cocktail (Shelf Stable), 64 fl oz
Fruit Punch, 64 fl oz
Grape White (Shelf Stable), 64 fl oz
Grapefruit (Shelf Stable), 64 fl oz
Lemon Juice from Concentrate (Shelf Stable), 32 fl oz
Lemon Juice Reconstituted (Shelf Stable), 15 fl oz
Lemonade
Limeade, 64 fl oz
Orange Juice - from Concentrate & Calcium Enriched, 1 gal
Organic Apple Juice, 33.8 fl oz
Organic Apricot Nectar, 33.8 fl oz
Organic Cranberry Juice, 33.8 fl oz
Organic Mango Nectar, 33.8 fl oz
Organic Orange Juice from Concentrate, 64 fl oz
Tomato Juice - 100% Juice (Shelf Stable from Concentrate), 46 fl oz
Welch's ⓘ
Welch's, All
Winn-Dixie 👁
Apple Cider
Apple Juice
Berry Punch
Cran Raspberry Juice
Cranberry Apple

Cranberry Juice Cocktail
Cranberry Raspberry
Fruit Punch, All
Fruit Punch Drink
Grape Cranberry
Grape Drink, All
Grape Juice
Grape Juice Cocktail
Grape Punch
Grapefruit Juices
Lemon Drink
Lemonade
Orange Drink, All
Orange Juice with Calcium
Orange Juices
Orange Punch
Pink Lemonade
Tropical Juices
White Grape Juice
Wyman's
Wyman's, All

MIXERS

Simply Enjoy (Stop & Shop) ✏ 👁
Cosmopolitan Mixer
Lemon Drop Martini Mixer
Margarita Cocktail Mixer
Mojito Cocktail Mixer
Watermelon Martini Mixer

PROTEIN POWDER

Bob's Red Mill ⓘ 👤
Soy Protein Powder, Item# 1512
Living Harvest
Protein Powders, All

SMOOTHIES & SHAKES

Bolthouse Farms
Bolthouse Farms, All
Concord Foods
Banana Smoothie
Banana Soy Shake
Chocolate Banana Smoothie
Chocolate Banana Soy Shake
Orange Smoothie
Strawberry Smoothie
Tropical Fruit Soy Shake
Tropical Pineapple Smoothie

Hy-Vee ✗ ◉
Peach Yogurt Smoothie, 10 oz
Raspberry Yogurt Smoothie, 10 oz
Strawberry Yogurt Smoothie, 10 oz
Tropical Yogurt Smoothie, 10 oz

Lucerne (Safeway) ✗ ◉
Smoothies - Light, All Flavors

Silk ✗
Silk, All

Tillamook
Yogurt Smoothies, All

V8 ◉
Orange Crème Splash Smoothies, All Sizes
Peach Mango Splash Smoothies, All Sizes
Strawberry Banana Splash Smoothies, All Sizes

WholeSoy & Co.
Smoothies, All

Winn-Dixie ◉
Low Fat Smoothies
Non Fat Smoothies

SPORTS

Gatorade
Gatorade Thirst Quencher, All Flavors

Ingles Markets ◉
Sports Drinks

MVP (Wegman's) ✗ ◉ ()
Blue Freeze Sport Drink, 8 pack
Blue Freeze Sport Drink, 32 fl oz
Fruit Punch Sport Drink, 8 pack
Fruit Punch Sport Drink, 32 oz
Grape Sport Drink, 8 pack
Grape Sport Drink, 32 fl oz
Green Apple Sport Drink, 32 fl oz
Lemon Lime Sport Drink, 8 pack
Lemon Lime Sport Drink, 32 fl oz
Orange Sport Drink, 8 pack
Orange Sport Drink, 32 fl oz
Raspberry Lemonade Sport Drink, 32 fl oz

POWERade
Mountain Blast

Propel
Propel, All Flavors

Select Brand (Safeway) ✗ ◉
Amazon Freeze Winners Thirst Quencher
Fruit Punch Winners Thirst Quencher
Glacier Wave Winners Thirst Quencher
Lemon Ice Winners Thirst Quencher
Lemon Lime Winners Thirst Quencher

Lemon Winners Thirst Quencher
Orange Winners Thirst Quencher
Tangerine Freeze Winners Thirst Quencher
Tropical Winners Thirst Quencher

Tampico
Tampico, All

Velocity Fitness Water (Wegman's) ✗ ◉ ()
Berry, 6 pack
Black Cherry, 6 pack
Grape, 6 pack
Kiwi Strawberry, 6 pack
Lemon, 6 pack

Zico
Zico, All

TEA & TEA MIXES

Adagio Teas
Teas, All

Alter Eco Fair Trade
Tea, All

Bigelow
Bigelow Tea, All BUT Blueberry Harvest, Chamomile Mango, Cinnamon Spice (formerly Sinfully Cinnamon) Herb Teas & Take-A-Break Loose Tea

Boston Tea
Boston Tea, All

Eden Foods
Kukicha Tea, UPC# 024182181234
Lotus Root Tea Powder, UPC# 024182181241
Mu 16 Herb Tea, UPC# 024182181258
Organic Chamomile Herb Tea, UPC# 024182181425
Organic Genmaicha Tea, UPC# 024182181562
Organic Hojicha Chai Roasted Green Tea, UPC# 024182181388
Organic Hojicha Tea, UPC# 024182181456
Organic Kukicha Tea - Loose (Recloseable Pouch), UPC# 024182181333
Organic Kukicha Twig Tea, UPC# 024182181203
Organic Matcha Tea Refill, UPC# 024182181265
Organic Sencha Ginger Green Tea, UPC# 024182181401
Organic Sencha Green Tea, UPC# 024182181371
Organic Sencha Green Tea, UPC# 024182181227
Organic Sencha Green Tea - Loose (Recloseable Pouch), UPC# 024182181326
Organic Sencha Mint Green Tea, UPC# 024182181418
Organic Sencha Rose Green Tea, UPC# 024182181395

Beverages

Equal Exchange ()
Tea, All

Health Market (Hy-Vee) ✗ ◉
Green Tea Extract, 50 count

Honest Tea
Beverages, All

Hy-Vee ✗ ◉
Decaffeinated Green Tea, 1.3 oz
Decaffeinated Tea Bags, 48 count
Family Size Tea Bags, 24 count
Green Tea, 3.75 oz
Tea Bags, 100 count

Laura Lynn (Ingle's) ◉
Cold Brew Tea, 22 count
Decaf Tea, 48 count
Family Decaf Tea, 24 count
Family Tea, 24 count
Green Tea, 48 count
Tagless Tea, 100 count
Tea Bags, 48 count

Midwest Country Fare (Hy-Vee) ✗ ◉
Tea Bags, 100 count

Mighty Leaf Tea ()
Teas, All

Nestea (Nestlé) ◉ ✗ ☖
Nestea, All Flavors

Oregon Chai
Oregon Chai, All

Original Ceylon Tea Company, The
Original Ceylon Tea Company, The, All

Red Rose
Red Rose Teas, All

Republic of Tea, The ⛌
Republic of Tea, The, All

Revolution Tea
Teas, All

Safeway ✗ ◉
Iced Tea Mix, All

Salada
100% Green Tea
Naturally Decaffeinated 100% Green Tea
Regular Black
Regular Black Decaf

Select Brand (Safeway) ✗ ◉
Chamomile Herbal Tea
Evening Delight Herbal Tea
Green Tea
Lemon Herbal Tea
Peppermint Herbal Tea

Stop & Shop ✗ ◉
Iced Tea Mix

Teance
Tea, All

Thai Kitchen
Thai Iced Tea - Leaves

Traditional Medicinals
Traditional Medicinals, All BUT PMS Tea & St. John's Good Mood

Turkey Hill ◉
Drink Products, All

Wegman's ✗ ◉ ()
Black Tea - Orange Pekoe & Pekoe Cut Black Tea, 100 tea bags
Chamomile Organic Tea, 20 bags - 0.7 oz
Decaffeinated Black Tea, 48 tea bags
Decaffeinated Green Tea, 48 tea bags - 2.79 oz
Decaffeinated Iced Tea Mix, 53 oz
Earl Grey Organic Tea, 20 bags - 1.4 oz
English Breakfast Organic Tea, 20 bags - 1.6 oz
Green Tea, 48 tea bags - 3.81 oz
Ice Tea Mix with Natural Lemon Flavor & Sugar, 26.5 oz
Iced Tea Mix, 53 oz
Iced Tea Mix with Natural Lemon Flavor & Sugar (Club Pack), 74.2 oz
Jasmine Green Organic Tea, 20 bags - 1.4 oz
Peppermint Organic Tea, 20 bags
Regular Tea Bags, 48 count
Rooibos Strawberry Cream Organic Tea, 1.4 oz - 20 bags

Winn-Dixie ◉
Decaffeinated Tea
Instant Tea
Sweet Tea
Tea
Tea with NutraSweet, All

Yogi Tea
Yogi Tea, All BUT Calming Tea, Fasting Tea, Kava Stress Relief Tea & Stomach Ease Tea

TEA DRINKS

AriZona
Tea, All

Enviga
Berry Sparkling Green Tea
Sparkling Green Tea

Fuze ()
Fuze, All

Hansen's
  Hansen's, All

Honest Tea
  Beverages, All

Hy-Vee ✗ 👁
  Thirst Splashers Raspberry Tea, 1 oz

Nature's Promise (Stop & Shop) ✗ 👁
  Organic Fair Trade Green Tea - Decaf, Lemon &
    Regular (Shelf Stable & Ready-to-Drink)

Nestea (Coca-Cola Company, The)
  Diet Nestea Lemon
  Diet Nestea Peach Green Tea
  Lemon Sweet (Hot Fill)
  Nestea Peach Green Tea
  Sweetened Lemon Tea

POM Wonderful ⓘ 💊
  Pom Tea

Snapple
  Snapple, All

Teas' Tea 🌅
  Teas' Tea, All

Thai Kitchen
  Thai Iced Tea (Can)

Wegman's ✗ 👁 ()
  Iced Tea, 20 fl oz & 2 L
  Iced Tea - Diet (Cans), 12 - 12 fl oz
  Iced Tea Cans, 12 - 12 fl oz

CANNED AND PRE-PACKAGED FOODS

ASIAN SPECIALTY ITEMS

Eden Foods
Arame, UPC# 024182154757
Bonito Flakes, UPC# 024182002164
Daikon Radish - Dried & Shredded, UPC# 024182300154
Hiziki, UPC# 024182150797
Instant Wakame Flakes, UPC# 024182151695
Kombu, UPC# 024182152739
Kombu Balls, UPC# 024182265606
Lotus Root, UPC# 024182300147
Mekabu Wakame, UPC# 021482151732
Nori, UPC# 024182157062
Organic Dulse Flakes, UPC# 024182151701
Pickled Daikon Radish, UPC# 024182300109
Sushi Nori, UPC# 024182157703
Sushi Nori, UPC# 024182157697
Toasted Nori Krinkles, UPC# 024182157079
Ume Plum Balls, UPC# 024182000856
Ume Plum Concentrate (Bainiku Ekisu), UPC# 024182263084
Umeboshi Paste, UPC# 024182300130
Umeboshi Plums, UPC# 024182300161
Wakame, UPC# 024182151718
Yansen Dandelion Root Concentrate, UPC# 024182263091

BEANS, BAKED

Amy's Kitchen ()
Vegetarian Baked Beans
B&M Baked Beans
B&M Baked Beans, All
Bush's Best 👁
Bush's Best, All BUT Chili Beans, Chili Magic Chili Starter & Homestyle Chili Lines
Eden Foods
Baked Beans with Sorghum & Mustard, UPC# 024182002850

Food You Feel Good About (Wegman's) 〆 👁 ()
Vegetarian Baked Beans, 28 oz
Health Market (Hy-Vee) 〆 👁
Organic Baked Beans, 15 oz
Hy-Vee 〆 👁
Home Style Baked Beans, 28 oz
Onion Baked Beans, 28 oz
Original Baked Beans, 28 oz
Stop & Shop 〆 👁
Brown Sugar & Bacon Baked Beans
Homestyle Baked Beans
Vegetarian Baked Beans
Wegman's 〆 👁 ()
Homestyle Baked Beans, 27 oz
Original Baked Beans, 27 oz

BEANS, OTHER

Bush's Best 👁
Bush's Best, All BUT Chili Beans, Chili Magic Chili Starter & Homestyle Chili Lines
Eden Foods
Aduki Beans, UPC# 024182002522
Baby Lima (Butter) Beans, UPC# 024182002584
Black Beans, UPC# 024182002652
Black Beans, UPC# 024182002539
Black Eyed Peas, UPC# 024182002591
Black Soybeans, UPC# 024182002201
Cannellini (White Kidney) Beans, UPC# 024182002669
Cannellini (White Kidney) Beans, UPC# 024182002560
Caribbean Black Beans, UPC# 024182002720
Garbanzo Beans (Chick Peas), UPC# 024182002638
Garbanzo Beans (Chick Peas), UPC# 024182002515
Great Northern Beans, UPC# 024182000870
Kidney Beans, UPC# 024182002645
Kidney Beans, UPC# 024182002546
Navy Beans, UPC# 024182002553

Pinto Beans, UPC# 024182002621
Pinto Beans, UPC# 024182002508
Rice & Cajun Small Red Beans, UPC# 024182002263
Rice & Caribbean Black Beans, UPC# 024182002256
Rice & Garbanzo Beans, UPC# 024182002232
Rice & Kidney Beans, UPC# 024182002225
Rice & Lentils, UPC# 024182002270
Rice & Pinto Beans, UPC# 024182002249
Small Red Beans, UPC# 024182002577

Fantastic Foods ()
Instant Black Beans

Health Market (Hy-Vee) ⚡ 👁
Organic Black Beans, 15 oz
Organic Dark Red Kidney Beans, 15 oz
Organic Garbanzo Beans, 15 oz
Organic Pinto Beans, 15 oz

Hormel 🍽 👁
Kid's Kitchen - Beans & Wieners

Hy-Vee ⚡ 👁
Baby Lima Beans, 16 oz
Black Beans, 15 oz
Black-Eyed Peas, 16 oz
Blue Lake Cut Green Beans, 14.5 oz
Butter Beans, 15 oz
Chili Style Beans, 30 oz
Chili Style Beans, 15 oz
Great Northern Beans, 32 oz
Great Northern Beans, 16 oz
Large Lima Beans, 16 oz
Lentils, 16 oz
Light Red Kidney Beans, 15 oz
Navy Beans, 16 oz
Pinto Beans, 32 & 64 oz
Pinto Beans, 16 oz
Pork & Beans, 30 oz
Pork & Beans, 15 oz
Red Beans, 15 oz
Red Kidney Beans, 16 oz

Ingles Markets 👁
Beans & Franks
Canned Black-Eye Peas
Canned Kidney Beans
Canned Lima Beans
Chili Beans
Pork & Beans

Italian Classics (Wegman's) ⚡ 👁 ()
Cannellini Beans, 15.5 oz
Garbanzo Beans, 7.5 oz
Garbanzo Beans, 15.5 oz

Joan of Arc
Black Beans

Butter Beans
Garbanzo Beans
Great Northern Beans
Light & Dark Red Kidney Beans
Pinto Beans
Red Beans

Midwest Country Fare (Hy-Vee) ⚡ 👁
Chili Style Beans, 15 oz
Pork & Beans, 15 oz

Safeway ⚡ 👁
Pork & Beans

San Carlos (Winn-Dixie) 👁
Black Beans

Stop & Shop ⚡ 👁
Beans
Black Beans
Black Eyed Peas
Chick Peas
Kidney Beans - Light & Dark Red
Lima Beans
Pink Beans
Pinto Beans
Red Beans
Romano Beans

Thrifty Maid 👁
Black Eye Peas
Butter Beans
Chili Beans
Kidney Beans
Lima Beans
Navy Beans

Wegman's ⚡ 👁 ()
Black Beans, 15 oz
Blackeye Peas, 15 oz
Butter Beans, 15 oz
Dark Kidney Beans, 40 oz
Dark Kidney Beans, 15.5 oz
Dark Red Kidney Beans - No Salt Added, 15.5 oz
Great Northern Beans, 15.5 oz
Light Kidney Beans, 32 & 40 oz
Light Kidney Beans, 15 oz
Lima Beans, 8.5 oz
Lima Beans, 15 oz
Pinto, 15 oz
Pork & Beans in Tomato Sauce, 41 oz
Pork & Beans in Tomato Sauce, 16 oz
Seasoned Chili Beans, 15.5 oz

Williams Foods ()
Williams Hot Chili Beans
Williams Medium Chili Beans
Williams Mild Chili Beans

Canned & Pre-Packaged Foods

Winn-Dixie 👁

Great Northern Beans

BEANS, REFRIED

Amy's Kitchen ()

Refried Beans with Green Chiles
Refried Black Beans
Refried Black Beans - Light in Sodium
Traditional Refried Beans
Traditional Refried Beans - Light in Sodium

Casa Fiesta 👁

Refried Beans, 08802 - 16 oz

Eden Foods

Refried Black Beans, UPC# 024182002997
Refried Black Soy & Black Beans, UPC#
  024182002973
Refried Kidney Beans, UPC# 024182002966
Refried Pinto Bean, UPC# 024182002980
Refried Spicy Black Beans, UPC# 024182002942
Refried Spicy Pinto Beans, UPC# 024182002959

Fantastic Foods ()

Instant Refried Beans

Health Market (Hy-Vee) 🖊 👁

Organic Refried Beans, 15 oz

Hy-Vee 🖊 👁

Fat Free Refried Beans, 15 & 31 oz
Traditional Refried Beans, 15 oz

Ingles Markets 👁

Fat Free Refried Beans
Refried Beans

Safeway 🖊 👁

Refried Beans

San Carlos (Winn-Dixie) 👁

Refried Beans

BOUILLON

Astor (Winn-Dixie) 👁

Beef Cubes

Edward & Sons Trading Company ⛄

Garden Veggie Bouillon Cubes
Not Beef Bouillon Cubes
Not Chick-n Bouillon Cubes
Reduced Sodium Bouillon Cubes

Herb-Ox Bouillon 👑 👁

Beef
Chicken
Garlic Chicken
Vegetable

Hy-Vee 🖊 👁

Beef Bouillon Cubes, 3.4 oz
Chicken Bouillon Cubes 2998, 3.4 oz
Instant Beef Bouillon, 4 oz
Instant Chicken Bouillon, 4 oz

Stop & Shop 🖊 👁

Beef Flavored Bouillon Cubes - Instant & Regular
Chicken Flavored Bouillon Cubes - Instant & Regular

Streit's

Soup Bases, All

Winn-Dixie 👁

Beef Bouillon

BROTH & STOCK

College Inn 🖊 👁

Garden Vegetable Broth

Food You Feel Good About (Wegman's) 🖊 👁 ()

Beef Flavored Culinary Stock - All Natural, 32 fl oz
Chicken Culinary Stock - All Natural, 32 fl oz
Thai Culinary Stock - All Natural, 32 fl oz
Vegetable Culinary Stock - All Natural, 32 fl oz

Kitchen Basics

Kitchen Basics, All

Manischewitz

Chicken Broth

Nature's Promise (Stop & Shop) 🖊 👁

All Natural Beef Broth
Organic Chicken Broth
Organic Vegetable Broth

Safeway 🖊 👁

Chicken Broth

Stop & Shop 🖊 👁

Beef Broth
Chicken Broth

Swanson Broth & Canned Poultry 👁

Lower Sodium Beef Broth, 14 oz
Natural Goodness Chicken Broth, All Sizes
Organic Broths, All Sizes
RTS Beef Broth, 145 oz
RTS Chicken Broth, 145 & 495 oz
Vegetable Broth, 14 oz

Wolfgang Puck's 👁

All Natural Roasted Chicken Stock
Organic Beef Broth
Organic Chicken Broth
Organic Vegetable Broth

Canned & Pre-Packaged Foods

CHILI & CHILI MIXES

Amy's Kitchen ()
Black Bean Chili
Medium Chili
Medium Chili - Light in Sodium
Medium Chili with Vegetables
Spicy Chili
Spicy Chili - Light in Sodium

Bush's Best 👁
Bush's Best, All BUT Chili Beans, Chili Magic Chili
  Starter & Homestyle Chili Lines

Dr. McDougall's Right Foods
Crowd Pleasing Chili Mix Pouch

Food You Feel Good About (Wegman's) 〰 👁 ()
Spicy Red Lentil Chili (Store Prepared), 16 oz

Healthy Advantage (Safeway) 〰 👁
Vegetarian Chili

Hormel 🐾 👁
Chili with Beans - Regular, Chunky & Hot

Hy-Vee 〰 👁
Chili with Beans, 15 oz
Hot Chili with Beans, 15 oz

Stagg 🐾 👁
Chunkero Chili
Classic Chili
Dynamite Hot Chili
Ranch House Chicken Chili
Silverado Beef Chili
Steak House Chili
Turkey Ranchero Chili
Vegetable Garden Chili
White Chicken Chili

Texas Pete
Chili No Bean
Hot Dog Chili

COCONUT MILK

Native Forest 🍸
Organic Coconut Milk
Organic Light Coconut Milk

Taste of Thai, A
Coconut Milk
Lite Coconut Milk

Thai Kitchen
Coconut Milk Lite - Thailand
Coconut Milk Lite Organic-Thailand
Premium Coconut Milk - Indonesia
Premium Coconut Milk - Thailand
Premium Coconut Milk Organic - Indonesia
Premium Coconut Milk Organic - Thailand

CRANBERRY SAUCE

Hy-Vee 〰 👁
Jellied Cranberry Sauce, 16 oz
Whole Berry Cranberry Sauce, 16 oz

Manischewitz
Cranberry Sauce

Ocean Spray ⓘ
Sauces, All

Safeway 〰 👁
Cranberry Sauce - Jellied & Whole

Stop & Shop 〰 👁
Cranberry Sauce - Jellied & Whole Berry

Thrifty Maid 👁
Jellied Cranberry Sauce

Wegman's 〰 👁 ()
Jellied Cranberry Sauce, 8 & 16 oz
Whole Berry Cranberry Sauce, 16 oz

FRUIT

Del Monte 〰 👁
Canned/Jarred Fruits, All

Food You Feel Good About (Wegman's) 〰 👁 ()
Apricots - Halved, 15 oz
Chunk Pineapple, 8 oz
Chunk Pineapple, 20 oz
Crushed Pineapple, 8 oz
Crushed Pineapple, 20 oz
Fruit Cocktail, 20 oz
Fruit Cocktail, 14.75 oz
Fruit Cocktail in Pear Juice, 8.25 oz
Half Pears - Lite, 15 oz
Halved Peaches, 29 oz
Halved Yellow Cling Peaches, 14.75 oz
Lite Grapefruit, 16 oz
Peaches - Sliced in Juice, 8.25 oz
Pear Halves, 29 oz
Pineapple Tidbits, 20 oz
Sliced Peaches, 20 oz
Sliced Peaches, 14.5 oz
Sliced Pears, 29 oz
Sliced Pears - Lite, 15 oz
Sliced Pineapple, 8 oz
Sliced Pineapple, 20 oz

Hy-Vee 〰 👁
Bartlett Pear Halves, 5.25 oz
Bartlett Pears, 8.5 oz
Bartlett Pears, 29 oz

Chunk Pineapple, 20 oz
Crushed Pineapple, 20 oz
Diced Peaches, 18 oz
Fruit Cocktail, 8.75 oz
Fruit Cocktail, 30 oz
Fruit Cocktail, 5.25 oz
Lite Chunk Mixed Fruit, 5.25 oz
Lite Fruit Cocktail, 15 oz
Lite Peach Halves, 15 oz
Lite Peach Slices, 15 oz
Lite Pears, 15 oz
Mandarin Oranges, 15 oz
Mandarin Oranges, 11 oz
Mixed Fruit, 18 oz
Natural Lite Diced Peaches, 18 oz
Natural Lite Diced Pears, 18 oz
Peach Halves, 29 oz
Peach Halves, 5.25 oz
Peach Slices, 8.75 oz
Peach Slices, 29 oz
Peach Slices, 5.25 oz
Purple Plums, 30 oz
Sliced Bartlett Pears, 15 oz
Sliced Pineapple, 20 oz
Unpeeled Apricot Halves, 8.75 & 30 oz
Unpeeled Apricot Halves, 15.25 oz
Yellow Cling Lite Sliced Peaches, 29 oz

Ingles Markets 👁

Canned Fruit Cocktail - Pears, Peaches & Mixed
  Fruit
Canned Pineapple

Knouse Foods (See Section 3 for Knouse Brands)

Dutch Baked Apples
Fried Apples
Red Tart Pitted Cherries
Sliced Apples
Spiced Apple Rings
Spiced Crab Apples

Midwest Country Fare (Hy-Vee) ⁄ 👁

Bartlett Pear Halves in Light Syrup, 29 oz
Bartlett Pear Halves in Light Syrup, 15.25 oz
Crushed Pineapple, 8 oz
Crushed Pineapple, 20 oz
Fruit Cocktail, 29 oz
Fruit Cocktail, 14.5 oz
Lite Peach Halves, 29 oz
Lite Peach Slices, 29 oz
Lite Peach Slices, 14.5 oz
Peach Slices, 29 oz
Peach Slices, 14.5 oz
Pineapple Chunks, 8 oz

Pineapple Chunks, 20 oz
Pineapple Slices, 20 oz
Pineapple Tidbits, 8 oz

Native Forest 🍸

Organic Mango Chunks
Organic Papaya Chunks
Organic Pineapple Chunks
Organic Pineapple Crushed
Organic Pineapple Mini Rings
Organic Pineapple Slices
Organic Tropical Fruit Salad

Oregon Fruit Products

Canned Fruit Products, All, 15 oz
Red Tart Cherries, 14.5 oz

S & W ⁄ 👁

Canned/Jarred Fruits, All

Safeway ⁄ 👁

Mixed Fruit & Peel
Red Tart Pitted Cherries
Sliced Peaches

Stop & Shop ⁄ 👁

Apricots - Heavy Syrup & Splenda
Bartlett Pear Halves - Heavy Syrup, Light Syrup, Pear
  Juice & Splenda
Fruit Cocktail - Heavy Syrup, Pear Juice & Splenda
Fruit Mix in Heavy Syrup
Island Apricots in Light Syrup
Peaches - Whole & Slices: Yellow Cling, Pear Juice &
  Heavy Syrup
Very Cherry Fruit Mix in Light Syrup
Whole Plums in Heavy Syrup

Thrifty Maid 👁

Apricot Halves
Fruit Cocktail
Fruit Mix
Mandarin Oranges
Peaches
Pears
Pineapple
Plums in Syrup
Triple Cherry Fruit Mix

Wegman's ⁄ 👁 ()

Fruit Cocktail in Heavy Syrup, 30 oz
Fruit Cocktail in Heavy Syrup, 14.5 oz
Grapefruit Light Syrup, 16 oz
Half Pears- Heavy Syrup, 15.25 oz
Halved Pears- Heavy Syrup, 8.5 oz
Mandarin Oranges, 15 oz
Mandarin Oranges, 11 oz
Sliced Peaches in Heavy Syrup, 29 oz
Sliced Pears - Heavy Syrup, 15.25 oz

Canned & Pre-Packaged Foods

Sliced Pears - Heavy Syrup, 29 oz
Sliced Pineapple - Heavy Syrup, 8.25 oz
Sliced Yellow Cling Peaches - Raspberry Flavor, 15 oz
Sliced Yellow Cling Peaches in Heavy Syrup, 15 oz
Triple Cherry Fruit Mix - Cherry Flavored & Light
   Syrup, 15 oz
Whole Segment Mandarin Oranges, 11 oz

Winn-Dixie 👁
Fruit Blast Fruits, All

Wyman's
Wyman's, All

Meals & Meal Starters

Annie's Homegrown
Gluten-Free & Wheat-Free Rice Pasta & Cheddar

Dinty Moore ☕ 👁
Microwave Meals - Rice with Chicken
Microwave Meals - Scalloped Potatoes & Ham

Gluten-Free Pantry, The
Gluten-Free Pantry, The, All

Hormel ☕ 👁
Beef Tamales
Completes Microwave Meals - BBQ Beef & Beans, 10
   oz
Completes Microwave Meals - Chicken & Rice, 10 oz
Completes Microwave Meals - Sweet & Sour Rice, 10
   oz
Microwave Trays - SW Style Black Beans & Rice, 10
   oz
Southwest Style Rice Microwave Cups

Mi Viejita
Mi Viejita, All

Tamarind Tree
Tamarind Tree Indian Dinners, All

Taste of India, A
Masala Rice & Lentils Quick Meal
Spiced Rice with Raisins Quick Meal

Taste of Thai, A
Coconut Ginger Noodles Quick Meal
Peanut Noodles Quick Meal
Red Curry Noodles Quick Meal
Spicy Peanut Bake

Thai Kitchen
Instant Rice Noodle Bowls - Lemongrass & Chili
Instant Rice Noodle Bowls - Mushroom
Instant Rice Noodle Bowls - Roasted Garlic
Instant Rice Noodle Bowls - Spring Onion
Instant Rice Noodle Bowls - Thai Ginger
Noodle Carts - Pad Thai
Noodle Carts - Roasted Garlic

Noodle Carts - Thai Peanut
Noodle Carts - Toasted Sesame
Stir-Fry Rice Noodle Meal Kit - Lemongrass & Chili
Stir-Fry Rice Noodle Meal Kit - Original Pad Thai
Stir-Fry Rice Noodle Meal Kit - Pad Thai with Chili
Stir-Fry Rice Noodle Meal Kit - Thai Peanut
Take-Out Boxes - Ginger & Sweet Chili
Take-Out Boxes - Original Pad Thai
Take-Out Boxes - Thai Basil & Chili

Meat

Hormel ☕ 👁
Black Label - Canned Hams
Breast of Chicken Chunk Meats
Chicken Chunk Meats
Corned Beef
Corned Beef Hash
Dried Beef
Ham Chunk Meats
Ham Patties
Pickled Pigs Feet
Pickled Pork Hocks
Pickled Tidbits
Turkey Chunk Meats
Vienna Sausage

Hy-Vee ✖ 👁
98% Fat Free Breast of Chicken, 5 & 10 oz

Safeway ✖ 👁
Corned Beef Hash

Spam ☕ 👁
Classic
Less Sodium
Lite
Oven Roasted Turkey
Smoked

Stop & Shop ✖ 👁
Premium Chunk Chicken Breast in Water

Swanson Broth & Canned Poultry 👁
Mixin' Chicken, 5 oz
Premium Chunk Chicken Breast in Water, All Sizes
Premium White & Dark Chunk Chicken, All Sizes

Thrifty Maid 👁
Canned Corned Beef
Chicken Vienna Sausage
Vienna Sausage

Underwood
Deviled Ham Spread

Canned & Pre-Packaged Foods

PIE FILLINGS

Comstock/Wilderness 👁
Pie Fillings

Food You Feel Good About (Wegman's) ✎ 👁 ()
Solid Pack Pumpkin, 15 & 29 oz

Hy-Vee ✎ 👁
100% Natural Pumpkin, 15 oz
More Fruit Apple Pie Filling or Topping, 21 oz
More Fruit Cherry Pie Filling or Topping, 21 oz
Pumpkin, 15 oz

Knouse Foods (See Section 3 for Knouse Brands)
Apple Pie Filling
Apricot Pie Filling
Banana Crème Pie Filling
Blackberry Pie Filling
Blueberry Pie Filling
Cherries Jubilee Pie Filling
Cherry Pie Filling
Chocolate Crème Pie Filling
Coconut Crème Pie Filling
Dark Sweet Cherry Pie Filling
Key Lime Pie Filling
Lemon Crème Pie Filling
Lemon Pie Filling
Lite Apple Pie Filling
Lite Cherry Pie Filling
Peach Pie Filling
Pineapple Pie Filling
Raisin Pie Filling
Strawberry Glaze Pie Filling
Strawberry Pie Filling
Vanilla Crème Pie Filling

Midwest Country Fare (Hy-Vee) ✎ 👁
Apple Pie Filling, 20 oz
Cherry Pie Filling, 21 oz

Safeway ✎ 👁
Canned Pumpkin

Thrifty Maid 👁
Apple Pie Filling
Blueberry Pie Filling
Cherry Pie Filling

SOUPS & SOUP MIXES

Amy's Kitchen ()
Black Bean Vegetable Soup
Chunky Tomato Bisque Soup
Chunky Tomato Bisque Soup - Light in Sodium
Chunky Vegetable Soup
Corn Chowder Soup
Cream of Tomato Soup
Cream of Tomato Soup - Light in Sodium
Fire Roasted Southwestern Vegetable Soup
Lentil Soup
Lentil Soup - Light in Sodium
Lentil Vegetable Soup
Lentil Vegetable Soup - Light in Sodium
Potato Leek Soup
Split Pea Soup
Split Pea Soup - Light in Sodium
Thai Coconut Soup
Tuscan Bean & Rice Soup

Campbell's 👁
Chicken Broccoli Cheese (Chunky Soup), 18 oz
Savory Lentil (Select Soup), 19 oz

Dr. McDougall's Right Foods
Black Bean & Lime Big Cup
Pad Thai Big Cup
Tamale Pie Big Cup
Tortilla Soup Big Cup
Tortilla Soup Mix Pouch

Eden Foods
Organic Genmai (Brown Rice) Miso, UPC# 024182134643

Ener-G
Ener-G, All BUT Low Protein Products

Fantastic Foods ()
Baja Black Bean Chipotle Soup Cup
Buckaroo Bean Chili Soup Cup
Creamy Potato Leek Soup Cup
Creamy Potato Simmer Soup
Great Lakes Cheddar Broccoli Soup Cup
Southwest Tortilla Bean Soup Cup
Split Pea Soup Cup
Summer Vegetable Rice Soup Cup

Food You Feel Good About (Wegman's) ✎ 👁 ()
Broccoli & Vermont White Cheddar Soup (Store Prepared), 16 oz
Caribbean Black Bean Soup (Store Prepared), 16 oz
Moroccan Lentil with Chick Pea Soup (Store Prepared), 16 oz

Hormel 🍲 👁
Microwave Bean & Ham Soup

Laura Lynn (Ingle's) 👁
Beefy Onion Soup Mix, 2.2 oz
Onion Soup Mix

Manischewitz
Borscht, All
Chicken Rice Cup of Soup
Chicken Soup

Condensed Clear Chicken Soup
Hearty Bean Cello Soup Mix
Homestyle Mediterranean Black Bean Soup Mix
Schav
Soup Mix
Split Pea Homestyle Soup Mix
Split Pea with Seasoning Cello Soup Mix
Tomato Vegetable Homestyle Soup Mix
Vegetable Soup & Dip Mix

Midwest Country Fare (Hy-Vee) ✏ ◉
Onion Soup, 1-3/8 oz

Miso-Cup 🎖
Japanese Restaurant Style
Organic Traditional with Tofu
Original Golden
Reduced Sodium

Nueva Cocina
Chipotle Black Bean Soup
Cuban Black Bean Soup
Red Bean Soup

OrgraN
Orgran, All

Safeway ✏ ◉
Chicken with Rice
Condensed Homestyle Chicken with Wild Rice
Onion Soup Mix

Select Brand (Safeway) ✏ ◉
Baked Potato Signature Soup
Black Bean & Rice Soup Mix ()
Black Bean Soup Cups ()
Fajita Chicken Signature Soup
Fiesta Chicken Tortilla Signature Soup
Potato Leek Soup Cups ()
Split Pea Soup Cups ()
Tex Mex Soup Cups ()
Toasted Corn Chowder Signature Soup
Tortilla Con Queso Soup Mix ()

Stop & Shop ✏ ◉
Condensed Chicken with Rice Soup
Ready to Serve Chunky Vegetable Soup

Taste of Thai, A
Coconut Ginger Soup Base

Thai Kitchen
Coconut Ginger Soup (Can)
Instant Rice Noodle Soup - Bangkok Curry
Instant Rice Noodle Soup - Garlic & Vegetable
Instant Rice Noodle Soup - Lemongrass & Chili
Instant Rice Noodle Soup - Spring Onion
Instant Rice Noodle Soup - Thai Ginger
Tom Yum Soup Mix

Wegman's ✏ ◉ ()
Lobster Bisque (Store Prepared), 16 oz
New England Clam Chowder (Store Prepared), 16 oz

Winn-Dixie ◉
Bean Soup with Ham

Wolfgang Puck's ◉
Chicken Tortilla
Hearty Lentil & Vegetables
Organic Chicken with Wild Rice
Organic Creamy Butternut Squash
Organic French Onion
Organic Spicy Bean
Organic Split Pea
Organic Thick Hearty Lentil & Vegetables
Organic Tortilla
Roast Chicken with Rice & Rosemary
Roast Chicken with Wild Rice
Spicy Seven Bean with Italian Sausage

STEWS

Dinty Moore 🏺 ◉
Beef Stew
Chicken Stew
Microwave Meals - Beef Stew

TOMATOES

Contadina ✏ ◉
Tomatoes & Tomato Products, All BUT Contadina Tomato Paste with Italian Herbs

Cucina Antica
Tomato Sauces, All

Del Monte ✏ ◉
Tomatoes & Tomato Products, All BUT Del Monte Spaghetti Sauce Flavored with Meat

Eden Foods
Crushed Tomatoes, UPC# 024182011159
Crushed Tomatoes, UPC# 024182011111
Crushed Tomatoes with Basil, UPC# 024182011203
Crushed Tomatoes with Basil, UPC# 024182011166
Crushed Tomatoes with Onion & Garlic, UPC# 024182011210
Diced Tomatoes, UPC# 024182011302
Diced Tomatoes, UPC# 024182011180
Diced Tomatoes with Basil, UPC# 024182011319
Diced Tomatoes with Green Chilies, UPC# 024182011357
Diced Tomatoes with Roasted Onion & Garlic, UPC# 024182011326
Whole Tomatoes - Peeled, UPC# 024182011128

Whole Tomatoes with Basil - Peeled, UPC# 024182011135

Food You Feel Good About (Wegman's) ✒ 👁 ()
Diced Tomatoes, 14.5 oz
Diced Tomatoes - Chili Style, 14.5 oz
Roasted Garlic & Onion (Diced Tomatoes), 14.5 oz

Hy-Vee ✒ 👁
Crushed Tomatoes, 28 oz
Diced Tomatoes, 28 oz
Diced Tomatoes, 14.5 oz
Diced Tomatoes - Chili Ready, 14.5 oz
Diced Tomatoes with Chilies, 14.5 oz
Diced Tomatoes with Garlic & Onion, 14.5 oz
Italian Style Diced Tomatoes, 14.5 oz
Italian Style Stewed Tomatoes, 14.5 oz
Italian Style Tomato Sauce, 8 oz
Mild Diced Tomatoes & Green Chilies, 10 oz
Original Diced Tomatoes & Green Chilies, 10 oz
Petite Cut Diced Tomatoes, 28 oz
Petite Diced Tomatoes, 14.5 oz
Stewed Tomatoes, 14.5 oz
Tomato Paste, 6 oz
Tomato Sauce, 8 & 29 oz
Tomato Sauce, 15 oz
Whole Peeled Tomatoes, 28 oz
Whole Peeled Tomatoes, 14.5 oz

Italian Classics (Wegman's) ✒ 👁 ()
Coarse Ground Tomatoes, 28 oz
Crushed with Herb, 28 oz
Whole Roma, 28 oz

Laura Lynn (Ingle's) 👁
Tomato Products

Midwest Country Fare (Hy-Vee) ✒ 👁
Tomato Sauce, 8 & 15 oz

Nature's Promise (Stop & Shop) ✒ 👁
Organic Crushed Tomatoes with Basil
Organic Diced Tomatoes
Organic Tomato Paste
Organic Tomato Sauce
Organic Whole Peeled Tomatoes

Red Gold ⓘ
Tomato Puree, All
Tomato Sauce, All
Whole, Diced & Crushed Tomatoes, All

Redpack ⓘ
Tomato Puree, All
Tomato Sauce, All
Whole, Diced & Crushed Tomatoes, All

S & W ✒ 👁
Tomatoes & Tomato Products, All

Safeway ✒ 👁
Canned Tomato Products, All

Stop & Shop ✒ 👁
Crushed Tomatoes - No Added Salt, Regular, & Italian Seasoning
Diced Tomato - Italian Seasoning, No Salt Added & Regular
Stewed Tomatoes - Italian Seasoning, Mexican Style, No Salt Added & Regular
Tomato Paste
Tomato Puree
Tomato Sauce - Regular & No Added Salt
Whole Peeled Tomatoes - Regular & No Added Salt

Thrifty Maid 👁
Diced Tomatoes
Tomato Paste
Tomato Sauces

Tuttorosso ⓘ
Tuttorosso, All

Wegman's ✒ 👁 ()
Crushed Tomatoes, 28 oz
Diced Tomatoes, 14.5 oz
Italian Style Diced Tomatoes, 14.5 oz
Italian Style Stewed Tomatoes, 14.5 oz
Italian Style Whole Tomatoes with Basil, 28 oz
Kitchen Cut with Basil, 28 oz
Peeled Whole Tomatoes, 14.5 oz
Stewed Tomatoes, 8 oz
Stewed Tomatoes, 14.5 oz
Tomato Paste, 6 & 18 oz
Tomato Paste, 12 oz
Tomato Puree, 29 oz
Tomato Sauce, 8 & 28 oz
Tomato Sauce, 15 oz
Whole Tomatoes, 28 oz
Whole Tomatoes - No Salt, 14.5 oz

Tᴜɴᴀ & Oᴛʜᴇʀ Sᴇᴀꜰᴏᴏᴅ

Bumble Bee
Canned Seafood Products, All BUT Teriyaki Steak & Crackers in the Ready-to-Eat Salads

Chicken of the Sea
Chicken of the Sea, All BUT Ahi Tuna Steak in Grilled Herb Marinade, Ahi Tuna Steak in Teriyaki Sauce, Crab-tastic! Imitation Crab, Salmon Steak in Mandarin Orange Glaze, Mandarin Orange Salmon Cups, Teriyaki Tuna Cups & Tuna Salad Kits

Food You Feel Good About (Wegman's) ✒ 👁 ()
Tuna - Low Sodium (No HVP), 6 oz
Tuna in Water, 4 pack - 24 oz

Canned & Pre-Packaged Foods

Grand Selections (Hy-Vee) ↗ ◉
  Solid White Albacore Tuna, 6 oz
Hy-Vee ↗ ◉
  Alaska Pink Salmon, 4.75 oz
  Alaska Red Salmon, 4.75 oz
  Light Chunk Tuna in Oil, 6 oz
  Light Chunk Tuna in Water, 6 oz
Ingles Markets ◉
  Chunk Tuna, 3 oz (3 pack), 6 & 12 oz
  Solid White Albacore Tuna, 6 oz
Kasilof
  Kasilof, All
King Oscar
  King Oscar, All
Midwest Country Fare (Hy-Vee) ↗ ◉
  Light Tuna Chunks Packed in Water, 6 oz
Safeway ↗ ◉
  Chunk Light Tuna
Select Brand (Safeway) ↗ ◉
  Tongol Tuna
StarKist Tuna ↗ ◉
  Starkist Tuna, All BUT Tuna Creations Herb &
    Garlic, Tuna Fillet Teriyaki & Lunch Kit Crackers
Underwood
  Sardines in Mustard Sauce
  Sardines in Soybean Oil
Winn-Dixie ◉
  Chunk Light Tuna in Water

VEGETABLES

Bruce Foods ◉
  Bruce's Cut Yams, 04321 - 15 oz
  Bruce's Whole Yams, 04311 - 16 oz
Cantaré Foods
  Cantaré Foods, All BUT Baked Brie & Brie hors
    d'Oeuvres
Cara Mia
  Artichoke Salad
  Artichokes - Marinated
  Artichokes - Water Packed
  Green Asparagus
  Shredded Carrots
  White Asparagus
Del Monte ↗ ◉
  Canned Vegetables, All
Food You Feel Good About (Wegman's) ↗ ◉ ()
  Cut Green Beans - No Salt, 14.5 oz
  French Style Green Beans, 8 oz
  French Style Green Beans, 16 oz

French Style Green Beans - No Salt, 14.5 oz
Harvard Beets, 16 oz
Sliced Beets - No Salt, 16 oz
Sliced Carrots - No Salt Added, 14.5 oz
Sliced Pickled Beets, 16 oz
Small Sweet Peas, 15 oz
Sweet Peas, 15 oz
Sweet Peas - No Salt Added, 15 oz
Whole Onions in Brine, 15 oz
Whole Pickled Beets, 16 oz
Grand Selections (Hy-Vee) ↗ ◉
  Crisp & Sweet Whole Kernel Corn, 15.25 oz
  Fancy Cut Green Beans, 14.5 oz
  Fancy Whole Green Beans, 14.5 oz
  Young, Early June Premium Peas, 15 oz
Health Market (Hy-Vee) ↗ ◉
  Organic Cut Green Beans, 14.5 oz
  Organic French Cut Green Beans, 14.5 oz
  Organic Sweet Peas, 15 oz
  Organic Whole Kernel Corn, 15.25 oz
Hy-Vee ↗ ◉
  Cream Style Corn, 8.5 oz
  Cream Style Corn, 15 oz
  Cut Green Beans, 8 oz
  Diced Green Chilies, 4 oz
  French Cut Green Beans, 14.5 oz
  Golden Hominy, 14.5 oz
  Green Split Peas, 16 oz
  Mixed Vegetables, 15 oz
  Mushrooms Stems & Pieces, 4 oz
  Sliced Water Chestnuts, 8 oz
  Sweet Peas, 8.5 oz
  Sweet Peas, 15 oz
  White Hominy, 14.5 oz
  Whole Green Beans, 14.5 oz
  Whole Kernel Corn, 8.5 oz
  Whole Kernel Corn, 15 oz
  Whole Kernel White Corn, 15 oz
Ingles Markets ◉
  Canned Spinach
  Canned Turnip Greens
  Canned Turnip Greens with Diced Turnips
  Chopped Mustard Greens
  Cream Style Corn
  Cut Asparagus
  Cut Beets
  Cut Sweet Potatoes
  French Style Green Beans
  Gold 'n White Corn
  Mixed Vegetables
  No Salt Cut Green Beans
  No Salt Mixed Vegetables

Canned & Pre-Packaged Foods

No Salt Whole Kernel Corn
Pole Beans
Sliced Beets
Sliced Carrots
Sliced Potatoes
Sweet Peas
Tiny June Peas
Vacuum Packed Corn
Whole Baby Carrots
Whole Potatoes
WK Corn

Italian Classics (Wegman's) ✗ ◉ ()
Artichoke Hearts in Brine, 13.75 oz

Laura Lynn (Ingle's) ◉
Cut Green Beans
Mushrooms, All

Mediterranean Organic
Mediterranean Organics, All

MiCasa (Stop & Shop) ✗ ◉
Para Micasa Minced Garlic in Water

Midwest Country Fare (Hy-Vee) ✗ ◉
Cream Style Corn, 15 oz
Cut Green Beans, 14.5 oz
French Style Green Beans, 14.5 oz
Mushrooms & Stems, 7 oz
No Salt Added Mushrooms & Stems, 4 oz
Sweet Peas, 15 oz
Whole Kernel Corn, 15 oz

Native Forest ♟
Artichoke Hearts - Marinated
Artichoke Hearts - Quartered
Artichoke Hearts - Whole
Green Asparagus Cuts & Tips
Green Asparagus Spears
Organic Hearts of Palm
White Asparagus Spears

Nature's Promise (Stop & Shop) ✗ ◉
Organic Corn
Organic Cut Green Beans
Organic Sweet Peas

S & W ✗ ◉
Canned Vegetables, All

Safeway ✗ ◉
Cream Style Corn (Canned)
Green Beans
White Hominy

Select Brand (Safeway) ✗ ◉
Organic Peas

Stop & Shop ✗ ◉
Beets - Whole & Sliced
Carrots

Cut Sweet Potatoes in Light Syrup
Golden Cut Wax Beans
Green Beans - French Style & No Added Salt
Mexican Style Corn
Mixed Vegetables - Regular & No Added Salt
Peas - No Salt Added
Peas & Carrots
Spinach - Regular & No Added Salt
Sweet Peas
Whole Kernel Corn
Whole Potatoes - Regular & No Added Salt

Thrifty Maid ◉
Asparagus
Beets
Carrots
Corn
Cream Style Corn
Field Peas
Green Beans
Hominy
Mix Vegetables
Mushrooms
Mustard Greens
Peas
Potatoes
Spinach
Turnip Greens
Yams/Sweet Potatoes

Trappey
Okra

Wegman's ✗ ◉ ()
Asparagus - Cut Green Spears & Tips, 14.5 oz
Bread & Butter Corn, 15.25 oz
Button Mushrooms, 4 oz
Creamed Corn, 8.75 oz
Creamed Corn, 15 oz
Crisp 'n Sweet Whole Kernel Corn, 15.25 oz
Cut Green Beans, 8 oz
Cut Green Beans, 14.5 oz
Marinated & Quartered Artichoke Hearts, 6.5 oz
Mixed Vegetables, 15 oz
Mushrooms - Pieces & Stems, 8 oz
Mushrooms - Pieces & Stems, 4 oz
Sliced Beets, 8.25 oz
Sliced Beets, 15 oz
Sliced Carrots, 8.25 oz
Sliced Carrots, 14.5 oz
Sliced Mushrooms, 4 oz
Sliced Potatoes, 16 oz
Small Sweet Peas, 8.5 oz
Spinach - Whole Leaf, 7.75 oz
Spinach - Whole Leaf, 14 oz

Canned & Pre-Packaged Foods

Sweet Peas, 8.5 oz
Veggi - Green Cut Green Beans, 14.5 oz
Wax Beans, 8 oz
Wax Beans, 14.5 oz
Whole Beets, 16 oz
Whole Kernel Corn, 8.75 oz
Whole Kernel Corn, 15 & 25 oz
Whole Potatoes, 16 oz
Whole Style Carrots, 14.5 oz

BAKING AISLE

BAKING MIXES

Bob's Red Mill ⓘ ♀
GF Brownie Mix, Item# 1612
GF Chocolate Cake Mix, Item# 1616
GF Chocolate Chip Cookie Mix, Item# 1615
GF Cinnamon Raisin Bread Mix, Item# 1604
GF Cornbread Mix, Item# 1609
GF Hearty Whole Grain Bread Mix, Item# 1603
GF Homemade Bread Mix, Item# 1602
GF Pancake Mix, Item# 1610
Wheat-Free Biscuit Mix, Item# 1334

Cherrybrook Kitchen
Wheat-Free/Gluten-Free Chocolate Cake
Wheat-Free/Gluten-Free Chocolate Chip Cookie
Wheat-Free/Gluten-Free Sugar Cookie

Chi-Chi's ⌚ ◉
Fiesta Sweet Corn Cake Mix

El Torito ⌚ ◉
Sweet Corn Cake Mix

Ener-G
Ener-G, All BUT Low Protein Products

Food-Tek
Food-Tek, All

Gluten-Free Pantry, The
Gluten-Free Pantry, The, All

Glutino
Glutino, All

Hodgson Mill
Apple Cinnamon Muffin Mix
Multi Purpose Baking Mix

Namaste Foods
Namaste Foods, All

OrgraN
Orgran, All

Pamela's Products
Amazing Bread Mix
Incredible Chocolate Chunk Cookie Mix
Irresistible Chocolate Brownie Mix

Luscious Chocolate Cake Mix
Ultimate Baking & Pancake Mix

BAKING POWDER

Bob's Red Mill ⓘ ♀
Baking Powder, Item# 1050

Clabber Girl
Baking Powder

Davis Baking Powder
Baking Powder

Hy-Vee ⟋ ◉
Double Acting Baking Powder, 10 oz

Laura Lynn (Ingle's) ◉
Baking Powder, 10 oz

Rumford
Baking Powder

Tone's, Durkee & Spice Islands
Baking Powder

Wegman's ⟋ ◉ ()
Baking Powder - Double Acting, 10 oz

BAKING SODA

Arm & Hammer
Baking Soda

Bob's Red Mill ⓘ ♀
Baking Soda, Item# 1055

Hy-Vee ⟋ ◉
Baking Soda, 16 oz

Laura Lynn (Ingle's) ◉
Baking Soda

Stop & Shop ⟋ ◉
Baking Soda

Tone's, Durkee & Spice Islands
Baking Soda

Winn-Dixie ◉
Baking Soda

CHOCOLATE CHIPS & OTHER CHIPS

Gluten-Free Pantry, The
Gluten-Free Pantry, The, All

Guittard
Guittard, All

Hy-Vee ✗ ◉
Butterscotch Chips, 12 oz
Milk Chocolate Chips, 11.5 oz
Peanut Butter Chips, 10 oz
Semi Sweet Chocolate Chips, 24 oz
Semi Sweet Chocolate Chips, 12 oz

Manischewitz
Chocolate Morsels

Midwest Country Fare (Hy-Vee) ✗ ◉
Chocolate Flavored Chips, 12 oz

Nestlé Toll House Morsels & Baking Ingredients
Semi-Sweet Morsels

Safeway ✗ ◉
Butterscotch Chips
Chocolate Chips - Milk Chocolate, Semi Sweet & Real Chocolate

Select Brand (Safeway) ✗ ◉
Chocolate Chips

Stop & Shop ✗ ◉
Semi-Sweet Chocolate Chips

Thrifty Maid ◉
Semi-Sweet Morsels

Wegman's ✗ ◉ ()
Chocolate Morsels - Semi-Sweet, 12 & 24 oz

Winn-Dixie ◉
Chocolate Chips

COCOA POWDER

Equal Exchange ()
Baking Cocoa

Guittard
Guittard, All

Hy-Vee ✗ ◉
Baking Cocoa, 8 oz

Laura Lynn (Ingle's) ◉
Cocoa

Stop & Shop ✗ ◉
Baking Cocoa

COCONUT

Hy-Vee ✗ ◉
Coconut, 14 oz
Flake Coconut, 7 oz

Laura Lynn (Ingle's) ◉
Coconut, 14 oz

Let's Do…Organic ⚥
Coconut Flakes
Creamed Coconut
Reduced Fat Shredded Coconut
Shredded Coconut

Safeway ✗ ◉
Sweetened Coconut

Wegman's ✗ ◉ ()
Coconut, 7 oz
Sweetened Flaked Coconut, 14 oz

Winn-Dixie ◉
Coconut Flakes

CORN SYRUP & OTHER SYRUP SWEETENERS

Brer Rabbit
Syrup Full
Syrup Light

Karo
Syrups, All

Lundberg Family Farms
Rice Syrup - Eco-Farmed Sweet Dreams
Rice Syrup - Organic Sweet Dreams

Wegman's ✗ ◉ ()
Light Corn Syrup, 16 oz

Wholesome Sweeteners ⚥
Organic Cane Syrups

Winn-Dixie ◉
Light Corn Syrup

CORNMEAL & OTHER MEALS

Bob's Red Mill ⓘ ⚥
Almond Meal/Flour, Item# 4999
Flaxseed Meal - Brown, Item# 1235
Hazelnut Meal/Flour, Item# 1811
Millet Grits/Meal, Item# 1297
Organic Flaxseed Meal - Brown, Item# 6032
Organic Golden Flaxseed Meal, Item# 6035

Hodgson Mill
Milled Flax Seed
Organic Golden Milled Flax Seed
Organic Yellow Corn Meal
White Corn Meal

Yellow Corn Meal, Plain

Safeway ✗ ◉

Yellow Corn Meal ()

FLOURS

Bob's Red Mill ⓘ ⅋

Amaranth Flour, Item# 1012
Black Bean Flour, Item# 1660
Brown Rice Flour, Item# 1460
Fava Bean Flour, Item# 1659
Garbanzo Bean Flour, Item# 1260
Garbanzo/Fava Bean Flour, Item# 1605
GF All Purpose Baking Flour, Item# 1600
Green Pea Flour, Item# 1666
Millet Flour, Item# 1296
Organic Brown Rice Flour, Item# 6072
Organic Buckwheat Flour, Item# 1090
Organic Coconut Flour, Item# 6135
Organic Quinoa Flour, Item# 1448
Organic White Rice Flour, Item# 6063
Potato Flour, Item# 1445
Sorghum Flour, Item# 2530
Sweet White Rice Flour, Item# 5038
Tapioca Flour, Item# 1532
Teff Flour, Item# 1534
White Bean Flour, Item# 1664
White Rice Flour, Item# 1461

Ener-G

Ener-G, All BUT Low Protein Products

Gluten-Free Pantry, The

Gluten-Free Pantry, The, All

Hodgson Mill

Brown Rice Flour
Buckwheat Flour
Organic Soy Flour
Soy Flour

Lundberg Family Farms

Rice Flours & Grinds, All

Tom Sawyer ⅋

All Purpose Gluten Free Flour

FOOD COLORING

Hy-Vee ✗ ◉

Assorted Food Coloring, 1.2 fl oz

Safeway ✗ ◉

Food Coloring - Assorted

Tone's, Durkee & Spice Islands

Food Coloring, All

FROSTING

Cherrybrook Kitchen

Wheat-Free/Gluten-Free Chocolate Frosting
Wheat-Free/Gluten-Free Vanilla Frosting

HONEY

Hy-Vee ✗ ◉

Honey, 16, 24 & 40 oz
Squeeze Bear Honey, 12 oz

Safeway ✗ ◉

Creamed Honey
Pure Honey

Wegman's ✗ ◉ ()

Honey - 100% Pure Clover, 40 oz
Honey - 100% Pure Clover, 32 oz
Honey - Clover, 80 oz
Honey - Orange Blossom, 16 oz
Honey - US Grade A Clover, 16 oz
Squeezable Bear Clover Honey - 100% Pure, 24 oz
Squeezable Bear Clover Honey - 100% Pure, 12 oz

Winn-Dixie ◉

Honey

MARSHMALLOWS

Hy-Vee ✗ ◉

Colored Miniature Marshmallows, 10.5 oz
Marshmallows, 16 oz
Marshmallows, 10 oz
Miniature Marshmallows, 16 oz
Miniature Marshmallows, 10.5 oz

Laura Lynn (Ingle's) ◉

Regular Marshmallows, 10 & 16 oz

Manischewitz

Marshmallows

Safeway ✗ ◉

Marshmallows - Large & Mini

Winn-Dixie ◉

Marshmallows

MILK - CONDENSED, EVAPORATED & POWDERED

DariFree

Original

Hy-Vee ✗ ◉

Evaporated Milk, 12 fl oz
Fat Free Evaporated Milk, 12 oz
Instant Non Fat Dry Milk, 8 qt
Instant Non Fat Dry Milk, 20 qt

Baking Aisle

Sweetened Condensed Milk, 14 oz

Laura Lynn (Ingle's) 👁
Evaporated Milk
Instant Dry Milk, 3 - 1 qt & 8 qt
Instant Dry Milk, 20 qt
Sweetened Condensed Milk, 14 oz

Meyenberg
Goat Milk Products, All

Safeway 𝄪 👁
Sweetened Condensed Milk

Stop & Shop 𝄪 👁
Instant Nonfat Dry Milk

Wegman's 𝄪 👁 ()
Evaporated Milk, 5 & 12 fl oz
Fat Free Evaporated Milk, 12 fl oz
Sweetened Condensed Milk (Can), 14 fl oz

Winn-Dixie 👁
Evaporated Milk
Fat Free Evaporated Skim Milk
Non Fat Dry Milk
Sweetened Condensed Milk

MOLASSES

Brer Rabbit
Molasses Blackstrap
Molasses Full
Molasses Mild
Syrup Full
Syrup Light

Crosby's Molasses
Molasses, All

Grandma's Molasses
Original
Robust

Wholesome Sweeteners 🍋
Organic Blackstrap Molasses

OIL & OIL SPRAYS

Annie's Naturals ()
Basil Flavored Olive Oil
Dipping Oil Herb Flavored Olive Oil
Organic Meyer Lemon Flavored Extra Virgin Olive Oil
Organic Sicilian Orange Flavored Extra Virgin Olive Oil
Roasted Garlic Flavored Extra Virgin Olive Oil
Roasted Pepper Flavored Olive Oil

Bragg
Bragg, All

Carapelli 🍋 👁
Olive Oil

Crisco
Crisco, All BUT No-Stick Flour Spray

Dynasty
Sesame Oil, #03263 & #03260

Eden Foods
Extra Virgin Olive Oil - Spanish, UPC# 024182000122
Extra Virgin Olive Oil - Spanish, UPC# 024182000139
Extra Virgin Olive Oil - Spanish, UPC# 024182000115
Hot Pepper Sesame Oil, UPC# 024182000245
Organic Safflower Oil, UPC# 024182000184
Organic Sesame Oil, UPC# 024182000276
Organic Sesame Oil, UPC# 024182000252
Organic Soybean Oil, UPC# 024182000146
Toasted Sesame Oil, UPC# 024182421293
Toasted Sesame Oil, UPC# 024182000283

Filippo Berio 🍋
Filippo Berio, All

Food You Feel Good About (Wegman's) 𝄪 👁 ()
Black Truffle Extra Virgin Olive Oil, 3.52 fl oz
Grapeseed Oil, 17 fl oz
Pumpkin Seed Oil, 8.4 fl oz
Sicilian Lemon Extra Virgin Olive Oil, 8.4 fl oz
Walnut Oil - Pure, 3.2 oz

Grand Selections (Hy-Vee) 𝄪 👁
100% Pure & Natural Olive Oil, 17 fl oz
Extra Virgin Olive Oil, 17 fl oz

House Of Tsang 🍋 👁
Hot Chili Sesame Oil
Mongolian Fire Oil
Sesame Oil
Wok Oil

Hy-Vee 𝄪 👁
100% Pure Canola Oil, 32 & 48 fl oz
100% Pure Canola Oil, 128 fl oz
100% Pure Corn Oil, 32 fl oz
100% Pure Vegetable Oil, 24, 32 & 48 fl oz
100% Pure Vegetable Oil, 128 fl oz
Natural Blend Oil, 48 fl oz

Ingles Markets 👁
Blended Oil, 48 oz
Canola Oil, 32 & 48 oz
Canola Oil, 128 oz
Corn Oil, 48 oz
Corn Oil, 24 oz
Peanut Oil, 48 oz
Peanut Oil, 128 oz

Baking Aisle

Vegetable Oil, 24, 48 & 64 oz
Vegetable Oil, 128 oz

Italian Classics (Wegman's) ⟋ ◉ ()
Campania Oil
Oil - Tuscany, 25.3 fl oz

La Tourangelle
Oils, All

Lapas
Lapas Olive Oil

Living Harvest
Oils, All

Manischewitz
Cooking Sprays, All Varieties
Vegetable Oil

Mazola
Oils, All
Sprays, All

MiCasa (Stop & Shop) ⟋ ◉
Corn Oil
Vegetable Oil

Midwest Country Fare (Hy-Vee) ⟋ ◉
100% Pure Vegetable Oil, 48 fl oz
Vegetable Oil, 32 fl oz

Montebello
Olive Oil

Newman's Own Organics ()
Olive Oil

Nunez de Prado
Olive Oil

Robert Rothschild Farm
Gourmet Dipping Oil
Italian Oil
Red Chili Pepper & Garlic Oil
Roasted Garlic Oil
Rosemary & Garlic Oil

Safeway ⟋ ◉
Cooking Spray - Butter Flavored
Oils - Edible

Simply Enjoy (Stop & Shop) ⟋ ◉
Flavored Extra Virgin Olive Oil - Basil, Garlic,
  Lemon, Orange & Pepper
Regional Extra Virgin Olive Oil - Apulian, Sicilian,
  Tuscan & Umbrian

Stop & Shop ⟋ ◉
Blended Oil
Butter Flavored Cooking Spray
Canola Cooking Spray
Canola Oil
Corn Oil
Extra Light Olive Oil

Garlic Flavored Cooking Spray
Grill Spray
Olive Oil Cooking Spray
Pure Olive Oil
Soybean Oil
Vegetable Cooking Spray
Vegetable Oil

Terrapin Ridge
Spicy Mustard Seed Oil

Villa Flor
Olive Oils

Wegman's ⟋ ◉ ()
100% Pure Olive Oil, 1 pt
Basting Oil, 8 fl oz
Basting Oil, 12 fl oz
Campania Style Extra Virgin Olive Oil, 16.9 fl oz
Canola Oil, 32 & 48 fl oz
Canola Oil, 128 fl oz
Canola Oil Cooking Spray, 6 oz
Corn Oil, 48 fl oz
Corn Oil Cooking Spray, 5 oz
Extra Virgin Olive Oil, 1 pt
Mild Olive Oil, 1 pt
Natural Butter Flavor, Canola Oil Cooking Spray, 6
  oz
Novello Unfiltered Extra Virgin Olive Oil, 16.9 fl oz
Oil - Puglia, 25.3 fl oz
Olive Oil - Extra Virgin, 34 fl oz
Olive Oil - Pure, 34 fl oz
Olive Oil Cooking Spray, 5 fl oz
Peanut Oil, 32 fl oz
Puglia Style Extra Virgin Olive Oil, 16.9 fl oz
Sicilian Style Extra Virgin Olive Oil, 16.9 fl oz
Submarine Sandwich Oil, 12.25 fl oz
Tuscany Style Extra Virgin Olive Oil, 16.9 fl oz
Vegetable Oil, 24 fl oz
Vegetable Oil - 100% Soybean, 48 fl oz
Vegetable Oil - 100% Soybean, 32 fl oz
Vegetable Oil - 100% Soybean Oil, 128 fl oz

Winn-Dixie ◉
Butter Cooking Spray
Canola Oil
Canola Oil Spray
Cooking Sprays
Corn Oil
Corn Oil Spray
Olive Oil
Olive Oil Spray
Peanut Oil
Vegetable Oil

SHORTENING & OTHER FATS

Crisco
Crisco, All BUT No-Stick Flour Spray

Empire Kosher
Rendered Chicken Fat

Hy-Vee ⚡ 👁
Vegetable Oil Shortening, 48 oz
Vegetable Shortening - Butter Flavor, 48 oz

Ingles Markets 👁
3# Vegetable Shortening
Shortening, 42 oz

Midwest Country Fare (Hy-Vee) ⚡ 👁
Pre-Creamed Shortening, 42 oz

Stop & Shop ⚡ 👁
Meat Fat/Vegetable Shortening
Vegetable Shortening

Wegman's ⚡ 👁 ()
Vegetable Shortening, 3 lb

Winn-Dixie 👁
Shortening
Vegetable Shortening

SPICE MIXES & SEASONINGS

Ac'cent
Ac'cent Flavor Enhancer

Bone Suckin' Sauce ⚕
Bone Suckin' Rib Rub

Bragg
Bragg, All

Cajun King 👁
Char-Grill Seasoning Mix, 02859 - 1.25 oz

Casa Fiesta 👁
Taco Seasoning Mix, 08122 - 1.25 oz

Chi-Chi's ☠ 👁
Fiesta Restaurante Seasoning Mix

Cholula Hot Sauce
Cholula, All

Concord Foods
Cole Slaw Mix
Extra Spicy Guacamole Mix
Guacamole Mix
Hollandaise Sauce Mix
Mashed Potato Seasoning Mix - Roasted Garlic & Herb
Roasted Potato Seasoning Mix - Original Recipe
Salsa Mixes - Mild & Hot
Stir Fry Mix
Sweet Potato & Yam Glaze

Daniel's Bar-B-Q
Daniel's Bar-B-Q, All

Durkee
California Style Blends - Garlic Salt
California Style Blends - Onion Salt

Dynasty
Chinese Five Spices, #03023

Eden Foods
Eden Shake (Furikake) Seasoning, UPC# 024182002027
Organic Garlic Gomasio (Sesame Salt), UPC# 024182002058
Organic Gomasio (Sesame Salt), UPC# 024182002010
Organic Seaweed Gomasio (Sesame Salt), UPC# 024182002096

Emeril's
Chicken Rub
Essence - Asian
Essence - Baby Bam
Essence - Bayou Blast
Essence - Italian
Essence - Original
Essence - Southwest
Fish Rub
Rib & Steak Rub

Gluten-Free Pantry, The
Gluten-Free Pantry, The, All

Hy-Vee ⚡ 👁
Chicken Grill Seasoning, 2 oz
Chili Powder, 4.38 oz
Garlic Salt, 9.5 oz
Italian Seasoning, 0.75 oz
Lemon Pepper, 2.38 oz
Season Salt, 16 oz
Seasoned Salt, 9 oz
Steak Grilling Seasoning, 3 oz

Laura Lynn (Ingle's) 👁
Steak Seasoning, 16 oz

Lydia's Organics ⚕
Lydia's Organics, All

Manischewitz
Brisket & Steak Seasoning
Fish Seasoning
Poultry Seasoning

McNess
Baked Potato Seasoning
Butter Flavored Salt
Chili Seasoning
Garlic Salt
Gourmet Seasoning

Hamburger Seasoning
Lemon Pepper
Onion Salt
Poultry Seasoning
Retro Spices - Apple Pie Spice
Retro Spices - Chili Seasoning
Retro Spices - Coleslaw
Retro Spices - Fried Chicken
Retro Spices - Garlic Mashed Potato
Retro Spices - Meatloaf Seasoning
Retro Spices - Potato Salad
Retro Spices - Pumpkin Pie Spice
Retro Spices - Sage Stuffing
Retro Spices - Soup Pot
Retro Spices - Wild Game

Mexene Chili ◉
Mexene Chili Powder Seasoning, 02202 - 3 oz

Midwest Country Fare (Hy-Vee) ⚡ ◉
Chili Powder, 2.15 oz
Italian Seasoning, 1 oz
Season Salt, 4.5 oz

Morton Salt ⚐
Hot Salt
Nature's Seasons Seasoning Blend
Tender Quick Mix

Mrs. Dash ()
Mrs. Dash Seasonings in the Shaker Bottles

Nueva Cocina
Seasonings, All

Safeway ⚡ ◉
Fajita Seasoning Mix ()

Spice Hunter ()
Spice Blends

Spice Islands
Beau Monde
Chili Powder
Crystallized Ginger
Fines Herbs
Garlic Pepper Seasoning
Grilling Gourmet & World Flavors, All
Italian Herb Seasoning
Summer Savory

Sunbird ()
Beef & Broccoli
Chinese Chicken Salad
Chop Suey
Chow Mein
Fried Rice
General Tso's Chicken
Honey Sesame Chicken
Honey Teriyaki

Hot & Spicy Fried Rice
Hot & Spicy Kung Pao
Hot & Spicy Szechwan
Lemon Chicken Stir Fry
New Hot & Sour Soup
Orange Beef
Oriental Vegetable Stir Fry
Phad Thai
Spare Rib
Stir Fry
Sweet & Sour
Thai Chicken
Thai Fried Rice
Thai Red Curry
Thai Spicy Beef
Thai Stir Fry

Taste of Thai, A
Chicken & Rice Seasoning

Tempo
Chili Mix
Sloppy Joe Mix

Tone's, Durkee & Spice Islands
Apple Pie Spice
Chicken & Rib Rub
Chicken Seasoning
Chili Powder
Crazy Dave's Lemon Pepper
Crazy Dave's Pepper & Spice
Crazy Dave's Salt & Spice
Curry Powder
Garlic Pepper
Garlic Salt
Italian Seasoning
Jamaican Jerk Seasoning
Lemon & Herb
Lemon Garlic Seasoning
Lemon Pepper
Lime Pepper
Mr. Pepper
Onion Salt
Oriental 5-Spice
Pickling Spice
Pizza Seasoning
Poultry Seasoning
Pumpkin Pie Spice
Rosemary Garlic Seasoning
Salt Free Garden Seasoning
Salt Free Garlic & Herb
Salt Free Lemon Pepper
Salt Free Original All-Purpose Seasoning
Salt Free Veg. Seasoning
Seasoned Pepper

Baking Aisle

Six Pepper Blend
Smokey Mesquite Seasoning
Spaghetti/Pasta Seasoning
Spicy Spaghetti Seasoning
Steak Seasoning

Tradiciones ()
Carne Adovada
Chimichurri
Green Mole
Guajillo Enchilada
Red Mole

Wagners ()
Wagners Hollandaise

Wegman's ⁄ ◉ ()
Herbes de Provence, 1 oz

Williams Foods ()
Oriental Classics Sweet & Sour Pork
Bag-N-Bake Chicken
Chili Makins
Chili with Onions
Chipotle Chili
Chipotle Taco
Country Store Chili Soup
Country Store Tortilla Soup
Original or Fancy Chili
Spaghetti
Taco
Tex-Mex Chili
Tex-Mex Taco - Hot
White Chicken Chili

Winn-Dixie ◉
Cinnamon Sugar
Curry Powder
Garlic Salt
Italian Seasoning
Onion Salt
Pumpkin Pie Spice

SPICES

B&G Foods
Capers

Durkee
California Style Blends - Garlic Powder
California Style Blends - Onion Powder

Eden Foods
Sea Salt - French Coast, UPC# 024182002003
Sea Salt - Portuguese Coast, UPC# 024182001990

Hy-Vee ⁄ ◉
Basil Leaf, 8.63 oz
Bay Leaves, 0.19 oz

Black Pepper, 4 oz
Chopped Onion, 6.25 oz
Dill Weed, 0.58 oz
Garlic Powder, 6.25 oz
Ground Cinnamon, 3.88 oz
Ground Cloves, 2 oz
Ground Mustard, 1.55 oz
Meat Tenderizer, 4 oz
Oregano Leaf, 0.56 oz
Paprika, 1.87 oz
Parsley Flakes, 1.13oz
Red Crushed Pepper, 1.27 oz
Rosemary, 1 oz
Thyme, 0.75 oz

Laura Lynn (Ingle's) ◉
Black Pepper, 4 oz

McNess
Black Pepper
Cinnamon
Garlic Grains
Minced Onion
Nutmeg

Midwest Country Fare (Hy-Vee) ⁄ ◉
Chopped Onion, 1.63 oz
Cinnamon, 2.38 oz
Garlic Powder, 2.5 oz
Garlic Salt, 4.25 oz
Ground Black Pepper, 4 oz
Ground Black Pepper, 2.15 oz
Onion Powder, 2.75 oz
Parsley Flakes, 0.38 oz

Morton Salt ☷
Coarse Kosher Salt
Iodized Salt
Lite Salt Mixture
Pickling & Canning Salt
Popcorn Salt
Salt & Pepper Shakers
Salt Substitute
Sea Salt
Seasoned Salt Substitute
Table Salt - Non-Iodized

No Salt Salt Substitute ◉
No Salt Salt Substitute

Polaner
Ready to Use Wet Spices - Basil
Ready to Use Wet Spices - Garlic
Ready to Use Wet Spices - Jalapenos

Select Brand (Safeway) ⁄ ◉
Capers

Baking Aisle

Spice Hunter ()
Spices, All

Spice Islands
Grilling Gourmet & World Flavors, All
Old Hickory Smoked Salt
Saffron
Salt-Free, All

Tone's, Durkee & Spice Islands
Allspice
Alum
Anise Seed
Basil
Bay Leaves
Caraway Seed
Cardamom
Cayenne Pepper
Celery Flakes
Celery Seed
Chives
Cilantro
Cinnamon
Cloves
Coriander
Cream of Tartar
Crushed Red Pepper
Cumin
Dill Seed/Weed
Fennel
Garlic Minced
Garlic Powder
Ginger
Hickory Smoke Salt
Mace
Marjoram
Meat Tenderizer
Mint Leaves
MSG
Mustard
Nutmeg
Onion - Minced
Onion Powder
Orange Peel
Oregano
Paprika
Parsley
Pepper - Black/White, All
Pepper - Green Bell
Poppy Seed
Rosemary
Sage
Sesame Seed
Tarragon

Thyme
Turmeric

Wegman's ⁄ ◉ ()
Cracked Pepper Blend, 2.9 oz
Fleur de Sel (Sea Salt), 3 oz
Lemon Pepper Seasoning, 3.2 oz
Pepper Black, 4 oz
Pepper Black, 2 oz

Winn-Dixie ◉
Basil Leaves
Caraway Seed
Cayenne Pepper
Celery Flakes
Celery Salt
Chives
Chopped Onion
Coarse Grind Black Pepper
Cream of Tartar
Crushed Red Pepper
Dill Seed
Dill Weed
Garlic & Parsley Salt
Garlic Pepper
Garlic Powder
Ground Allspice
Ground Black Pepper
Ground Cinnamon
Ground Cloves
Ground Coriander
Ground Cumin
Ground Ginger
Ground Mace
Ground Marjoram
Ground Nutmeg
Ground Red Pepper
Ground Sage
Ground Thyme
Meat Tenderizer
Minced Garlic
Minced Onion
Mustard Seed
Onion Powder
Oregano
Paprika
Parsley Flakes
Peppermill Black Pepper
Poppy Seed
Rosemary Leaves
Rubbed Sage
Salt & Pepper Twin Pack
Sesame Seed
Thyme Leaves

Baking Aisle

Turmeric
White Pepper
Whole Allspice
Whole Bay Leaves
Whole Black Pepper
Whole Celery Seed
Whole Cinnamon Sticks
Whole Cloves
Whole Nutmeg
Whole Oregano Leaves

SPRINKLES

Laura Lynn (Ingle's) 👁
Chocolate Sprinkles Toppings
Rainbow Sprinkles Toppings
Let's Do... ⚇
Carnival Sprinkelz
Chocolaty Sprinkelz
Confetti Sprinkelz
Safeway ⚡👁
Sprinkles - Easter, Halloween, Holiday, Sand Sugar
Party & Valentines

STARCHES

Argo
Corn Starch
Bob's Red Mill ⓘ ⚇
Arrowroot Starch, Item# 1030
Cornstarch, Item# 1146
Potato Starch, Item# 1444
Clabber Girl
Corn Starch
Eden Foods
Organic Kuzu Root Starch, UPC# 024182300116
Hy-Vee ⚡👁
Cornstarch, 16 oz
Kingsford
Corn Starch
Laura Lynn (Ingle's) 👁
Corn Starch, 16 oz
Let's Do...Organic ⚇
Tapioca Starch
Manischewitz
Potato Starch
Rumford
Corn Starch
Safeway ⚡👁
Corn Starch

Streit's
Potato Starch
Tone's, Durkee & Spice Islands
Arrowroot

SUGAR & SUGAR SUBSTITUTES

Alter Eco Fair Trade
Unrefined Sugar
Dixie Crystal
Dixie Crystals, All
Equal ()
Equal
Hy-Vee ⚡👁
Aspartame Sweetener, 3.52 oz
Confectioners Powdered Sugar, 32 oz
Dark Brown Sugar, 32 oz
Light Brown Sugar, 32 oz
Pure Cane Sugar, 4 lb
Pure Cane Sugar, 10 lb
Saccharin Sugar Substitute, 3.52oz
Imperial Sugar
Imperial Sugar, All
Ingles Markets 👁
Brown Sugar
Confectioner's Sugar
Sugar
Safeway ⚡👁
Aspartame Sweetener
Sugar - Brown, Granulated & Powdered
Splenda
Splenda Brand Sweetener Products, All
Stop & Shop ⚡👁
Granulated Sugar
Sucralose
Sweet Measure
Sweet 'N Low
Sweet'n Low
Wegman's ⚡👁 ()
Dark Brown Sugar, 2 lb bag
Granulated Sugar, 10 lb
Granulated White Sugar, 5 lb
Light Brown Sugar, 2 lb bag
Sugar Substitute with Saccharin, 250 packets
Sugar Substitute with Saccharin, 100 packets
Sweetener with Aspartame, 50 & 200 packets
Sweetener with Aspartame, 100 packets
Wholesome Sweeteners ⚇
Blends, All Types
Dark Muscovado Sugar

Baking Aisle

Demerara Sugar
Evaporated Cane Juice, All Types
Inverts
Light Muscovado Sugar
Organic Evaporated Cane Juice, All Types
Organic Sucanat, All Types
Organic Sucanat with Honey
Sucanat, All Types

Winn-Dixie ◉
Confectioners Sugar
Sugars

VANILLA EXTRACT & OTHER FLAVORINGS

Hy-Vee ✗ ◉
Imitation Vanilla, 6 oz

McNess
Almond Extract
Champion Vanilla
Ginger Extract
Lemon Extract
Lemon Flavor
Maple Flavor
Peppermint Extract
Pure Vanilla Extract
Uncolored Vanilla
Vanilla, Butter & Nut Flavor
Wonder Flavor

Midwest Country Fare (Hy-Vee) ✗ ◉
Imitation Vanilla Flavor, 6 oz

Rodelle
Gourmet Vanilla, 8 oz
Organic Pure Vanilla Extract, 4 oz
Pure Vanilla Extract, 8 oz
Pure Vanilla Extract, 4 oz
Pure Vanilla Paste, 4 oz
Vanilla Bean, 2 count
Vanilla Flavor Alcohol Free All Natural, 4 oz

Spice Islands
Vanilla Bean

Tone's, Durkee & Spice Islands
Liquid Extracts, All

Wegman's ✗ ◉ ()
Vanilla Extract, 2 oz

Wright's
Liquid Smoke - Hickory
Liquid Smoke - Mesquite

YEAST

Bakipan ⚇
Active Dry Yeast (ADY), 4 & 7 oz Jar
Active Dry Yeast (ADY), 3 - 7g Envelopes
Bread Machine Yeast, 4 oz Jar
Instant Yeast, 4 & 7 oz Jar
Instant Yeast, 3 - 7g Envelopes

Bob's Red Mill ⓘ ⚇
Yeast - Active Dry, Item# 1590
Yeast - Nutritional T6635 Lg Flake, Item# 1594

Fleischmann's Yeast
Yeasts, All

Hodgson Mill
Active Dry Yeast
Fast Rise Yeast

Red Star Yeast ⚇
Active Dry Yeast (ADY), 4 oz Jar
Active Dry Yeast (ADY), 3 - 7 g Envelopes
Bread Machine Yeast, 4 & 7 oz Jar
Nutritional Yeast Flakes - Vegetarian Support
  Formula
Quick Rise Yeast, 4 oz Jar
Quick Rise Yeast, 3 - 7 g Envelopes

SAF ⚇
Active Dry Yeast (ADY), 3 - 7 g Envelopes
Bread Machine Yeast, 4 oz Jar
Perfect Rise, 3 - 7 g Envelopes

MISCELLANEOUS

Bob's Red Mill ⓘ ⚇
Guar Gum, Item# 1598
Organic Textured Soy Protein, Item# 7023
Rice Bran, Item# 1464
Soy Lecithin, Item# 1280
Textured Vegetable Protein (TVP), Item# 1545
Xanthan Gum, Item# 1599

I.M. Healthy ⚇
Southern Homestyle Corn Crumbs

Let's Do…Organic ⚇
Tapioca Granules
Tapioca Pearls

Williams Foods ()
Williams Jel Ease - Pectin

Baking Aisle

CEREAL

BREAKFAST CEREALS

Barbara's Bakery ()
  Brown Rice Crisps
  Corn Flakes
  Honey Rice Puffins

Ener-G
  Ener-G, All BUT Low Protein Products

Enjoy Life Foods ☘
  Enjoy Life Foods, All

Envirokidz () ⓘ
  Amazon Frosted Flakes
  Gorilla Munch
  Koala Crisp
  Peanut Butter Panda Puffs

Erewhon
  Aztec
  Corn Flakes
  Crispy Brown Rice - Gluten Free
  Crispy Brown Rice with Mixed Berries
  Rice Twice

Gluten-Free Pantry, The
  Gluten-Free Pantry, The, All

Glutino
  Glutino, All

Lydia's Organics ☘
  Lydia's Organics, All

Malt-O-Meal 👁
  Fruity Dyno-Bites

Nature's Path () ⓘ
  Crispy Rice
  Fruit Juice Cornflakes
  Honey'D Cornflakes
  Mesa Sunrise Flakes

New Morning
  Cocoa Crispy Rice

OrgraN
  Orgran, All

Perky's
  Cereals, All

Safeway ⚡ 👁
  Cocoa Astros Cereal ()
  Fruity Nuggets Cereal ()
  Puffed Corn Cereal ()

Wegman's ⚡ 👁 ()
  Fruity Rice Crisps, 13 oz
  Organic Strawberry Corn Flakes, 10.6 oz

Winn-Dixie 👁
  Corn Puffs
  Fruity Nuggets Cereal

HOT CEREALS

Bob's Red Mill ⓘ ☘
  Brown Rice Farina, Item# 1463
  GF Mighty Tasty Hot Cereal, Item# 1187
  Organic Brown Rice Farina, Item# 6071
  Organic Creamy Buckwheat Cereal, Item# 1095
  Soy Grits, Item# 1519

Erewhon
  Brown Rice Cream

Lundberg Family Farms
  Hot Cereal - Purely Organic

OrgraN
  Orgran, All

Winn-Dixie 👁
  Butter or Plain Grits
  Instant Grits - Butter & Original

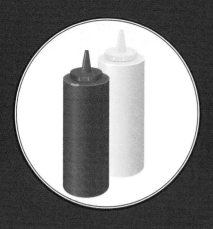

CONDIMENTS, SAUCES & DRESSINGS

BARBEQUE SAUCE

Annie's Naturals ()
Organic BBQ Sauce - Original
Organic BBQ Sauce - Spicy

Bone Suckin' Sauce 🏅
Bone Suckin' Sauce - Hiccuppin' Hot
Bone Suckin' Sauce - Hot
Bone Suckin' Sauce - Hot Thicker Style
Bone Suckin' Sauce - Regular
Bone Suckin' Sauce - Thicker Style

Cattlemen's Barbecue 👁
Cattlemen's Barbecue Sauces, All BUT Honey Flavor

Daniel's Bar-B-Q
Daniel's Bar-B-Q, All

Dynasty
Chinese-Style Barbecue Sauce, #09636

Gold's
BBQ Sauce, All

Homestyle Meals
Original BBQ Sauce, Item# 00950 - 15 oz
Smoked Chipotle BBQ Sauce, Item# 00951 - 15 oz

Hy-Vee ✗ 👁
Hickory BBQ Sauce, 18 oz
Honey Smoke BBQ Sauce, 18 oz
Original BBQ Sauce, 18 oz

K.C. Masterpiece
Classic Blend BBQ Sauce

Midwest Country Fare (Hy-Vee) ✗ 👁
Hickory BBQ Sauce, 18 oz
Honey BBQ Sauce, 18 oz
Original BBQ Sauce, 18 oz

Select Brand (Safeway) ✗ 👁
Hickory Smoked BBQ Sauce
Honey Mustard BBQ Sauce
Honey Smoked BBQ Sauce
Original BBQ Sauce

Stop & Shop ✗ 👁
BBQ Sauce - Original & Hickory Smoke

Wegman's ✗ 👁 ()
Memphis Style BBQ Sauce, 19 oz
Tropical BBQ Sauce, 19 oz

Winn-Dixie 👁
BBQ Sauce

COCKTAIL SAUCE

Cains
Seafood Cocktail Sauce FS

Captains Choice (Safeway) ✗ 👁
Cocktail Sauce

Gold's
Cocktail Sauce, All

Hy-Vee ✗ 👁
Cocktail Sauce for Seafood, 12 oz

Laura Lynn (Ingle's) 👁
Cocktail Sauce, 12 oz

Safeway ✗ 👁
Cocktail Sauce

Stop & Shop ✗ 👁
Seafood Cocktail Sauce

FRUIT BUTTERS & CURDS

Eden Foods
Apple Butter, UPC# 024182000696
Apple Cherry Butter, UPC# 024182000740
Cherry Butter, UPC# 024182000788

Fischer & Wieser
Texas Pecan Apple Butter
Texas Pecan Peach Butter

Knouse Foods (See Section 3 for Knouse Brands)
Apple Butter

Manischewitz
Apple Butter Spreads

Robert Rothschild Farm
  Apricot Pumpkin Butter
  Brandied Blackberry Butter
  Cinnamon Cranberry Butter
  Cinnamon Peach Butter
  Key Lime Curd Sauce
  Lemon Curd
  Pumpkin Curd

GRAVY & GRAVY MIXES

Streit's
  Gravy Mix

HORSERADISH

Boar's Head 👁 ⓘ
  Condiments, All
Di Lusso 🔆 👁
  Horseradish Sauce
Eden Foods
  Wasabi Powder, UPC# 024182002188
Gold's
  Horseradish, All
Manischewitz
  Horseradish, All
Robert Rothschild Farm
  Horseradish Sauce
  Raspberry Cranberry Horseradish Sauce
Terrapin Ridge
  Cranberry Horseradish Squeeze
Wegman's ✔ 👁 ()
  Horseradish Cream Sauce, 8 oz
  Prepared Horseradish, 8.5 oz

HOT SAUCE

Butcher's Cut (Safeway) ✔ 👁
  Jazz N Spicy Buffalo Wing Sauce
Cholula Hot Sauce
  Cholula, All
Di Lusso 🔆 👁
  Buffalo Wing Sauce
Emeril's
  Kick It Up Green Pepper Sauce
  Kick It Up Red Pepper Sauce
  Wing Sauce
Frank's RedHot 👁
  Frank's Original RedHot Sauce
  Frank's RedHot Buffalo Wing Sauce
  Frank's RedHot Chile 'n Lime Hot Sauce

  Frank's Xtra RedHot Sauce
Gillian's Foods
  Gillian's Foods, All
Hy-Vee ✔ 👁
  Chili Sauce, 12 oz
Laura Lynn (Ingle's) 👁
  Chili Sauce, 12 oz
Louisiana Gold Pepper Sauce 👁
  Louisiana Gold Pepper Sauce, 02333 - 2 oz
Louisiana Hot Sauce 👁
  Louisiana Hot Sauce, 02147 - 1.25 oz
Moore's Marinades ⚥
  Buffalo Wing Sauce
Nance's Mustards & Condiments
  Chili Sauce
  Mild & Hot Wing Sauces
Stop & Shop ✔ 👁
  Chili Sauce
Tabasco ⚥
  Tabasco Brand Pepper Sauces, All
Taste of Thai, A
  Sweet Red Chili Sauce
Texas Pete
  Buffalo Chicken Wing Sauce
  Hot Sauce
  Pepper Sauce
Thai Kitchen
  Roasted Red Chili Paste
  Spicy Thai Chili Sauce
  Sweet Red Chili Sauce
Trappey
  Hot Sauces
Wegman's ✔ 👁 ()
  Chili Sauce, 12 oz
Wizard's, The ⚥
  Organic Hot Stuff

ICE CREAM & DESSERT SAUCES

Eden Foods
  Apple Cherry Sauce, UPC# 024182000603
  Apple Cherry Sauce - Single Serve, UPC#
    024182000566
  Apple Cinnamon Sauce - Single Serve, UPC#
    024182000542
  Apple Strawberry Sauce, UPC# 024182000573
  Apple Strawberry Sauce (Single Serve), UPC#
    024182000559
Fischer & Wieser
  Fredericksburg Peach Dessert Sauce

Condiments, Sauces & Dressings

Hill County Strawberry Dessert Sauce

Hy-Vee ✔ 👁
Strawberry Syrup, 22 oz

Litehouse
Blueberry Dessert Glaze
Peach Dessert Glaze
Strawberry Dessert Glaze
Sugar Free Strawberry Dessert Glaze

Mrs. Richardson's Toppings
Mrs. Richardson's Toppings, All

Robert Rothschild Farm
Butter Rum Dessert Sauce & Dip
Cherry Almond Gourmet Sauce
Cinnamon Bun Caramel Dessert Sauce & Dip
Old Fashioned Caramel Sauce
Old Fashioned Hot Fudge Sauce
Red Raspberry Gourmet Sauce

Terrapin Ridge
Coconut Lime Dessert Squeeze
Passion Vanilla Dessert Squeeze
Red Raspberry Dessert Squeeze
Two Cherry Dessert Squeeze

Wegman's ✔ 👁 ()
Creamy Caramel Dessert Sauce, 11 oz
Milk Chocolate Dessert Sauce, 10 oz
Mint Chocolate Dessert Sauce, 10 oz
Raspberry Chocolate Dessert Sauce, 10 oz
Triple Chocolate Dessert Sauce, 10 oz

JAMS, JELLIES & PRESERVES

Crofter's Food
Jam, All

Crosby's Molasses
Jelly Mix, All

Deep South (Winn-Dixie) 👁
Jams
Jellies
Marmalades
Preserves

Fischer & Wieser
Apricot Orange Marmalade
Brazos Blackberry Jam
Cinnamon-Orange Tomato Preserves
Old Fashioned Peach Preserves
Raspberry Apricot Pecan Preserves
Rhubarb Strawberry Preserves
Texas Amaretto Peach Pecan Preserves
Whole Lemon Fig Marmalade
Wilde Berry Preserves

Garner
Jams, Jellies & Preserves

Ingles Markets 👁
Apple Jelly
Apricot Preserves
Grape Jam
Grape Jelly
Orange Marmalade
Peach Preserves
Peanut Butter & Grape Jelly Spread
Peanut Butter & Strawberry Jelly Spread
Red Raspberry Preserves
Strawberry Preserves

Knouse Foods (See Section 3 for Knouse Brands)
Fruit Spread

Nature's Promise (Stop & Shop) ✔ 👁
Organic Grape Jelly
Organic Raspberry Fruit Spread
Organic Strawberry Fruit Spread

Polaner
All Fruit - Sugar Free Jams
All Fruit - Sugar Free Jellies
All Fruit - Sugar Free Preserves

Robert Rothschild Farm
Hot Pepper Berry Patch Preserves
Hot Pepper Peach Preserves
Hot Pepper Raspberry Preserves
Jalapeno & Ancho Chili Pepper Jam
Peach Pie Jam
Red Pepper Jelly
Red Raspberry Preserves
Seedless Raspberry Preserves
Strawberry Rhubarb Preserves
Triple Berry Preserves
Wild Maine Blueberry Preserves

Safeway ✔ 👁
Jams
Jellies

Select Brand (Safeway) ✔ 👁
Jams
Jellies

Simply Enjoy (Stop & Shop) ✔ 👁
Balsamic Sweet Onion Preserves
Blueberry Preserves
Raspberry Champagne Peach Preserves
Red Pepper Jelly
Roasted Garlic & Onion Jam
Spiced Apple Preserves
Strawberry Preserves

Condiments, Sauces & Dressings

Stop & Shop ✔ ◉
Apple Jelly
Apricot Preserves
Apricot Spread
Blueberry Spread
Concord Grape Jelly (Squeezable & Spreadable)
Currant Jelly
Grape Preserves
Mint Jelly
Orange Marmalade
Peach Preserves
Pineapple Preserves
Red Raspberry Preserves
Seedless Blackberry Preserves
Strawberry Preserves
Strawberry Spread
Sugar Free Preserves - Apricot, Red Raspberry, Blackberry & Strawberry

Wegman's ✔ ◉ ()
Apple Jelly, 12 oz
Apricot Preserves, 18 oz
Apricot, Peach & Passion Fruit Spread, 20 oz
Blackberry (Seedless) Preserves, 12 oz
Blackberry Jelly, 12 oz
Blueberry, Cherry & Raspberry Fruit Spread, 20 oz
Cherry Jelly, 12 oz
Cherry Preserves, 12 oz
Grape Jelly, 32 oz
Grape Jelly, 18 oz
Grape Preserves, 18 oz
Just Fruit Apricot Spread, 10 oz
Just Fruit Blueberry Spread, 10 oz
Just Fruit Red Raspberry Spread, 10 oz
Just Fruit Strawberry Spread, 10 oz
Mint Apple Jelly, 12 oz
Orange Marmalade, 18 oz
Peach Preserves, 18 oz
Pineapple Preserves, 12 oz
Raspberry, Strawberry & Blackberry Fruit Spread, 20 oz
Raspberry, Wild Blueberry & Blackberry Fruit Spread, 20 oz
Red Currant Jelly, 12 oz
Red Raspberry Jelly, 12 oz
Red Raspberry Preserves, 32 oz
Red Raspberry Preserves, 18 oz
Strawberry Jelly, 12 oz
Strawberry Preserves, 18 & 32 oz
Strawberry Preserves, 12 oz
Strawberry, Plum & Raspberry Fruit Spread, 20 oz
Sugar Free Fruit Spread - Apricot, Peach & Passion Fruit, 14 oz
Sugar Free Fruit Spread - Raspberry, Wild Blueberry & Blackberry, 14 oz
Sugar Free Fruit Spread - Strawberry, Plum & Raspberry, 14 oz

Welch's ⓘ
Welch's, All

Winn-Dixie ◉
Jellies
Preserves

KETCHUP

Del Monte ✔ ◉
Tomatoes & Tomato Products, All BUT Del Monte Spaghetti Sauce Flavored with Meat

Food You Feel Good About (Wegman's) ✔ ◉ ()
Organic Tomato Ketchup, 24 oz

Heinz ☼
Hot & Spicy Kick'rs
Ketchup, All
No Sodium Added Ketchup
One Carb Ketchup
Organic Ketchup

Hy-Vee ✔ ◉
Ketchup, 64 oz
Squeezable Ketchup, 24, 36 & 46 oz
Squeezable Ketchup, 20 oz

Manischewitz
Ketchup

Midwest Country Fare (Hy-Vee) ✔ ◉
Ketchup, 24 & 36 oz

Red Gold ⓘ
Ketchup, All

Redpack ⓘ
Ketchup, All

Safeway ✔ ◉
Ketchup

Streit's
Ketchup

Terrapin Ridge
Smoked Apple Catsup

Winn-Dixie ◉
Ketchup

MARASCHINO CHERRIES

Hy-Vee ✔ ◉
Green Maraschino Cherries, 6 oz
Red Maraschino Cherries, 6 oz
Red Maraschino Cherries, 10 oz

Condiments, Sauces & Dressings

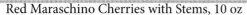

Red Maraschino Cherries with Stems, 10 oz

Midwest Country Fare (Hy-Vee) ✗ ◉

Maraschino Cherries, 10 oz

Safeway ✗ ◉

Maraschino Cherries

Thrifty Maid ◉

Maraschino Cherries

Wegman's ✗ ◉ ()

Jumbo Maraschino Cherries without Stems, 12 oz
Maraschino Cherries with Stems, 16 oz
Maraschino Cherries without Stems, 16 oz
Maraschino Cherries without Stems, 10 oz

MARINADES & COOKING SAUCES

Annie's Naturals ()

Baja Lime Marinade
Lemon Pepper Marinade
Roasted Garlic & Balsamic Marinade
Southwestern with Smoked Chipotles Marinade
Tropical Grill Marinade

Di Lusso 🌱 ◉

Sweet Onion Sauce

Emeril's

Herbed Lemon Pepper Marinade
Hickory Maple Chipotle Marinade & Grilling Sauce
Lemon Rosemary & Gaaahlic Marinade
Orange Herb with Poppy Seed Marinade
Roasted Vegetable Marinade

Fischer & Wieser

Mango Ginger Habanero Sauce
Original Roasted Raspberry Chipotle Sauce, The
Papaya Lime Serrano Sauce
Texas 1015 Onion Glaze

Hy-Vee ✗ ◉

Citrus Grill Marinade, 12 fl oz
Herb & Garlic Marinade, 12 fl oz
Lemon Pepper Marinade, 12 fl oz
Mesquite Marinade, 12 fl oz

Italian Classics (Wegman's) ✗ ◉ ()

Lemon & Caper Sauce, 11 oz
Mushroom Marsala Sauce, 11 oz

Jack Daniel's EZ Marinader 🌱

Garlic & Herb Variety

Moore's Marinades 🎖

Original Marinade

Olde Cape Cod

Cranberry Grilling Sauce
Honey Orange Grilling Sauce
Lemon Ginger Grilling Sauce

Sweet & Sour Grilling Sauce (Sweet & Bold)

Robert Rothschild Farm

Anna Mae's Sweet Smoky Chipotle Oven & Grill
Sauce
Anna Mae's Sweet Smoky Oven & Grill Sauce
Apricot Ginger Oven & Grill Sauce
Apricot Mango Wasabi Sauce
Asian Sesame Oven & Grill Sauce
Blackberry Chipotle Oven & Grill Sauce
Ginger Wasabi Sauce
Hot Pepper Raspberry Chipotle Sauce
Lemon Dill & Capers Sauce
Lemon Dill Sauce
Lemon Wasabi Sauce
Mushroom Trio Simmer Sauce & Marinade
Raspberry Pineapple Oven & Grill Sauce
Raspberry Seafood Sauce

Terrapin Ridge

Apple Dill & Rosemary Sauce
Balsamic Green Peppercorn Sauce
Curry Mint Marinade
Moroccan Spice Pomegranate Marinade
Orange Mango with Lemongrass Sauce
Raspberry Honey & Lime Marinade

Wegman's ✗ ◉ ()

Chicken BBQ Marinade, 16 fl oz
Citrus Dill Marinade, 16 fl oz
Fajita Marinade, 16 fl oz
Greek Marinade, 16 fl oz
Honey Mustard Marinade, 16 fl oz
Lemon & Garlic Marinade, 16 fl oz
Rosemary Balsamic Marinade, 16 fl oz
Spiedie Marinade, 16 fl oz
Steakhouse Peppercorn Marinade, 16 fl oz
Sweet & Sour Sauce, 12 fl oz
Tangy Marinade, 16 fl oz
Zesty Savory Marinade, 16 fl oz
Zesty Thai Marinade, 16 fl oz

Winn-Dixie ◉

Hollandaise Sauce
Meat Marinade

MAYONNAISE

Cains

All Natural Mayonnaise
Fat Free Mayonnaise Dressing
Light Reduced Calorie Mayonnaise
Reduced Fat Mayonnaise Dressing

Enlighten (Safeway) ✗ ◉

Mayonnaise

Condiments, Sauces & Dressings

DON'T SEE YOUR FAVORITE BRAND? LOOK IT UP IN SECTION 3!

French's 👁
Gourmayo - Creamy Dijon
Gourmayo - Sun Dried Tomato
Gourmayo - Wasabi Horseradish

Hellmann's 👁
Mayonnaise Products & Spreads, All

Hy-Vee 🖊 👁
Mayonnaise, 32 oz
Squeezable Mayonnaise, 18 fl oz

Laura Lynn (Ingle's) 👁
Fat Free Mayonnaise, 32 oz
Mayonnaise, 16 oz

Manischewitz
Mayonnaise

Nasoya
Dijon Nayonaise, UPC# 2548400039
Fat Free Nayonaise, UPC# 2548400043
Nayonaise, UPC# 2548400041
Nayonaise, UPC# 2548400040

Select Brand (Safeway) 🖊 👁
Mayonnaise - Fat Free Distilled with Wood, Reduced Fat & Regular

Streit's
Mayonnaise

Vegenaise
Expeller
Grapeseed
Organic
Original

Wegman's 🖊 👁 ()
Classic Mayonnaise, 32 & 48 fl oz
Mayonnaise, 16 fl oz

Winn-Dixie 👁
Lite Mayonnaise
Mayonnaise

MUSTARD

Boar's Head 👁 ⓘ
Condiments, All

Bone Suckin' Sauce ⚱
Bone Suckin' Mustard

Di Lusso 🍴 👁
Chipotle Mustard
Cranberry Honey Mustard
Deli Style Mustard
Dijon Mustard
Honey Mustard
Jalapeno Mustard

Eden Foods
Brown Mustard (Squeeze Bottle), UPC# 024182002089
Organic Brown Mustard, UPC# 024182002195
Organic Brown Mustard, UPC# 024182002126
Organic Yellow Mustard (Squeeze Bottle), UPC# 024182002119
Yellow Mustard - Organic, UPC# 024182002102

Emeril's
Dijon Mustard
Kicked Up Horseradish Mustard
NY Deli Style Mustard
Smooth Honey Mustard

Food You Feel Good About (Wegman's) 🖊 👁 ()
Spicy Brown Mustard, 12 oz

French's 👁
Honey Mustard
Prepared Mustards

Gold's
Mustard, All

Hy-Vee 🖊 👁
Dijon Mustard, 12 oz
Honey Mustard, 12 oz
Mustard, 9 & 24 oz
Mustard, 16 oz
Spicy Brown Mustard, 12 oz

Laura Lynn (Ingle's) 👁
Mustards

McNess
Dusseldorf Mustard

Midwest Country Fare (Hy-Vee) 🖊 👁
Mustard, 16 oz

Olde Cape Cod
Mustards

Robert Rothschild Farm
Anna Mae's Smoky Mustard
Apricot Ginger Mustard
Champagne Garlic Mustard
Horseradish Mustard
Raspberry Honey Mustard
Raspberry Wasabi Mustard

Safeway 🖊 👁
Mustard - including Stone Ground Horseradish

Select Brand (Safeway) 🖊 👁
Mustard - Classic/Country Dijon, Spicy Brown & Stone Ground Horseradish

Stop & Shop 🖊 👁
Creamy Dijon Mustard
Deli Mustard
Dijon Mustard

Condiments, Sauces & Dressings

Honey Mustard
Old Grainy Mustard
Raspberry Grainy Mustard
Spicy Brown Mustard
Tarragon Dijon Mustard
Yellow Mustard

Terrapin Ridge
Balsamic Herb Mustard
Cracked Pepper, Lemon & Thyme Mustard
Natural Wasabi Mustard
Orange Cranberry Mustard
Pipin' Hot Pepper Mustard
Sweet Beet Horseradish Mustard
Wasabi Lime Mustard

Texas Pete
Honey Mustard Sauce (Ensure Best By 11/06 and
    Later)

Wegman's ⚡ ◉ ()
Classic Yellow Mustard, 9 & 16 oz
Dijon - Whole Grain Mustard, 9.2 oz
Dijon Traditional Mustard, 9.2 oz
Honey Mustard, 16 oz
Horseradish Mustard, 9 oz
Mustard Sauce, 8 oz

Winn-Dixie ◉
Yellow Mustard

OLIVES

B&G Foods
Black Olives
Green Olives

Di Lusso ♨ ◉
Green Ionian Olives
Mediterranean Mixed Olives

Hy-Vee ⚡ ◉
Chopped Ripe Olives, 4.25 oz
Large Ripe Black Olives, 6 oz
Manzanilla Olives, 5.75 oz
Manzanilla Olives, 21 oz
Medium Ripe Black Olives, 6 oz
Queen Olives, 7 oz
Sliced Ripe Black Olives, 3.8 oz
Sliced Ripe Black Olives, 2.25 oz
Sliced Salad Olives, 10 oz

Ingles Markets ◉
Olives - Green & Ripe, All

Mediterranean Organic
Mediterranean Organics, All

Midwest Country Fare (Hy-Vee) ⚡ ◉
Large Ripe Black Olives, 6 oz

Sliced Ripe Black Olives, 2.25 oz

Peloponnese ♨ ◉
Kalamata Olives

Safeway ⚡ ◉
Black Olives
Manzanilla Olives

Stop & Shop ⚡ ◉
Manzanilla Olives - Stuffed & Sliced
Pitted Black Ripe Olives - Jumbo, Large, Medium &
    Small: Chopped, Whole & Sliced
Stuffed Queen Olives

Wegman's ⚡ ◉ ()
Manzanilla with Pimento, 5.75, 7, 10 & 21 oz
Pitted Ripe Olives - Colossal, 5.75 oz
Pitted Ripe Olives - Medium, 6 oz
Queen Stuffed Olives, 7 fl oz
Ripe Olives - Sliced, 2.25 oz
Ripe Olives - X-Large, 6 oz
Salad Olives, 10 oz
Spanish Salad Olives - Sliced, 5.75 oz

Winn-Dixie ◉
Olives

PANCAKE & MAPLE SYRUP

Aunt Jemima
Syrups

Eggo
Kellogg's Eggo Syrup

Food You Feel Good About (Wegman's) ⚡ ◉ ()
Pure Maple Syrup - Club Pack, 64 fl oz
Pure Maple Syrup - Dark Amber, 32 fl oz
Pure Maple Syrup - Dark Amber, 12.5 fl oz

Grand Selections (Hy-Vee) ⚡ ◉
100% Pure Maple Syrup, 8 oz

Hy-Vee ⚡ ◉
Butter Flavor Syrup, 24 oz
Lite Pancake Syrup, 36 oz
Lite Syrup, 36 fl oz
Lite Syrup, 24 fl oz
Pancake & Waffle Syrup, 36 fl oz
Pancake & Waffle Syrup, 24 fl oz
Pancake Syrup, 36 oz

Laura Lynn (Ingle's) ◉
Butter Pancake & Waffle Syrup, 24 oz
Lite Pancake & Waffle Syrup, 24 oz
Pancake & Waffle Syrup, 24 & 32 oz
Pancake & Waffle Syrup, 12 oz

Log Cabin () ◉
Country Kitchen Syrup

Condiments, Sauces & Dressings

Manischewitz
Pancake Syrup

Michele's
Michele's, All

Midwest Country Fare (Hy-Vee) ✗ ◉
Pancake & Waffle Syrup, 24 oz

Robert Rothschild Farm
Maple Praline Syrup
Raspberry Syrup
Roasted Pecan Syrup

Safeway ✗ ◉
Syrup - Butter Light, Light, Old Fashioned & Original and Pure Maple

Select Brand (Safeway) ✗ ◉
Pure Maple Syrup, All

Vermont Maid
Syrup - Sugar Free
Syrup - Sugar Free Butter

Wegman's ✗ ◉ ()
Light Reduced Calorie Pancake Syrup - Buttery Flavor, 24 fl oz
Maple Syrup - Organic, 12 fl oz
Maraschino Cherry Flavored Syrup, 12.7 fl oz
Pancake Lite Syrup, 12 fl oz
Pancake Syrup - Buttery Flavor, 24 fl oz
Pancake Syrup Made with 2% Real Maple Syrup, 12 fl oz
Pancake Syrup Made with 2% Real Maple Syrup (Club Pack), 64 fl oz
Pancake Syrup with 2% Real Maple Syrup, 24 fl oz

Wholesome Sweeteners ⚇
Organic Pancake & Waffle Syrup

Winn-Dixie ◉
Lite Syrup
Syrup

PASTA & PIZZA SAUCE

Amy's Kitchen ()
Family Marinara Pasta Sauce
Family Marinara Pasta Sauce - Light in Sodium
Garlic Mushroom Pasta Sauce
Puttanesca Sauce
Roasted Garlic Pasta Sauce
Tomato Basil Pasta Sauce

Classico ☖
Pasta Sauces, All

Contadina ✗ ◉
Tomatoes & Tomato Products, All BUT Contadina Tomato Paste with Italian Herbs

Del Monte ✗ ◉
Tomatoes & Tomato Products, All BUT Del Monte Spaghetti Sauce Flavored with Meat

Eden Foods
Pizza Pasta Sauce, UPC# 024182001174
Spaghetti Sauce, UPC# 024182001143
Spaghetti Sauce - No Salt Added, UPC# 024182001150

Emeril's
Home Style Marinara Pasta Sauce
Kicked Up Tomato Pasta Sauce
Mushroom & Onion Pasta Sauce
Puttanesca Pasta Sauce
Roasted Gaahlic Pasta Sauce
Roasted Red Pepper Pasta Sauce
Sicilian Gravy Pasta Sauce
Vodka Pasta Sauce

Food You Feel Good About (Wegman's) ✗ ◉ ()
Chunky Marinara Pasta Sauce, 26 oz
Chunky Pizza Sauce, 14 oz
Four Cheese, 26 oz
Garden Vegetable Pasta Sauce - Grilled Flavor, 26 oz
Onion & Mushroom Pasta Sauce - Grilled Flavor, 26 oz
Roasted Garlic Pasta Sauce, 26 oz
Smooth Marinara, 26 oz
Tomato & Basil, 26 oz

Gillian's Foods
Gillian's Foods, All

Health Market (Hy-Vee) ✗ ◉
Tomato Basil Sauce, 25 oz

Hy-Vee ✗ ◉
3 Cheese Spaghetti Sauce, 26 oz
Mushroom Spaghetti Sauce, 26 oz
Pizza Sauce, 15 oz
Spaghetti Sauce with Meat, 26 oz
Traditional Spaghetti Sauce, 26 oz

Italian Classics (Wegman's) ✗ ◉ ()
Bolognese Sauce, 17 oz
Diavolo Sauce, 26 oz
Sun Ripened Dried Tomato, 26 oz
Tomato with Italian Sausage, 26 oz
Vodka Sauce, 16.5 oz
White Clam Sauce, 10.5 oz

Manischewitz
Pasta Sauce, All
Tomato & Mushroom Sauce

Mom's
Pasta Sauces, All

Condiments, Sauces & Dressings

Nature's Promise (Stop & Shop) ✎ 👁
   Organic Pasta Sauce - Garden Vegetable & Parmesan
   and Plain
Newman's Own ✎
   Bombolina (Basil)
   Cabernet Marinara
   Diavolo (Spicy Simmer Sauce)
   Five Cheese
   Marinara (Venetian)
   Marinara with Mushrooms
   Pesto & Tomato
   Roasted Garlic & Peppers
   Sockarooni - Mushrooms, Onions & Peppers
   Sweet Onion & Roasted Garlic
   Tomato & Roasted Garlic
   Vodka Sauce
Prego 👁
   Mushroom, 4 lb 3 oz
   Organic Sauces, All
   Three Cheese Sauce, 26 oz
   Traditional Sauce, All Sizes
Robert Rothschild Farm
   Artichoke Pasta Sauce
   Roasted Portabella & Roma Tomato Pasta Sauce
   Vodka Pasta Sauce
Safeway ✎ 👁
   Meat Spaghetti Sauce
   Mushroom Spaghetti Sauce
   Traditional Spaghetti Sauce
Select Brand (Safeway) ✎ 👁
   Classic Pesto Refrigerated Pasta Sauce
   Creamy Parmesan Basil Refrigerated Pasta Sauce
   Garden Vegetable & Herb Refrigerated Pasta Sauce
   Light Alfredo Refrigerated Pasta Sauce
   Mushroom/Onion Refrigerated Pasta Sauce
   Roasted Garlic & Mushroom Refrigerated Pasta
   Sauce
Simply Enjoy (Stop & Shop) ✎ 👁
   Fra Diavolo Sauce
   Marinara Sauce
   Roasted Garlic Sauce
   Sicilian Eggplant Sauce
   Tomato Basil Sauce
   Vodka Sauce
Thrifty Maid 👁
   Garlic & Herb Spaghetti Sauce
   Mushroom Spaghetti Sauce
   Traditional Spaghetti Sauce
Timpone's Organic
   Pasta Sauces, All

Tuttorosso ⓘ
   Tuttorosso, All
Wegman's ✎ 👁 ()
   Marinara Pasta Sauce - Organic, 25 oz
   Roasted Garlic Pasta Sauce - Organic, 25 oz
   Tomato Basil Pasta Sauce - Organic, 25 oz
Winn-Dixie 👁
   Classic Style Home-Style Pasta Sauce
   Classic Style Marinara Sauce Fine Pasta
   Classic Style Tomato Basil Fine Pasta Sauce
   Fat Free Fine Pasta Sauce
   FraDiavolo Fine Pasta Sauce
   Peppers & Onions Fine Pasta Sauce
   Pizza Sauce
   Select Recipe Double Garlic Pasta Sauce
   Select Recipe Fine Diablo Pasta Sauce
   Spaghetti Sauce with Mushroom
   Spaghetti Thick & Zesty Sauce
   Vodka Cream Fine Pasta Sauce

PEANUT & OTHER NUT BUTTERS

Fisher Nuts
   Peanut Butter - Chunky & Creamy
Food You Feel Good About (Wegman's) ✎ 👁 ()
   Natural Peanut Butter - Creamy, 16 oz
   Natural Peanut Butter - Crunchy, 16 oz
Hy-Vee ✎ 👁
   Creamy Peanut Butter, 28 & 40 oz
   Creamy Peanut Butter, 18 oz
   Crunchy Peanut Butter, 28 & 40 oz
   Crunchy Peanut Butter, 18 oz
   Reduced Fat Peanut Butter, 18 oz
I.M. Healthy ⚇
   Soynut Butter, All
MaraNatha Natural & Organic Nut Butters
   MaraNatha Natural & Organic Nut Butters, All
Midwest Country Fare (Hy-Vee) ✎ 👁
   Creamy Peanut Butter, 40 oz
   Creamy Peanut Butter, 18 oz
   Crunchy Peanut Butter, 40 oz
   Crunchy Peanut Butter, 18 oz
Nature's Promise (Stop & Shop) ✎ 👁
   Cashew Butter
   Organic Almond Butter - Smooth & Unsalted
   Organic Peanut Butter, All
Safeway ✎ 👁
   Peanut Butter - Regular & Reduced Fat Creamy and
   Crunchy
Simple Food
   Organic Soynut Butters, All

Condiments, Sauces & Dressings

Stop & Shop ⋏ ◉
All Natural Smooth Peanut Butter - Regular, No Added Salt & Reduced Fat
Peanut Butter - Crunchy, Creamy & Smooth

Wegman's ⋏ ◉ ()
Creamy Peanut Butter, 28 oz
Creamy Peanut Butter, 18 oz
Creamy Peanut Butter (Club Pack), 64 oz
Creamy Peanut Spread - Reduced Fat, 18 oz
Crunchy Peanut Butter, 28 oz
Crunchy Peanut Butter, 18 oz
Organic Natural Creamy Peanut Butter with Peanut Skins, 16 oz
Organic Natural Crunchy Peanut Butter with Peanut Skins, 16 oz

Winn-Dixie ◉
Crunchy Peanut Butter
Smooth Peanut Butter

PEPPERS

B&G Foods
Peppers
Bruce Foods ◉
Nacho Sliced Jalapeños, 08732 - 8 oz
Cara Mia
Piquillo Peppers (Strips)
Piquillo Peppers (Whole)
Casa Fiesta ◉
Whole Green Chilies, 08706 - 26 oz
Di Lusso ☼ ◉
Roasted Red Peppers
Hy-Vee ⋏ ◉
Whole Green Chilies, 4 oz
Peloponnese ☼ ◉
Roasted Sweet Peppers
Trappey
Peppers
Vlasic () ◉
Peppers
Winn-Dixie ◉
Banana Pepper Rings - Hot & Mild
Jalapenos

PICKLES

B&G Foods
Pickles
Hy-Vee ⋏ ◉
Bread & Butter Sandwich Slices, 16 fl oz

Bread & Butter Sweet Chunk Pickles, 24 fl oz
Bread & Butter Sweet Slices, 24 fl oz
Bread & Butter Sweet Slices, 16 fl oz
Dill Kosher Sandwich Slices, 16 fl oz
Fresh Pack Kosher Baby Dills, 32 fl oz
Hamburger Dill Slices, 32 & 46 fl oz
Hamburger Dill Slices, 16 fl oz
Kosher Baby Dills, 16 fl oz
Kosher Cocktail Dills, 24 fl oz
Kosher Dill Pickles, 32 fl oz
Kosher Dill Spears, 24 fl oz
Polish Dill Pickles, 32 fl oz
Polish Dill Spears, 24 fl oz
Refrigerated Kosher Dill Halves, 32 oz
Refrigerated Kosher Dill Sandwich Slices, 32 oz
Refrigerated Kosher Dill Spears, 24 oz
Refrigerated Kosher Dill Whole Pickles, 32 oz
Special Recipe Baby Dills, 24 fl oz
Sweet Gherkins, 16 fl oz
Whole Dill Pickles, 46 fl oz
Whole Sweet Pickles, 16 fl oz
Zesty Kosher Dill Spears, 24 fl oz
Zesty Sweet Chunks, 24 fl oz

Ingles Markets ◉
Pickles, All
Midwest Country Fare (Hy-Vee) ⋏ ◉
Dill Pickles, 32 oz
Hamburger Dill Pickle Slices, 32 oz
Kosher Dill Pickles, 32 oz
Whole Sweet Pickles, 16 oz
Mt. Olive Pickle Company ⓘ
Mount Olive Pickle Company, All (Ensure "Best If Used by Date" of July 2008 or later for: 12 oz Hot Dog Relish, 16 oz No Sugar Added Sweet Gherkins & 16 oz Sweet India Relish)
Safeway ⋏ ◉
Pickles, All
Vlasic () ◉
Pickles
Wegman's ⋏ ◉ ()
Fresh Pack Polish Dill Spears, 24 fl oz
Fresh Pack Sweet Bread & Butter Chips, 16 fl oz
Hamburger Dill Slices, 16 fl oz
Kosher Dill Pickles - Sandwich Slices, 20 fl oz
Kosher Dill Spears (Fresh Pack), 24 fl oz
Kosher Dills (Fresh Whole Pack), 32 fl oz
Polish Dills - Whole (Fresh Pack), 46 fl oz
Refrigerated Kosher Dill Pickles Halves, 32 fl oz
Sweet Bread & Butter Chips (Fresh Pack), 24 fl oz
Sweet Gherkins, 16 fl oz
Sweet Midgets, 16 fl oz

Condiments, Sauces & Dressings

Sweet Sandwich Slices (Fresh Pack), 16 fl oz

Winn-Dixie 👁
- Dill Pickles

RELISH

B&G Foods
- Relishes

Hy-Vee ⚡ 👁
- Dill Relish, 10 fl oz
- Squeeze Sweet Relish, 1.5 fl oz
- Sweet Relish, 10 fl oz

Midwest Country Fare (Hy-Vee) ⚡ 👁
- Sweet Pickle Relish, 16 oz

Mt. Olive Pickle Company ⓘ
- Mount Olive Pickle Company, All (Ensure "Best If Used by Date" of July 2008 or later for: 12 oz Hot Dog Relish, 16 oz No Sugar Added Sweet Gherkins & 16 oz Sweet India Relish)

Nance's Mustards & Condiments
- Corn Relish

Terrapin Ridge
- Pickle Pepper Relish

Wegman's ⚡ 👁 ()
- Dill Relish, 10 oz
- Hamburger Relish, 10 fl oz
- Hot Dog Pickle Relish, 10 oz
- Relish Sweet, 16 oz
- Relish Sweet, 10 oz

Winn-Dixie 👁
- Relish

SALAD DRESSING & DRESSING MIXES

Annie's Naturals ()
- Balsamic Vinaigrette Dressing
- Caesar with Parmesan & Romano Dressing
- Italian with Parmesan Cheese Dressing
- Mango Fat Free Dressing
- Raspberry & Balsamic Fat Free Dressing
- Strawberry & Balsamic Fat Free Dressing

Bragg
- Bragg, All

Brianna's ⚡
- Brianna's, All BUT Asiago Caesar, Chipotle Cheddar, Ginger Mandarin, Lemon Tarragon, Monterey Ranch & Thousand Island

Cains
- Bell Pepper Italian (Pouch)
- Caesar (Pouch)
- Chipotle Ranch Dressing
- Country Blue Cheese (Pouch)
- Country Peppercorn & Parm (Pouch)
- Country Thousand Island (Pouch)
- County Ranch (Pouch)
- Creamy French (Pouch)
- Creamy Garlic Italian (Pouch)
- Creamy Italian Dressing
- Fat Free Italian Dressing
- Fat Free Raspberry Vinaigrette Dressing
- French Dressing
- Golden Italian (Pouch)
- Greek Deluxe (Pouch)
- Italian Dressing
- Italian Light Cains (Pouch)
- Light Caesar (Pouch)
- Light Caesar Dressing
- Light French Dressing
- Light Italian Dressing
- Light Raspberry Vinaigrette Dressing
- Lite Ranch Cains (Pouch)
- Low Fat Caesar (Pouch)
- Mayo Cains with EDTA (Pouch)
- Peppercorn Dressing
- Peppercorn Parmesan Dressing
- Raspberry Vinaigrette (Pouch)
- Robust Italian Dressing
- White Balsamic & Honey Vinaigrette Dressing

Caroline's
- Sweet Blue Onion
- Sweet Celery Dressing
- Sweet French Onion
- Sweet Orange Dressing
- Sweet Razzmataz

Drew's All Natural
- Buttermilk Ranch Dressing/Marinade
- Garlic Italian Dressing/Marinade
- Honey Dijon Dressing/Marinade
- Kalamata Olive & Caper Dressing/Marinade
- Poppy Seed Dressing/Marinade
- Raspberry Dressing/Marinade
- Roasted Garlic & Peppercorn Dressing/Marinade
- Romano Caesar Dressing/Marinade
- Rosemary Balsamic Dressing/Marinade
- Smoked Tomato Dressing/Marinade

El Torito 🛎 👁
- Cilantro Pepita Dressing
- Serrano Ranch Dressing

Emeril's
- Balsamic Vinaigrette
- Blush Wine Vinaigrette
- Caesar Dressing
- Dijon Vinaigrette

Honey Mustard Dressing
House Herb Vinaigrette Dressing
Italian Vinaigrette
Kicked Up French Dressing
Raspberry Balsamic Vinaigrette

Enlighten (Safeway) ✔ 👁

Balsamic & Red Wine Vinaigrette
Garden Italian Dressing
Honey Mustard Salad Dressing
Roasted Sweet Pepper & Garlic Vinaigrette Dressing

Follow Your Heart

Caesar Dressing
Caesar with Parmesan Dressing
Creamy Garlic Dressing
Honey Mustard Dressing
Lemon Herb Dressing
Low Fat Ranch Dressing
Organic Balsamic Vinaigrette Dressing
Organic Chipotle Lime Ranch Dressing
Organic Chunky Bleu Cheese Dressing
Organic Creamy Caesar Dressing
Organic Creamy Miso Ginger Dressing
Organic Creamy Ranch Dressing
Organic Italian Vinaigrette Dressing
Sesame Dijon Dressing
Sesame Miso Dressing
Spicy Southwest Ranch Dressing
Thousand Island Dressing

Food You Feel Good About (Wegman's) ✔ 👁 ()

Fat Free Red Wine Vinegar, 16 fl oz
Fat Free Roasted Red Pepper, 16 fl oz

Health Market (Hy-Vee) ✔ 👁

Organic Creamy Caesar Dressing, 12 fl oz
Organic Honey Mustard Dressing, 12 fl oz
Organic Raspberry Vinaigrette, 12 fl oz

Hy-Vee ✔ 👁

Chunky Blue Cheese Salad Dressing, 16 fl oz
French Dressing, 24 fl oz
French Dressing, 16 fl oz
Italian Dressing, 24 oz
Italian Dressing, 16 fl oz
Light French Salad Dressing, 16 fl oz
Light Italian Dressing, 24 fl oz
Light Italian Salad Dressing, 16 fl oz
Light Ranch Dressing, 24 fl oz
Light Ranch Salad Dressing, 16 fl oz
Light Thousand Island Dressing, 16 fl oz
Lite Salad Dressing, 32 oz
Ranch Dressing, 24 fl oz
Ranch Dressing, 16 fl oz
Salad Dressing, 32 oz

Salad Dressing, 16 oz
Squeezable Salad Dressing, 18 fl oz
Thousand Island Dressing, 24 fl oz
Thousand Island Dressing, 16 fl oz
Zesty Italian Dressing, 16 fl oz

Laura Lynn (Ingle's) 👁

1000 Island Dressing, 8 & 24 oz
1000 Island Dressing, 16 oz
Buttermilk Dressing, 16 oz
California French Dressing, 16 oz
California Honey French Dressing, 16 oz
Chunky Blue Cheese Dressing, 16 oz
Creamy Cucumber Dressing, 16 oz
Creamy Italian Dressing, 16 oz
Fat Free Italian Dressing, 16 oz
Fat Free Ranch Dressing, 16 oz
French Dressing, 8 oz
French Dressing, 16 oz
Garlic Ranch Dressing, 16 oz
Italian Dressing, 8 & 24 oz
Italian Dressing, 16 oz
Lite Ranch Dressing, 16 oz
Peppercorn Ranch Dressing, 16 oz
Poppy Seed Dressing, 16 oz
Ranch Dressing, 8 & 24 oz
Ranch Dressing, 16 oz
Ranch Dressing Mix
Red Wine Vinegar & Oil Dressing, 16 oz
Salad Dressing, 32 oz
Zesty Italian

Litehouse

Balsamic Vinaigrette
Big Bleu
Bleu Cheese Vinaigrette
Caesar Dressing
Caesar Sensation
Chunky Bleu Cheese
Chunky Garlic Caesar
Coleslaw Dressing
Cranberry Vinaigrette
Garlic Caesar
Gourmet Caesar
Greek Dressing
Homestyle Ranch
Honey Mustard
Huckleberry Vinaigrette
Idaho Bleu Bleu Cheese Crumbles
Jalapeno Ranch Dressing
Lite Bleu Cheese
Lite Honey Dijon
Lite Ranch
Original Bleu Cheese

Peppercorn Ranch
Pomegranate Blueberry
Ranch Dressing
Raspberry Walnut Vinaigrette
Red Wine Olive Oil Vinaigrette
Rustic Ranch
Salsa Ranch
Spinach Dressing
Sweet Herb French
Thousand Island Dressing

Manischewitz
Fat Free Italian Dressing
Garlic Ranch Salad Dressing

Midwest Country Fare (Hy-Vee) ◢ ◉
Ranch Dressing, 16 fl oz

Nasoya
Creamy Dill Vegi Dressing, UPC# 2548400053
Creamy Italian Dressing, UPC# 2548400620
Creamy Italian Vegi Dressing, UPC# 2548400054
Garden Herb Vegi Dressing, UPC# 2548400050
Lemongrass Ginger Vinaigrette, UPC# 2548400619
Peppercorn Parm, UPC# 2548400621
Sesame Garlic Vegi Dressing, UPC# 2548400052
Tangy Blue, UPC# 2548400618
Thousand Island, UPC# 2548400616
Thousand Island Vegi Dressing, UPC# 2548400055
Wasabi Ranch, UPC# 2548400617

Nature's Promise (Stop & Shop) ◢ ◉
Ranch

Newman's Own ◢
Balsamic Vinaigrette
Caesar
Creamy Caesar
Creamy Italian (Parmesanio Italianio)
Light Balsamic Vinaigrette
Light Caesar Dressing
Light Cranberry & Walnut
Light Honey Mustard
Light Italian
Light Lime Vinaigrette
Light Raspberry & Walnut
Light Red Wine & Vinegar
Light Sun Dried Tomato
Olive Oil & Vinegar
Parmesan & Roasted Garlic
Ranch Dressing
Red Wine & Vinegar
Three Cheese Balsamic Vinaigrette
Two Thousand Island

Olde Cape Cod
Blue Cheese & Chive Dressing

Garlic & Herb Dressing
Lite Raspberry Vinaigrette Dressing
Lite Sweet & Sour Poppyseed Dressing
Sundried Tomato Lite Dressing

Organicville
Organicville, All

Robert Rothschild Farm
Peanut Ginger Dressing & Marinade
Raspberry Dressing
Raspberry Wasabi Dressing

Safeway ◢ ◉
Creamy Italian Dressing
Fat Free 1000 Island Dressing
Italian Dressing Mix
Light Ranch Dressing
Light Zesty Italian Salad Dressing
Ranch Dressing Mix
Ranch with Bacon Dressing
Regular 1000 Island Dressing
Regular Ranch Dressing
Regular Zesty Italian Dressing

Select Brand (Safeway) ◢ ◉
Basil Ranch Salad Dressing
Blue Cheese Dressing
Cranberry/Orange Dressing
Harvest Vegetable Dressing
Italian Salad Dressing Mix
Ranch Dressing
Raspberry Vinaigrette
Red Wine Balsamic Dressing
Roasted Red Pepper & Garlic Vinaigrette
Tuscan Basil Herb Dressing

Stop & Shop ◢ ◉
Balsamic Vinaigrette
Blue Cheese
Caesar
French - Regular & Creamy
Italian - Creamy, Fat Free & Lite
Ranch - Regular & Fat Free
Raspberry Vinaigrette
Thousand Island

Taste of Thai, A
Peanut Salad Dressing Mix

Terrapin Ridge
Black Walnut Dressing
Lavender Honey Dressing
Poblano Lime Dressing

Wegman's ◢ ◉ ()
Balsamic Delight Dressing, 16 fl oz
Balsamic Vinaigrette - Organic, 12 fl oz
Basil Vinaigrette Salad Dressing, 16 fl oz

Caramelized Onion & Bacon Dressing, 16 fl oz
Cracked Pepper Ranch Dressing, 16 fl oz
Creamy Caesar Dressing - Organic, 12 fl oz
Creamy Curry & Roasted Red Pepper Dressing, 16 fl oz
Creamy Italian Dressing, 16 fl oz
Creamy Ranch Dressing, 16 fl oz
Creamy Ranch, Dressing, 24 fl oz
Fat Free Parmesan Italian, 16 fl oz
Honey Mustard Dressing - Organic, 12 fl oz
Italian Dressing - Organic, 12 fl oz
Light Garlic Italian Dressing, 16 fl oz
Light Golden Caesar Dressing, 16 fl oz
Light Parmesan Peppercorn Ranch Dressing, 16 fl oz
Light Ranch Dressing, 16 fl oz
Maple Dijon, 16 fl oz
Parmesan Italian Dressing, 16 fl oz
Poppyseed Delight Dressing, 16 fl oz
Raspberry Vinaigrette - Organic, 12 fl oz
Roasted Red Bell Pepper & Garlic, 16 fl oz
Roasted Tomato & Cheddar Dressing, 16 fl oz
Salad Dressing - Whip, 32 fl oz
Sun-Dried Tomato Vinaigrette - Organic, 12 fl oz
Tarragon Vinaigrette, 16 fl oz
Thousand Island, 16 fl oz
Three Spice Garden French, 16 fl oz
Toasted Sesame & Ginger, 16 fl oz
Traditional Italian, 16 fl oz
Traditional Italian Dressing, 24 fl oz

Winn-Dixie 👁
Italian Salad Dressing Mix

SAUERKRAUT

B&G Foods
Sauerkraut
Eden Foods
Sauerkraut, UPC# 024182011005
Food You Feel Good About (Wegman's) ⁄ 👁 ()
Sauerkraut, 8, 16 & 27 oz
Hy-Vee ⁄ 👁
Shredded Kraut, 14 & 27 oz
Ingles Markets 👁
Sauerkraut
Safeway ⁄ 👁
Sauerkraut
Stop & Shop ⁄ 👁
Sauerkraut
Thrifty Maid 👁
Sauerkraut

Vlasic () 👁
Sauerkraut

SLOPPY JOE SAUCE

Hy-Vee ⁄ 👁
Sloppy Joe Sauce, 15.5 & 26.5 oz
Ingles Markets 👁
Sloppy Joe Sauce
Not-So-Sloppy-Joe ☠ 👁
Sloppy-Joe Sauce
Safeway ⁄ 👁
Sloppy Joe
Thrifty Maid 👁
Sloppy Joe Sauce

SOY & TAMARI SAUCE

Eden Foods
Organic Tamari, UPC# 024182011593
Organic Tamari, UPC# 024182011586
Hy-Vee ⁄ 👁
Soy Sauce, 10 fl oz
San-J ☃ ()
Organic Wheat Free Tamari (Gold Label)
Organic Wheat Free Tamari Reduced Sodium Tamari (Platinum Label)

STEAK SAUCE

Hy-Vee ⁄ 👁
Classic Steak Sauce, 10 oz
Ingles Markets 👁
Elmer Ingle 1922 Sauce, 10 oz
Laura Lynn (Ingle's) 👁
Steak Sauce, 11 & 17 oz
Select Brand (Safeway) ⁄ 👁
Steak Sauce
Wegman's ⁄ 👁 ()
Steak Sauce - Regular, 10 oz

TACO & OTHER MEXICAN SAUCES

Chi-Chi's ☠ 👁
Taco Sauce
Hy-Vee ⁄ 👁
Medium Taco Sauce, 16 oz
Mild Enchilada Sauce, 15 oz
Mild Taco Sauce, 16 oz

Ingles Markets 👁
Sauce & Taco Sauce

Las Palmas
Crushed Tomatillos
Red Chile Sauce
Red Enchilada Sauce

Pace 👁
Enchilada Sauces, All
Red Sauces, All

Select Brand (Safeway) 〰 👁
Fiesta Fajita Sauce

Stop & Shop 〰 👁
Para Micasa Adobo - Regular & with Pepper

TARTAR SAUCE

Cains
Tartar Sauce

Laura Lynn (Ingle's) 👁
Squeeze Tarter Sauce, 11.25 oz

Wegman's 〰 👁 ()
Tartar Sauce, 8 fl oz

TERIYAKI & OTHER ASIAN SAUCES

Dynasty
Hoisin Sauce, #09627
Plum Sauce, #09630

Eden Foods
Mirin (Rice Cooking Wine), UPC# 024182000481
Tekka (Miso Condiment), UPC# 024182002171

Jack Daniel's EZ Marinader 🐾
Teriyaki Variety

Marukan ☿ 🐾
Ponzu Sudachi Citrus Marinade

Masala Maza
Chutneys, All
Korma Simmer Sauce 🐾
Madras Coconut Curry 🐾
Tandoori Grill Sauce 🐾

Moore's Marinades ☿
Teriyaki Marinade

Premier Japan ☿
Organic Wheat-Free Hoisin
Organic Wheat-Free Teriyaki

Taste of Thai, A
Fish Sauce
Garlic Chili Pepper Sauce
Green Curry Paste
Panang Curry Paste

Peanut Satay Sauce
Peanut Sauce Mix
Red Curry Paste
Yellow Curry Paste

Thai Kitchen
Fish Sauce
Green Curry Paste
Lemongrass Sauce - Choice Crop
Lemongrass Splash Sauce
Less Sodium Fish Sauce
Original Pad Thai Sauce
Peanut Satay Sauce
Plum Sauce
Red Curry Paste
Spicy Peanut Satay Sauce

VINEGAR

Barengo
Red & Balsamic Vinegars

Bragg
Bragg, All

Di Lusso 🐾 👁
Red Wine Vinegar

Eden Foods
Organic Apple Cider Vinegar, UPC# 024182000634
Organic Apple Cider Vinegar, UPC# 024182000627
Organic Brown Rice Vinegar, UPC# 024182422160
Organic Brown Rice Vinegar, UPC# 024182422177
Organic Brown Rice Vinegar, UPC# 024182420869
Red Wine Vinegar, UPC# 024182000610
Red Wine Vinegar, UPC# 024182000597
Ume Plum Vinegar, UPC# 024182425888
Ume Plum Vinegar, UPC# 024182425895
Ume Plum Vinegar, UPC# 024182424195

Four Monks
Vinegars, All

Grand Selections (Hy-Vee) 〰 👁
Balsamic Vinegar of Modena, 17 fl oz
Red Wine Vinegar, 17 fl oz
White Wine Vinegar, 17 oz

Heinz 🐾
Apple Cider Flavored Vinegar
Apple Cider Vinegar
Distilled White Vinegar
Red Wine Vinegar

Hy-Vee 〰 👁
Apple Cider Flavored Distilled Vinegar, 16 & 32 fl oz
Apple Cider Flavored Distilled Vinegar, 128 fl oz
White Distilled Vinegar, 16, 32 & 64 fl oz
White Distilled Vinegar, 128 fl oz

Condiments, Sauces & Dressings

Condiments, Sauces & Dressings

Italian Classics (Wegman's) ✗ 👁 ()
Balsamic - 12 Year, 8.5 fl oz
Balsamic - 8 Year, 8.45 fl oz
Balsamic Vinegar (Aged Up to 3 Yrs), 17 fl oz
Chianti Red Wine Vinegar, 16.9 fl oz
Tuscan White Wine Vinegar, 16.9 fl oz

Knouse Foods (See Section 3 for Knouse Brands)
Apple Cider Vinegar
White Distilled Vinegar

Lorenzi
Balsamic Vinegar

Manischewitz
Apple Cider Vinegar
White Vinegar

Marukan 👄 ☀
Genuine Brewed Rice Vinegar
Organic Rice Vinegar
Organic Seasoned Rice Vinegar
Rice Vinegar Dressing (Sushi-Su)
Seasoned Gourmet Rice Vinegar
Seasoned Gourmet Rice Vinegar Lite Dressing

Nakano
Natural & Seasoned Rice Vinegars

Newman's Own Organics ()
Balsamic Vinegar

Regina
Vinegar, All

Select Brand (Safeway) ✗ 👁
Vinegar, All BUT Malt Vinegar

Simply Enjoy (Stop & Shop) ✗ 👁
Balsamic Vinegar of Modena
White Balsamic Vinegar

Stop & Shop ✗ 👁
Cider Vinegar
White Vinegar
Wine Vinegar

Wegman's ✗ 👁 ()
Apple Cider Vinegar, 16 fl oz
Red Wine Vinegar, 16 fl oz
Vinegar Cider, 32 fl oz
Vinegar Cider, 128 fl oz
White Distilled Vinegar, 16, 32 & 64 fl oz
White Distilled Vinegar, 128 fl oz

Winn-Dixie 👁
Vinegar

WORCESTERSHIRE SAUCE

French's 👁
Worcestershire Sauce

Hy-Vee ✗ 👁
Worcestershire Sauce, 10 fl oz

Lea & Perrins ☀
Lea & Perrins, All Varieties

Safeway ✗ 👁
Worcestershire Sauce

Winn-Dixie 👁
Worcestershire Sauce

Wizard's, The 👄
Organic Wheat-Free Vegan Worcestershire

MISCELLANEOUS

Boar's Head 👁 ⓘ
Condiments, All

Bragg
Bragg, All

Cedar's Mediterranean Foods
Bruschetta

Concord Foods
Potato Topping

Di Lusso ☀ 👁
Sandwich Spread

Gold's
Duck Sauce, All

Hy-Vee ✗ 👁
Sandwich Spread, 16 oz

Manischewitz
Tehina - Ready to Serve

Robert Rothschild Farm
Caramelized Onion Balsamic Spread

Simply Enjoy (Stop & Shop) ✗ 👁
Smoked Salmon Dill Sandwich Spread

Terrapin Ridge
Kalamata Feta Squeeze
Roasted Yellow Pepper Squeeze
Spicy Chipotle Squeeze

Texas Pete
Seafood Sauce

Wegman's ✗ 👁 ()
Remoulade Sauce, 8 oz

Winn-Dixie 👁
Sweet Salad Cubes

Snacks & Convenience Foods

APPLESAUCE

Eden Foods
Apple Sauce, UPC# 024182000665
Apple Sauce (Single Serve), UPC# 024182000535

Food You Feel Good About (Wegman's) ✗ ◉ ()
Chunky Natural Applesauce, 23.5 oz
Natural Applesauce, 50 oz & 6 - 4 oz cups
Natural Applesauce, 25 oz

Hy-Vee ✗ ◉
Applesauce, 25 oz & 6 pack - 24 oz
Applesauce, 50 oz
Cinnamon Applesauce, 6 pack - 24 oz
Cinnamon Applesauce, 25 oz
Natural Style Applesauce, 50 oz & 6 pack - 24 oz
Natural Style Applesauce, 25 oz

Knouse Foods (See Section 3 for Knouse Brands)
Apple-Cherry Sauce
Apple-Grape Sauce
Apple-Green Apple Sauce
Apple-Orange-Mango Sauce
Apple-Peach Sauce
Apple-Raspberry Sauce
Apple-Strawberry Sauce
Cinnamon Apple Sauce
Golden Delicious Sauce
Granny Smith Sauce
McIntosh Sauce
Red Delicious Sauce
Sweetened Apple Sauce
Unsweetened Apple Sauce

Midwest Country Fare (Hy-Vee) ✗ ◉
Applesauce with Cinnamon, 50 oz
Applesauce with Cinnamon, 24 oz
Applesauce with Peaches, 24 oz
Applesauce with Raspberries, 24 oz
Applesauce with Strawberries, 24 oz
Home Style Applesauce, 50 oz

Home Style Applesauce, 24 oz
Natural Applesauce, 50 oz
Natural Applesauce, 24 oz

Mott's
Sauces, All BUT Mr & Mrs T Pina Colada & Clamato

Safeway ✗ ◉
Applesauce - Cups, Natural & Sweetened

Stop & Shop ✗ ◉
Applesauce - Chunky
Applesauce - Cinnamon
Applesauce - Mixed Berry
Applesauce - Natural
Applesauce - Regular
Applesauce - Strawberry

Thrifty Maid ◉
Applesauce

Wegman's ✗ ◉ ()
Applesauce - Mixed Berry, 6 - 4 oz cups
Applesauce - Peach Mango, 6 - 4 oz cups
Applesauce - Sweetened with Calcium & Vitamin C, 25 oz
Applesauce Cinnamon, with Calcium & Vitamin C, 25 oz
Applesauce with Calcium & Vitamin C (Sweetened), 25 oz
Chunky, Sweetened Applesauce, 25 oz
Cinnamon Applesauce, 50 oz
Cinnamon Applesauce, 25 oz
Cinnamon Applesauce (Snack Pack), 6 - 4oz cups
MacIntosh Applesauce - Sweetened, 25 oz
Sweetened Applesauce, 25 & 50 oz
Sweetened Applesauce, 15 oz
Sweetened Applesauce (Snack Pack), 6 - 4oz cups

BARS

Arico Natural Food Company
Arico Natural Food Company, All

BumbleBar
  Bumblebar, All
Envirokidz ◖◗ ⓘ
  Crispy Rice Bars - Berry, Peanut Butter & Chocolate
Frankly Natural Bakers
  Gluten Free Apricot Energy Bar
  Gluten Free Date Nut Energy Bar
  Gluten Free Raisin Energy Bar
  Gluten Free Tropical Energy Bar
Glucerna ♨
  Caramel Nut Glucerna Snack Bar ◖◗
  Lemon Crunch Glucerna Snack Bar ◖◗
Glutino
  Glutino, All
Jocalat ♀
  Jocalat, All
Lärabar ♀
  Larabar, All
Lydia's Organics ♀
  Lydia's Organics, All
OrgraN
  Orgran, All
PureFit
  Purefit, All
ZonePerfect ◖◗
  Chocolate Almond Raisin Bar
  Chocolate Caramel Cluster Bar, Old bars are NOT
    GF; newer, GF bars will have packaging that reads
    "Excellent Source of Protein," "Excellent Source of
    Calcium" and "Good Source of Fiber"
  Chocolate Coconut Crunch Bar
  Chocolate Peanut Butter Bar, Old bars are NOT
    GF; newer, GF bars will have packaging that reads
    "Excellent Source of Protein," "Excellent Source of
    Calcium" and "Good Source of Fiber"
  Chocolate Raspberry Bar
  Fudge Graham Bar
  Mango Orange Delight Bar
  Peanut Toffee Bar

BEEF JERKY & OTHER MEAT SNACKS

Hy-Vee ✗ ◉
  Original Beef Jerky, 4 oz
Oberto Natural Style Beef Jerky
  Hickory (Red Bag), 4 oz
  Original (Red Bag), 4 oz
  Peppered (Red Bag), 4 oz
Rustler's ◖◗ ◉
  Beef Jerky

  Spicy Flavor Beef Stick
Safeway ✗ ◉
  Original Beef Jerky
  Peppered Beef Jerky
Wellshire Farms
  Matt's Select Pepperoni Sticks - Original, Item# 00170
    - 4.87oz
  Turkey Tom Toms - Hot & Spicy, Item# 00166 - 4.87
    oz
  Turkey Tom Toms - Original, Item# 00165 - 4.87 oz
Wild Ride Beef Jerky
  All-Natural Gallopin Pepper, 4 oz
  Hormone Free Gallopin Pepper, 4 oz
  Hot & Spicy Beef Sticks, 1 oz
  Pepperoni Beef Sticks, 1 oz
Winn-Dixie ◉
  Beef Jerky
  Peppered Beef Jerky

BROWNIES

Frankly Natural Bakers
  Gluten Free Carob Almondine Brownie
  Gluten Free Cherry Berry Brownie
  Gluten Free Java Jive Brownie
  Gluten Free Misty Mint Brownie
  Gluten Free Wacky Walnut Nut Brownie

CANDY

Alter Eco Fair Trade
  Chocolate Bars
Andes ♀
  Andes
Baby Ruth ✗ ♨ ◉
  Baby Ruth
  Baby Ruth Crème Egg (Seasonal, Easter)
Before & After Candy
  Before & After Mints, All
Bit-O-Honey ✗ ♨ ◉
  Bit-O-Honey
Blow Pops ♀
  Blow Pops
  Super Blow Pops
Bottle Caps ✗ ♨ ◉
  Bottle Caps
Butterfinger ✗ ♨ ◉
  Butterfinger, EXCEPT Butterfinger Crisp &
    Butterfinger Stixx
  Butterfinger Crème Eggs (Seasonal, Easter)
  Butterfinger Nesteggs (Seasonal, Easter)

Snacks & Convenience Foods

Milk Chocolate with Butterfinger Hearts (Seasonal, Valentines)
Milk Chocolate with Butterfinger Tigger (Seasonal, Valentines)

Caramel Apple Pops
Caramel Apple Pops

Cella's
Cella's Dark Chocolate Covered Cherries
Cella's Milk Chocolate Covered Cherries

Charleston Chew
Charleston Chew

Charms
Candy Carnival
Pops
Sour Balls
Squares

Child's Play
Child's Play

Clark Bars
Clark Bars

Concord Foods
Candy Apple Kit
Caramel Apple Kit
Caramel Apple Wrap

Crows
Crows

Dots
Dots

Dove
Dove Chocolate, All BUT Milk & Dark Chocolate Covered Almonds

Endangered Species Chocolate
Endangered Species Chocolate, All

Equal Exchange
Chocolate, All

Fisher Nuts
Almond Bark - Both Kinds

Fluffy Stuff Cotton Candy
Fluffy Stuff Cotton Candy

Frooties
Frooties

Fruit Rolls
Fruit Rolls

Fruit Smoothie Pops
Fruit Smoothie Pops

Gobstoppers
Candy Canes (Seasonal, Christmas)
Chewy
Eggbreakers (Seasonal, Easter)
Heartbreakers (Seasonal, Valentines)

Original
Snowballs (Seasonal, Christmas)

Goobers
Goobers

Guittard
Guittard, All

Haviland
Peppermint Patties
Thin Mints
Wintergreen Patties

Hint Mint
Hint Mint, All

Hot Tamales
Hot Tamales
Hot Tamales Fire
Hot Tamales Ice
Snack Pack & Variety Pack Bags

Hy-Vee
Assorted Gum Balls, 5 oz
Butterscotch Buttons, 6.75 oz
Chocolate Caramel Clusters, 12 oz
Chocolate Covered Raisins, 12 oz
Chocolate Peanut Clusters, 12 oz
Chocolate Stars, 12 oz
Cinnamon Imperials, 6 oz
Circus Peanuts, 4.75 oz
Double Dipped Chocolate Covered Peanuts, 12 oz
Dum Dum Suckers, 3.75 oz
Gum Drops, 11 oz
Gummi Bears, 5.25 oz
Gummi Peach Rings, 5 oz
Gummi Sour Squiggles, 4.5 oz
Gummi Squiggles, 5.25 oz
Lemon Drops, 7 oz
Milk Chocolate Peanut Butter Cups, 12 oz
Milk Kraft Caramels, 4.5 oz
Orange Slices, 11 oz
Smarties, 4.75 oz
Spice Drops, 11 oz
Starlight Kisses, 6.75 oz
Tootsie Flavored Rolls, 4.75 oz
Tootsie Pops, 2.75 oz
Wax Bottles, 3.5 oz

Jelly Belly
Jelly Beans, All

Junior Caramels
Junior Caramels

Junior Mints
Junior Mints

Just Born
Jelly Beans

Laffy Taffy ✐ ⊠ ◉
- Laffy Taffy
- Laffy Taffy Rope

Laura Lynn (Ingle's) ◉
- Bag Candy (2/$3.00), All

Let's Do...Organic ⦿
- Classic Gummi Bears
- Fruity Gummi Feet
- Jelly Gummi Bears
- Super Sour Gummi Bears

Lifesavers
- Lifesavers Products

Lik-M-Aid Fun Dip ✐ ⊠ ◉
- Lik-M-Aid Fun Dip

M&M'S ◉
- M&M's, All BUT M&M's Crispy

Mamba ⦿ ◠
- Mamba

Manischewitz
- Caramel Cashew Patties
- Chocolate Frolic Bears
- Chocolate Lollycones
- Dark Chocolate Coins
- Fruit Slices
- Hazelnut Truffles
- Mallo Cups
- Milk Chocolate Coins
- Mini Sour Fruit Slices
- Peppermint Patties
- Swiss Chocolate Mints
- Viennese Crunch

Marshmallow Peeps ✐
- Chicks & Bunnies
- Christmas Trees & Snowmen
- Cocoa Cats
- Holiday Cookie Flavored Cutouts
- Marshmallow Peeps Inside a Milk Chocolate Egg
- Non-Flavored Hearts
- Orange Creme Flavored Eggs
- Pumpkins, Spooky Cats & Ghosts
- Strawberry & Vanilla Creme Flavored Hearts

Mary Janes
- Mary Jane Peanut Butter Kisses
- Mary Janes

Mike and Ike ✐
- Berry Blast
- Jelly Beans
- Jolly Joes Grape & Tangy Twister
- Original Fruits
- Snack Pack & Variety Pack Bags
- Tropical Typhoon

Milkfuls ⦿ ◠
- Milkfuls

Milky Way ◉
- Milky Way, All BUT Milky Way Bar

Necco
- Banana Split Chews
- Canada Mint & Wintergreen Lozenges
- Candy Eggs (Easter)
- Candy Stix
- Mint Julep Chews
- Necco Wafers
- Squirrel Nut Caramels
- Squirrel Nut Zippers
- Talking Pumpkins (Halloween)
- Ultramints

Nerds ✐ ⊠ ◉
- Nerds
- Nerds Gumballs
- Nerds Rope

Nestlé Milk Chocolate ✐ ⊠ ◉
- Nestlé Milk Chocolate

Nestlé Treasures ✐ ⊠ ◉
- Nestlé Treasures - Includes Treasures Bars

Nestlé Turtles ✐ ⊠ ◉
- Crème Egg (Seasonal, Easter)
- Dark Chocolate
- Milk Chocolate
- Sugar Free

Newman's Own Organics ◠
- Chocolate Bars, All BUT Crisp Rice
- Chocolate Cups, All

Nips ✐ ⊠ ◉
- Regular
- Sugar Free

Oh Henry! ✐ ⊠ ◉
- Oh Henry!

Peanut Chews ✐
- Peanut Chews

Peeps ✐
- Cocoa Bunnies
- Sugar-Free Chicks

Pez Candy ⊠ ✐ ⦿
- Pez Candy

Pixy Stix ✐ ⊠ ◉
- Pixy Stix

Pops Galore ⦿
- Pops Galore

Raisinets ✐ ⊠ ◉
- Raisinets

Snacks & Convenience Foods

Reed's
- Candy, All

Riesen � ()
- Riesen

Runts ✒ ☀ ◉
- Chewy
- Freckled Eggs (Seasonal, Easter)
- Hearts (Seasonal, Valentine)
- Regular

Safeway ✒ ◉
- Dessert Mints
- Spice Drops
- Star Light Mints

Scharffen Berger �
- Chocolate

Select Brand (Safeway) ✒ ◉
- Butterscotch Truffles
- Chocolate/Raspberry Truffles
- Milk Chocolate Truffles
- Mocha Truffles

Simply Enjoy (Stop & Shop) ✒ ◉
- Chocolates
- Dark Chocolate Amaretto Coated Cranberries
- Dark Chocolate Cappuccino Crunch Bits
- Dark Chocolate Caramel Squares
- Dark Chocolate Covered Cherries
- Dark Chocolate Covered Coffee Beans
- Dark Chocolate Covered Cranberries
- Dark Chocolate Covered Kona Almond Coffee Beans
- Dark Chocolate Covered Strawberries
- Dark Chocolate Raspberry Sticks
- Milk Chocolate Butter Toffee Squares
- Milk Chocolate Coated Cashews
- Milk Chocolate Cocoa Almonds
- Milk Chocolate Covered Cashews
- Milk Chocolate Covered Cherries
- Milk Chocolate Covered Peanuts
- Milk Chocolate Covered Raisins
- Milk Chocolate Pecan Caramel Patties
- White Chocolate Coated Coffee Nuggets
- Whole Chocolate Covered Raspberries
- Yogurt Coated Cranberries

Skittles ◉
- Skittles Bite-Sized Candies

Skybar
- Skybars

Sno-Caps ✒ ☀ ◉
- Sno-Caps

Sour Patch Kids
- Sour Patch Kids

Spangler Candy Company
- Candy Canes
- Cane Classics
- Circus Marshmallow Peanuts
- Disney Candy Canes
- Disney Marshmallow Treats
- Disney Winnie the Pooh Saf-T-Pops
- Dum Dum Candy Canes
- Dum Dums
- Jelly Belly Candy Canes
- Marshmallow Treats
- Saf-T-Pops
- Swirl Saf-T-Pops

Spree ✒ ☀ ◉
- Candy Canes (Seasonal, Christmas)
- Spree

Starburst ◉
- Starburst, All

Stop & Shop ✒ ◉
- Assorted Fruit Filled Candy
- Assorted Star Drops
- Assorted Starlights
- Blue Gummi Sharks
- Butter Toffee
- Butterscotch Disks
- Canada Wintergreen
- Candy Corn
- Candy Necklaces
- Cinnamon Starlights
- Circus Peanuts
- Gum Balls
- Gum Drops
- Gummi Bears
- Jelly Beans
- Kiddie Mix
- Lemon Drops
- Neon Sour Crawlers
- Orange Slices
- Pastel Mints
- Peach Rings
- Pina Colada Coated Cashews
- Red Ju Ju Coins
- Red Ju Ju Fish
- Root Beer Barrels
- Royal Mix
- Silver Mints
- Smarties
- Soft Peppermints
- Sour Balls
- Sour Gummi Worms
- Spearmint Leaves
- Spearmint Starlights

Don't see your favorite brand? Look it up in Section 3!

Spice Drops
Starlight Mints
Strawberry Buds
Watermelon Hard Candy

Sugar Babies 🍼
Sugar Babies

Sugar Daddy Pops 🍼
Sugar Daddy Pops

Sugar Mama Caramels 🍼
Sugar Mama Caramels

Super Blow Pops 🍼
Super Blow Pops

Sweetarts ⚞ ⛱ ◉
Sweetarts
Sweetarts Candy Canes (Seasonal, Christmas)
Sweetarts Lollipops (Seasonal, Valentines)

Sweethearts
Sweethearts Conversation Hearts (Valentines Only)

Teance
Tea Chocolates, All

Teenee Beanee ⚞
Jelly Beans, All

Teuscher ⛱
Marzipan, All
Praline, All
Truffles, All

Toffifay 🍼 ⚭
Toffifay

Tootsie Pops 🍼
Tootsie Peppermint Pops
Tootsie Pops

Tootsie Rolls 🍼
Tootsie Rolls

Tropical Dots 🍼
Tropical Dots

Tropical Stormz Pops 🍼
Tropical Stormz Pops

Wegman's ⚞ ◉ ⚭
Virginia Peanuts - Chocolate Covered, 20 oz

Werther's 🍼 ⚭
Chocolates
Original Chewy
Original Hard
Original Hard Sugar Free

WildBerry Dots 🍼
WildBerry Dots

Zip-A-Dee-Mini Pops 🍼
Zip-A-Dee-Mini Pops

Zours ⚞
Zours

CHEESE PUFFS & CURLS

Baked! Cheetos ⚭ ◉
Crunchy Cheese Flavored Snacks
Flamin' Hot Cheese Flavored Snacks

Barbara's Bakery ⚭
Jalapeño Cheese Puff
Original Bakes Cheese Puff
Original Cheese Puff
White Cheddar Bakes Cheese Puff

Cheetos ⚭ ◉
Asteroids Flamin' Hot Mini Cheese Flavored Snacks
Asteroids Mini Cheese Flavored Snacks
Cheddar Jalapeno Cheese Flavored Snacks
Crunchy Cheese Flavored Snacks
Flamin' Hot Cheese Flavored Snacks
Flamin' Hot Limon Cheese Flavored Snacks
Jumbo Puffs Cheese Flavored Snacks
Jumbo Puffs Flamin' Hot Cheese Flavored Snacks
Mix & Move Cheese Flavored Snacks
Natural White Cheddar Puffs Cheese Flavored Snacks
Puffs Cheese Flavored Snacks
Reduced Fat Cheese Flavored Snacks
Twisted Cheese Flavored Snacks

EatSmart
Cheddairs

Herr's ⚭
Cheese Curls
Honey Cheese Curls
Hot Cheese Curls

Laura Lynn (Ingle's) ◉
Baked Cheese Curls, 7 oz
Cheese Krunchy, 7 oz

Michael Season's
Lite Cheddar Cheese Curls ⚭
Lite Cheddar Cheese Puffs ⚭
Ultimate Cheddar Cheese Curls ⚭
Ultimate Cheddar Cheese Puffs ⚭
Ultimate White Cheese Puffs ⚭

Safeway ⚞ ◉
Cheese Curls
Puffed Cheese Snacks

Stop & Shop ⚞ ◉
Crunchy Cheese Corn Snacks
Puff Cheese Corn Snacks

Utz
Cheese Ball Barrell

Cheese Balls
Cheese Curls
Cheese Variety Sack, #349-13 count
Crunchy Cheese Curls
White Cheddar Cheese Curls

Winn-Dixie 👁
Crunchy Cheese Curls
Puffed Curls

CHIPS & CRISPS, NON-POTATO

Chester's ⓞ 👁
Flamin' Hot Flavored Fries
EatSmart
Cheddar Jalapeno Veggie Crisps
Garlic, Parmesan & Olive Oil Soy Crisps
Sundried Tomato Pesto Veggie Crisps
Tomato, Romano & Olive Oil Soy Crisps
Veggie Chips
Eden Foods
Brown Rice Chips, UPC# 024182511741
Enjoy Life Foods ⚥
Enjoy Life Foods, All
French's 👁
Potato Sticks - Barbecue Flavor
Potato Sticks - Cheezy Cheddar
Potato Sticks - Original Flavor
Funyuns ⓞ 👁
Onion Flavored Rings
Herr's ⓞ
Potato Stix - Regular
Veggie Crisp
Kitchen Table Bakers
Kitchen Table Bakers, All
Lundberg Family Farms
Rice Chips - Fiesta Lime
Rice Chips - Honey Dijon
Rice Chips - Nacho Cheese
Rice Chips - Pico De Gallo
Rice Chips - Santa Fe Barbecue
Rice Chips - Sea Salt
Rice Chips - Sesame & Seaweed
Rice Chips - Wasabi
Masuya
Rice Sembei Snacks, All Flavors
Michael Season's
Soy Protein Chip - Original ⓞ
Nature's Promise (Stop & Shop) 〰 👁
Soy Crisps - BBQ & Ranch

Newman's Own Organics ⓞ
Barbeque Soy Crisps
Cinnamon Sugar Soy Crisps
Lightly Salted Soy Crisps
White Cheddar Soy Crisps
Stop & Shop 〰 👁
BBQ Rice Crisps
Cheddar Rice Crisps
Ranch Rice Crisps

COOKIES

Arico Natural Food Company
Arico Natural Food Company, All
Ener-G
Ener-G, All BUT Low Protein Products
Enjoy Life Foods ⚥
Enjoy Life Foods, All
Envirokidz ⓞ ⓘ
Vanilla Animal Cookies
Gillian's Foods
Gillian's Foods, All
Gluten-Free Pantry, The
Gluten-Free Pantry, The, All
Glutino
Glutino, All
Manischewitz
Banana Split Macaroons
Cappuccino Chip Macaroons
Chocolate Chip Macaroons
Chocolate Chunk Cherry Macaroons
Chocolate Macaroons
Cinnamon Raisin Macaroons
Coconut Macaroons
Coffee Flavored Macaroons
Dark Chocolate Covered Macaroons
Fudgey Nut Brownie Macaroons
Honey Nut Macaroons
Maple Pecan Macaroons
Meringues, All
Rocky Road Macaroons
Tender Coconut Patties
Toffee Crunch Macaroons
Ultimate Triple Chocolate Macaroons
OrgraN
Orgran, All
Pamela's Products
Almond Anise Biscotti
Butter Shortbread Traditional Cookies
Chocolate Chip Walnut Traditional Cookies
Chocolate Chunk Pecan Shortbread Organic Cookies

Snacks & Convenience Foods

Chocolate Walnut Biscotti
Chunky Chocolate Chip Traditional Cookies
Dark Chocolate-Chocolate Chunk Organic Cookies
Espresso Chocolate Chunk Organic Cookies
Ginger with Almonds Traditional Cookies
Lemon Almond Biscotti
Lemon Shortbread Traditional Cookies
Old Fashioned Raisin Walnut Organic Cookies
Peanut Butter Chocolate Chip Organic Cookies
Peanut Butter Traditional Cookies
Pecan Shortbread Traditional Cookies
Shortbread Swirl Traditional Cookies
Simplebites Chocolate Chip Mini Cookies
Simplebites Mini Ginger Snapz
Spicy Ginger with Crystallized Ginger Organic Cookies

Streit's
Macaroons ♀

Walkers Shortbread
Meringue Nests

CRACKERS

Blue Diamond Growers ◊ ♀
Nut-Thins Crackers

Brown Rice Snaps ♀
Black Sesame (with Organic Brown Rice) Brown Rice Snaps
Cheddar (with Organic Brown Rice) Brown Rice Snaps
Onion Garlic Brown Rice Snaps
Salsa (with Organic Brown Rice) Brown Rice Snaps
Tamari Seaweed Brown Rice Snaps
Tamari Sesame Brown Rice Snaps
Toasted Onion (with Organic Brown Rice) Brown Rice Snaps
Unsalted Plain (with Organic Brown Rice) Brown Rice Snaps
Unsalted Sesame Brown Rice Snaps
Vegetable (with Organic Brown Rice) Brown Rice Snaps

Eden Foods
Brown Rice Crackers, UPC# 024182513417
Nori Maki Rice Crackers, UPC# 024182502503

Ener-G
Ener-G, All BUT Low Protein Products

Glutino
Glutino, All

Lydia's Organics ♀
Lydia's Organics, All

Mary's Gone Crackers
Mary's Gone Crackers, All

OrgraN
Orgran, All

DIP & DIP MIXES

Cedar's Mediterranean Foods
Hommus, All

Chi-Chi's ☖ ◉
Con Queso

Concord Foods
Chocolate Fudge Fruit Dips
Creamy Caramel Apple Dips
Fat Free Caramel Apple Dip
Organic Caramel Apple Dip

EatSmart
Sweet Salsa Dip
Three Bean Dip

Fantastic Foods ◊
Garlic Herb Dip
Onion & Mushroom Dip
Onion Soup & Dip
Original Hummus
Vegetable Soup & Dip

Fritos ◊ ◉
Bean Dip
Chili Cheese Dip
Hot Bean Dip
Jalapeno & Cheddar Flavored Cheese Dip
Mild Cheddar Flavor Cheese Dip

Guiltless Gourmet
Dips, All
Hummous, All

Heluva Good Dips
Bodacious Onion
Buttermilk Ranch
Creamy Salsa
Dinosaur Bbque
French Onion
New England Clam
Ranch

Hy-Vee ✓ ◉
Bacon & Cheddar Dip, 8 oz
French Onion Snack Dip, 8 oz
French Onion Snack Dip, 16 oz
Ranch with Dill Dip, 8 oz
Salsa Dip, 8 oz
Toasted Onion Snack Dip, 8 oz
Vegetable Party Dip, 8 oz

Laura Lynn (Ingle's) 👁
Ranch Dip Mix, 1 oz
Refrigerated Dips, All

Lay's () 👁
Creamy Ranch Dip
French Onion Dip
French Onion Flavored Dry Dip Mix
Green Onion Flavored Dry Dip Mix
Ranch Flavored Dry Dip Mix

Litehouse
Avocado Dip
Chocolate Caramel Dip
Chocolate Dip
Chocolate Yogurt Fruit Dip
Dilly of a Dip
Lowfat Caramel Dip
Onion Dip
Original Caramel Dip
Ranch Dip
Roasted Garlic Dip
Southwest Ranch Dip
Strawberry Yogurt Fruit Dip
Toffee Caramel Dip
Vanilla Crème Dip
Vanilla Yogurt Fruit Dip

Lucerne (Safeway) ⁄ 👁
Avocado Dip
Bacon Onion Dip
Clam Dip
French Onion Dip
Green Onion Dip
Guacamole Dip
Ranch Dip

Manischewitz
Hummus (Ready to Serve)

Robert Rothschild Farm
Artichoke Dip
Blackberry Honey Mustard Pretzel Dip
Chocolate Mint Dessert Sauce & Dip
Cinnamon Apple Caramel Fruit Dip
Honey Chipotle Dip
Jalapeno Pepper Dip
Onion Blossom Horseradish Dip
Onion Dill Vegetable Dip
Raspberry Chocolate Pretzel Dip
Raspberry Honey Mustard Pretzel Dip
Roasted Pineapple & Habanero Dip
Roasted Red Pepper and Onion Dip & Relish
Sesame Honey Mustard Pretzel Dip
Southwest Dip
Sun Dried Tomato Bread Dipper

Sun Dried Tomato Vegetable Dip
Sweet Heat Pretzel Dip
Toasted Garlic Horseradish Dip

Ruffles () 👁
French Onion Dry Dip Mix
Ranch Dry Dip Mix

Safeway ⁄ 👁
Nacho Cheese (Casa del Pueblo)

Select Brand (Safeway) ⁄ 👁
Cook N' Grill Plum Gourmet Dipping Sauce
Honey Mustard Gourmet Dipping Sauce

Snyder's of Hanover
Cheddar Cheese Dip

Stop & Shop ⁄ 👁
Refrigerated French Onion Dip
Refrigerated Ranch Dip
Refrigerated Veggie Dip

Tostitos () 👁
Creamy Southwestern Ranch Dip
Creamy Spinach Dip
Monterey Jack Queso
Reduced Fat Zesty Cheese Dip
Salsa Con Queso
Spicy Queso Supreme

Tribe Mediterranean Foods
Hummus, All Flavors

Utz
Jalapeno/Cheddar Dip (Can)
Mild Cheddar Dip (Can)

Wegman's ⁄ 👁 ()
French Onion Dip, 8 oz
Salsa Con Queso (Cheddar Cheese Dip), 15.5 oz

Winn-Dixie 👁
Dips (Refrigerated)

DRIED FRUIT

Craisins ⓘ
Cherry
Orange
Original

Crunchies
Crunchies, All

Eden Foods
Dried Montmorency Tart Cherries, UPC#
024182001006
Dried Montmorency Tart Cherries, UPC#
024182000795
Organic Dried Cranberries, UPC# 024182000900
Organic Dried Wild Blueberries, UPC#

Snacks & Convenience Foods

024182000887

Organic Wild Berry Mix, UPC# 024182000924

Food You Feel Good About (Wegman's) ✗ ◉ ()

Raisins, 6 - 1.5 oz boxes, 15 oz box & 24 oz canister

Hy-Vee ✗ ◉

Banana Chips, 6 oz

California Sun Dried Raisins, 15 & 24 oz

California Sun Dried Raisins, 6 count - 1.5 oz

Dried Apples, 4.5 oz

Dried Apricots, 6 oz

Dried Blueberries, 4 oz

Dried Cherries, 5 oz

Dried Cranberries, 6 oz

Dried Mixed Berries, 5 oz

Dried Mixed Fruit, 6 oz

Dried Pineapple, 6 oz

Navitas Naturals

Superfood Products, All

Safeway ✗ ◉

Dried Fruit - Apples

Dried Fruit - Apricots

Dried Fruit - Cherries

Dried Fruit - Peaches

Dried Fruit - Prunes

Raisins

Sensible Foods

Sensible Foods, All

Stretch Island Fruit Company

Stretch Island Fruit Company, All

Thrifty Maid ◉

Raisins

Wegman's ✗ ◉ ()

Dried Plums (Pitted Prunes), 24 oz

Welch's ①

Welch's, All

Winn-Dixie ◉

Raisins

Seedless Raisins

FRUIT CUPS

Del Monte ✗ ◉

Fruit Snack Cups (Metal & Plastic), All

Hy-Vee ✗ ◉

Diced Peaches Fruit Cups, 1 lb

Mandarin Orange Fruit Cups, 1 lb

Mixed Fruit - Fruit Cups, 1 lb

Pineapple Tidbit Fruit Cup, 1 lb

Tropical Fruit Cups, 1 lb

FRUIT SNACKS

Hy-Vee ✗ ◉

Dinosaurs Fruit Snacks, 5.4 oz

Fruit Snacks (Variety Pack), 5.4 oz

Rescue Heroes Fruit Snacks, 5.4 oz

Sharks Fruit Snacks, 5.4 oz

Snoopy Fruit Snacks, 5.4 oz

Strawberry Fruit Rolls, 4.5 oz

Veggie Tales Fruit Snacks, 5.4 oz

Kellogg's

Fruit Flavored Snacks

Yogos

Laura Lynn (Ingle's) ◉

Aliens Fruit Snacks

Animal Fruit Snacks

Creepy Fruit Snacks

Dinosaur Fruit Snacks

Safeway ✗ ◉

Fruit Snacks, All

Stop & Shop ✗ ◉

Build a Bear Fruit Snacks

Curious George Fruit Snacks

Dinosaur Fruit Snacks

Justice League Fruit Snacks

Peanuts Fruit Flavored Snacks

Sharks Fruit Snacks

Tom & Jerry Fruit Snacks

Underwater World Fruit Snacks

Variety Pack Fruit Snacks

Veggie Tales Fruit Snacks

GELATIN & GELATIN MIXES

Eden Foods

Agar Agar Bars, UPC# 024182159004

Agar Agar Flakes, UPC# 024182159318

Hy-Vee ✗ ◉

Cherry Gelatin, 3 oz

Cranberry Gelatin, 3 oz

Lemon Gelatin, 3 oz

Lime Gelatin, 3 oz

Orange Gelatin, 3 oz

Raspberry Gelatin, 3 oz

Strawberry Gelatin, 3 oz

Sugar Free Cherry Gelatin, 0.44 oz

Sugar Free Cranberry Gelatin, 0.44 oz

Sugar Free Orange Gelatin, 0.44 oz

Sugar Free Raspberry Gelatin, 0.44 oz

Sugar Free Strawberry Gelatin, 0.44 oz

Laura Lynn (Ingle's) ◉

Gelatins RTE Dairy, All

Safeway ✗ ◉
Gelatin Mix, All
Instant Gelatins - Regular & Sugar Free
Pineapple Lime Gel Cups

Stop & Shop ✗ ◉
Cherry Gelatin Mix
Cranberry Gelatin Mix
Orange Gelatin Mix
Raspberry Gelatin Mix
Refrigerated Gelatin Fun Pack
Refrigerated Rainbow Fruit Gelatin
Refrigerated Rainbow Parfait
Refrigerated Sugar Free Gelatin Fun Pack

Wegman's ✗ ◉ ()
Orange & Raspberry Gelatin Variety Pack, 6 - 3.5 oz snack cups
Strawberry Gelatin, 6 - 3.5 oz snack cups
Sugar Free Cherry & Black Cherry Gelatin, 6 snack cups - 19.5 oz
Sugar Free Orange & Raspberry Gelatin, 6 snack cups - 19.5 oz
Sugar Free Strawberry Gelatin, 6 snack cups - 19.5 oz

GUM

Big Red
Big Red Gum

Bubblicious
Bubblicious Gum

Chiclets
Chiclets Gum

Clorets
Clorets Gum

Dentyne
Dentyne Gum

Doublemint
Doublemint Gum

Eclipse
Eclipse Gum

Extra
Extra Gum

Freedent
Freedent Gum

Hy-Vee ✗ ◉
Dubble Bubble Gum, 5.25 oz

Juicy Fruit
Juicy Fruit Gum

Orbit
Orbit Gum
Orbit White Gum

Trident
Trident Gum

Wegman's ✗ ◉ ()
Sugar Free Peppermint Gum, 0.88 oz

Winterfresh
Winterfresh Gum

Wrigley
Wrigley's Spearmint Gum

NUTS & TRAIL MIXES

Carole's Soycrunch
Cinnamon Raisins
Coconut
Original
Toffee

Eden Foods
All Mixed Up, UPC# 024182000832
All Mixed Up Too, UPC# 024182000825
Organic Pumpkin Seeds - Roasted & Salted, UPC# 024182000849
Organic Tamari Roasted Almonds, UPC# 024182000801
Organic Tamari Roasted Spicy Pumpkin Seeds, UPC# 024182000818

Fisher Nuts
Almonds
Butter Toffee Peanuts
Cashews
Dry Roasted Sunflower Kernels
Fusions Brand Snack Mixes - Country Honey
Fusions Brand Snack Mixes - Martini Mix
Fusions Brand Snack Mixes - Trail Blazer
Honey Roasted Peanuts - Oil Roasted (Can)
Hot & Spicy Peanuts
Macadamia Nuts
Mixed Nuts
Nature's Nut Mix
Nuts & Fruits Brand Snack Mixes - Raisin/Cranberry
Nuts & Fruits Brand Snack Mixes - Trail Style
Party Peanuts
Pecans
Pine Nuts
Pistachios
Salad Buddies (No Salt) Sunflower Kernels
Salted In-Shell Sunflower Seeds
Spanish Peanuts
Unsalted Golden Roast Peanuts
Walnuts

Food You Feel Good About (Wegman's) ✗ ◉ ()
Peanuts - Unsalted & in the Shell, 48 oz

Snacks & Convenience Foods

Frito Lay ( ) 👁
Cashews
Deluxe Mixed Nuts
Flamin' Hot Flavored Sunflower Seeds
Honey Roasted Cashews
Honey Roasted Peanuts
Hot Peanuts
Original Trail Mix
Ranch Sunflower Seeds
Salted Almonds
Salted Peanuts
Smoked Almonds
Sunflower Seed Kernels
Sunflower Seeds

Hy-Vee ✗ 👁
Black Walnuts, 2 oz
Chocolate & Nut Trail Mix, 32 oz
Chocolate Nut Trail Mix, 10 oz
English Walnut Pieces, 6 oz
English Walnut Pieces, 2 oz
English Walnuts, 16 oz
Natural Almonds, 2 oz
Natural Sliced Almonds, 2 oz
Pecan Pieces, 6 oz
Pecan Pieces, 2 oz
Pecans, 12 oz
Raisin & Nut Trail Mix, 32 oz
Raisin Nut Trail Mix, 10 oz
Raw Spanish Peanuts, 16 oz
Salted Blanched Peanuts, 16 oz
Salted Spanish Peanuts, 16 oz
Slivered Almonds, 2 oz
Tropical Trail Mix, 7 oz

I.M. Healthy 😕
Roasted Sweet Corn, All

Kountry Fresh (Winn-Dixie) 👁
Deluxe Mixed Nuts
Dry Roasted Sunflower Kernels
Lightly Salted Cashew Halves & Pieces
Mixed Nuts
Party Peanuts
Salted Cashew Halves & Pieces
Spanish Peanuts
Whole Cashews

Laura Lynn (Ingle's) 👁
Cashew Halves, 16 oz
Cashew Halves, 10 oz
Deluxe Mixed Nuts, 10 oz
Dry Roast Nuts, 24 oz
Dry Roast Nuts, 16 oz
Honey Roast Peanuts, 16 oz
Honey Roast Peanuts, 12 oz

Light Salt Cashews, 10 oz
Light Salt Dry Roast Nuts, 16 oz
Light Salt Mixed Nuts, 12 oz
Light Salt Peanuts, 12 oz
Mixed Nuts, 12 oz
Party Peanuts, 16 oz
Party Peanuts, 12 oz
Roasted Almonds, 9 oz
Smoked Almonds, 9 oz
Spanish Peanuts, 12 oz
Sunflower Seeds, 7.25 oz
Unsalted Dry Roast Nuts, 16 oz
Whole Cashews, 10 oz

Living Harvest
Seeds, All

Lydia's Organics 😕
Lydia's Organics, All

Navitas Naturals
Superfood Products, All

Nut Harvest ( ) 👁
Natural Honey Roasted Peanuts
Natural Lightly Roasted Almonds
Natural Nut & Fruit Mix
Natural Sea Salted Peanuts
Natural Sea Salted Whole Cashews

Sabritas ( ) 👁
Picante Peanuts
Salt & Lime Peanuts

Safeway ✗ 👁
Cashews - Halves and Pieces & Whole
Nuts, All Varieties from S3012
Sunflower Seed Kernels
Trail Mix with Candy Pieces

Select Brand (Safeway) ✗ 👁
Baking Almonds

Sensible Foods
Sensible Foods, All

Thrifty Maid 👁
Boiled Peanuts

Wegman's ✗ 👁 ( )
Cashews - Salted
Cashews - Unsalted
Dry Roasted Macadamias, 6.75 oz
Dry Roasted Sunflower Kernels, Seasoned, 7.25 oz
Dry Roasted, Seasoned Peanuts, 40 oz
Dry Roasted, Unsalted Peanuts, 40 oz
Dry Roasted, Unsalted Peanuts, 16 oz
Honey Roasted Peanuts, 12 oz
Honey Roasted Whole Cashews, 10 oz
Marcona Almonds - Roasted & Salted, 16 oz
Natural Whole Almonds, 10.25 oz

Party Peanuts - Roasted & Salted, 12 oz
Peanuts - Salted & in the Shell, 48 oz
Peanuts Dry Roasted - Lightly Salted, 16 oz
Peanuts Dry Roasted - Seasoned, 16 oz
Roasted Almonds - Salted, 9 oz
Roasted Cashew Halves & Pieces - Salted, 34 oz
Roasted Cashew Halves & Pieces - Salted, 9 oz
Roasted Deluxe Mixed Nuts with Macadamias - Salted, 12 oz
Roasted Jumbo Cashew Mix with Almonds, Brazils & Pecans, 10 oz
Roasted Jumbo Cashews, 10 oz
Roasted Mixed Nuts with Peanuts - Lightly Salted, 38 oz
Roasted Mixed Nuts with Peanuts - Lightly Salted, 12 oz
Roasted Party Mixed Nuts with Peanuts, 12 oz
Roasted Party Mixed Nuts with Peanuts - Salted, 38 oz
Roasted Party Peanuts - Lightly Salted, 12 oz
Roasted Spanish Peanuts, 12 oz
Roasted Whole Cashews - Salted, 38 oz
Roasted Whole Cashews - Unsalted, 38 oz
Virginia Peanuts - Salted, 20 oz
Virginia Peanuts - Salted, 10 snack packs

POPCORN

Chester's () ◉
Butter Flavored Puffcorn Snacks
Cheese Flavored Puffcorn Snacks

Cracker Jack () ◉
Original Caramel Coated Popcorn & Peanuts

Eden Foods
Organic Popcorn, UPC# 024182000863

Fiddle Faddle ◉ ()
Fiddle Faddle, All BUT Honey Nut

Food You Feel Good About (Wegman's) ∥ ◉ ()
Yellow Popcorn, 32 oz

Herr's ()
Hulless Cheese Popcorn
Lite Popcorn
Original (Butter) Popcorn
White Cheddar Ranch Popcorn

Hy-Vee ∥ ◉
94% Fat Free Butter Microwave Popcorn, 9 oz
Butter Microwave Popcorn, 12 pack
Butter Microwave Popcorn, 3.5, 21 & 63 oz
Butter Microwave Popcorn, 10.5 oz
Extra Butter Lite Microwave Popcorn, 9 oz
Extra Butter Microwave Popcorn, 3.5, 21, 42 & 63 oz

Extra Butter Microwave Popcorn, 10.5 oz
Kettle Microwave Popcorn, 21 oz
Kettle Microwave Popcorn, 10.5 oz
Light Butter Microwave Popcorn, 9, 18 & 54 oz
Light Butter Microwave Popcorn, 12 pack - 42 oz
Natural Flavor Microwave Popcorn, 3 pack
White Popcorn, 64 oz
White Popcorn, 2 lb
Yellow Popcorn, 4 lb
Yellow Popcorn, 2 lb

Jolly Time
Jolly Time, All

Laura Lynn (Ingle's) ◉
Popcorn, All

Newman's Own Organics ()
Butter Flavored Pop's Corn
Light Butter Pop's Corn
No Butter/No Salt Pop's Corn

Poppycock ◉ ()
Poppycock, All BUT Indulgence Line's Nights in White Chocolate

Ricos
Flavored Popcorn

Safeway ∥ ◉
Microwave Popcorn, All
Popcorn - Light Butter Microwave
Popcorn - Yellow & Kettle

Smartfood () ◉
Reduced Fat White Cheddar Cheese Flavored Popcorn
White Cheddar Cheese Flavored Popcorn

Snyder's of Hanover
Butter Popcorn

Stop & Shop ∥ ◉
Microwave Popcorn - 94% Fat Free Butter
Microwave Popcorn - Butter Flavored
Microwave Popcorn - Butter Light
Microwave Popcorn - Kettle Corn
Microwave Popcorn - Movie Theater Butter Flavored
Microwave Popcorn - Natural Light
Microwave Popcorn - Sweet & Buttery
Yellow Popcorn

Utz
Butter Popcorn
Cheese Popcorn
Hulless Caramel Puff'n Corn
Hulless Cheese Puff'n Corn
Hulless Original Puff'n Corn
White Cheddar Popcorn

Wegman's ∥ ◉ ()
Kettle Corn Microwave Popcorn, 6 - 3.5 oz bags

Snacks & Convenience Foods

Microwave Popcorn - 94% Fat Free, Butter Flavor, 6 - 3 oz bags
Microwave Popcorn - Butter Flavor, 6 - 3.5 oz bags
Microwave Popcorn - Butter Flavor, 18 - 3.5 oz bags
Microwave Popcorn - Colossal Butter, 10.5 oz
Microwave Popcorn - Light, 3 - 3 oz bags
Microwave Popcorn - Light Butter Flavor, 6 pack - 18 oz
Microwave Popcorn - Movie Theater Butter, 6 - 3.5 oz bags
Movie Theatre Popcorn, 3 - 3.5 oz bags
Natural Popcorn, 10.5 oz

Winn-Dixie 👁
Butter Popcorn
Double Butter Popcorn
Gourmet Kettle Popcorn
Light Butter Popcorn
Microwave Popcorn - No Butter
Natural Flavor Popcorn
Popcorn - Plain & Barbeque
Salt Free Butter Popcorn

PORK SKINS & RINDS

Baken-Ets () 👁
Chile Limon Fried Pork Skins
Fried Pork Cracklins
Fried Pork Skins
Hot 'N Spicy Flavored Pork Cracklins
Hot 'N Spicy Flavored Pork Skins
Salt & Vinegar Fried Pork Skins

Herr's ()
Pork Rinds - Original

Winn-Dixie 👁
Hot Pork Rinds
Pork Rinds Plain

POTATO CHIPS & CRISPS

Baked! Lay's () 👁
Cheddar & Sour Cream Flavored Potato Crisps
Original Potato Crisps
Sour Cream & Onion Artificially Flavored Potato Crisps

Baked! Ruffles () 👁
Cheddar & Sour Cream Flavored Potato Crisps
Original Potato Crisps

Barbara's Bakery ()
No Salt Added Potato Chips
Regular Potato Chips
Ripple Potato Chips

Yogurt & Green Onion Potato Chips
Cheetos ()👁
Fantastiix! Chili Cheese Flavored Baked Corn/Potato Snack
EatSmart
Jalapeno Cheddar Potato Crisps
Sweet Potato Crisps
Zesty Ranch Potato Crisps
Herr's ()
Cheddar & Sour Cream
Honey BBQ Potato Chips
Ketchup Potato Chips
Kettle Cooked Jalapeno Chips
Kettle Russett Potato Chips
Lightly Salted Added Potato Chips
No Salt Potato Chips
Old Bay Potato Chips
Old Fashioned Potato Chips
Original (Crisp & Tasty) Potato Chips
Red Hot Potato Chips
Ripple Potato Chips
Salt & Pepper Potato Chips
Salt & Vinegar Potato Chips
Smoky BBQ Potato Chips
Kettle Brand 🍴
Kettle Brand Potato Chips, All BUT Multi-Grain Tortilla Chips & Bakers Pretzel & Pita Chips
Laura Lynn (Ingle's) 👁
Regular Potato Chips, 5.5 & 12 oz
Ripple Potato Chips, 5.5 oz
Sour Cream & Onion Potato Chips, 5.5 oz
Wavy Potato Chips, 12 oz
Lay's () 👁
Cheddar & Sour Cream Artificially Flavored Potato Chips
Chile Limon Potato Chips
Classic Potato Chips
Dill Pickle Flavored Potato Chips
Hot'n Spicy K.C. Masterpiece BBQ Flavored Potato Chips
Italian Rosemary & Herb Flavored Potato Chips
Kettle Cooked Jalapeno Flavored Extra Crunchy Potato Chips
Kettle Cooked Mesquite BBQ Flavored Extra Crunchy Potato Chips
Kettle Cooked Regular Potato Chips
Light Original Potato Chips
Lightly Salted Potato Chips
Limon Tangy Lime Flavored Potato Chips
Natural Country BBQ Thick Cut Potato Chips
Natural Sea Salt Thick Cut Potato Chips

Snacks & Convenience Foods

Salt & Vinegar Artificially Flavored Potato Chips
Sour Cream & Onion Artificially Flavored Potato Chips
Wavy Au Gratin Flavored Potato Chips
Wavy Hickory BBQ Flavored Potato Chips
Wavy Regular Potato Chips

Lay's Stax ☸ ◉
Cheddar Flavored Potato Crisps
Hidden Valley Ranch Flavored Potato Crisps
Hot'n Spicy Barbecue Flavored Potato Crisps
Jalapeno Cheddar Flavored Potato Crisps
K.C. Masterpiece BBQ Flavored Potato Crisps
Mesquite Barbecue Flavored Potato Crisps
Original Flavored Potato Crisps
Pizza Flavored Potato Crisps
Ranch Flavored Potato Crisps
Salt & Vinegar Flavored Potato Crisps
Sour Cream & Onion Flavored Potato Crisps
Spicy Buffalo Wings Flavored Potato Crisps

Manischewitz
Potato Chips, All Varieties

Maui Style () ◉
Regular Potato Chips
Salt & Vinegar Flavored Potato Chips

Michael Season's
Lite Baked Potato Crisps - BBQ
Lite Baked Potato Crisps - Lightly Salted
Lite Baked Potato Crisps - Sour Cream & Onion
Reduced Fat Kettle Style Potato Chip - Lightly Salted
Reduced Fat Kettle Style Potato Chip - Sea Salt & Balsamic Vinegar
Reduced Fat Kettle Style Potato Chip - Sea Salt & Cracked Pepper
Reduced Fat Lightly Salted Chips
Reduced Fat Potato Honey Barbecue Chips ()
Reduced Fat Potato Ripple Chips
Reduced Fat Potato Salt & Pepper Chips
Reduced Fat Potato Unsalted Chips
Reduced Fat Potato Yogurt & Green Onion Chips ()

Miss Vickie's () ◉
Jalapeno Flavored Potato Chips
Lime & Black Pepper Potato Chips
Mesquite BBQ Flavored Potato Chips
Original Potato Chips

Munchos () ◉
Regular Potato Crisps

O'Keely's () ◉
Cheddar & Bacon Potato Skins Flavored Potato Crisps

Pringles ◉
Original Fat Free Pringles

Sour Cream & Onion Fat Free Pringles

Ruffles () ◉
Cheddar & Sour Cream Flavored Potato Chips
K.C. Masterpiece BBQ - Mesquite BBQ Flavor Potato Chips
Light Cheddar & Sour Cream Flavored Potato Chips
Light Original Potato Chips
Natural Reduced Fat Regular Sea Salted Potato Chips
Reduced Fat Potato Chips
Regular Potato Chips
Sour Cream & Onion Flavored Potato Chips

Sabritas () ◉
Adobadas Tomato & Chile Flavored Potato Chips

Snyder's of Hanover
Cheddar Jalapeno Potato Crisps
Regular Potato Chips - Seasoned
Ripple Potato Chips - Not Seasoned
Sweet Potato Crisps

Stop & Shop ✗ ◉
Kettle Cooked Potato Chips
Plain Potato Chips
Rippled Potato Chips
Salt & Vinegar Potato Chips
Sour Cream & Onion Chips
Wavy Cut Potato Chips

Utz
BBQ Potato Chips
BBQ Potato Chips Sack, #048-6 count
Carolina BBQ Potato Chips
Cheddar & Sour Cream Potato Chips
Grandma Utz BBQ Kettle Potato Chips
Grandma Utz Regular Kettle Potato Chips
Homestyle Regular Kettle Potato Chips
Kettle Classic Dark Russet Potato Chips
Kettle Classic Jalapeno Potato Chips
Kettle Classic Potato Chips
Kettle Classic Smokin' Sweet Potato Chips
Kettle Classic Sour Cream & Chive Potato Chips
Kettle Classic Sweet Potato Chips
Mystic Dark Russet Kettle Potato Chips
Mystic Regular Kettle Potato Chips
Mystic Sea Salt & Vinegar Kettle Potato Chips
Natural Dark Russet Kettle Potato Chips
Natural Gourmet Medley Kettle Potato Chips
Natural Lightly Salted Kettle Potato Chips
Natural Sea Salt & Vinegar Kettle Potato Chips
No Salt Potato Chips
Red Hot Potato Chips
Reduced Fat Regular Potato Chips
Reduced Fat Ripple Potato Chips
Regular Potato Chip Sack, #194-12 count

Snacks & Convenience Foods

Regular Potato Chip Sack, #008-6 count
Regular Potato Chips
Ripple Potato Chips
Salt & Pepper Potato Chips
Salt & Vinegar Potato Chips
Sour Cream & Onion Potato Chips
Wavy Potato Chips

Wegman's ⚊ ◉ ()
BBQ Potato Chips, 11.5 oz
Cracked Pepper Potato Chips - Organic, 5 oz
Kettle Potato Chips - BBQ-Flavored, 8.5 oz
Kettle Potato Chips - Original, 8.5 oz
Kettle Potato Chips - Salt & Pepper, 8.5 oz
Krinkle Potato Chips, 5.5 oz
Krinkle Potato Chips, 12 oz
Regular Potato Chips, 5.5 oz
Regular Potato Chips, 12 oz
Roasted Garlic & Onion Potato Chips - Organic, 5 oz
Rosemary & Thyme Potato Chips - Organic, 5 oz
Salt & Vinegar Potato Chips, 14.5 oz
Sea Salt Potato Chips - Organic, 5 oz
Sour Cream & Onion Potato Chips, 11.5 oz
Wavy Potato Chips, 12 oz

Winn-Dixie ◉
Barbeque Chips
Dill Pickle Chips
Hot Potato Chips
Original Potato Chips
Salt & Vinegar Chips
Sour Cream & Onion Chips
Unsalted Potato Chips
Wavy Cheddar & Sour Cream Chips
Wavy Potato Chips

PRETZELS

Ener-G
Ener-G, All BUT Low Protein Products
Glutino
Glutino, All

PUDDING AND PUDDING & PIE MIXES

Concord Foods
Banana Cream Pie Mix
Banana Creme Pudding & Pie Filling
Crosby's Molasses
Pudding Mix, All
Food You Feel Good About (Wegman's) ⚊ ◉ ()
Homestyle Chocolate Pudding, 22 oz
Homestyle Rice Pudding, 22 oz

Homestyle Tapioca Pudding, 22 oz
Hy-Vee ⚊ ◉
Butterscotch Pudding Cups, 14 oz
Chocolate Fudge Pudding Cups, 14 oz
Chocolate Pudding Cups, 4 pack - 14 oz
Cooked Chocolate Pudding, 3.5 oz
Cooked Vanilla Pudding, 3.12 oz
Fat Free Chocolate Pudding Cups, 4 pack - 14 oz
Instant Butterscotch Pudding, 3.4 oz
Instant Chocolate Pudding, 3.9 oz
Instant Fat Free/Sugar Free Chocolate Pudding, 1.5 oz
Instant Fat Free/Sugar Free Vanilla Pudding, 1.34 oz
Instant Lemon Pudding, 3.4 oz
Instant Pistachio Pudding, 3.4 oz
Instant Vanilla Pudding, 5.1 oz
Instant Vanilla Pudding, 3.4 oz
Tapioca Pudding Cups, 4 pack - 14 oz
Vanilla Pudding Cups, 4 pack - 14 oz
Kozy Shack
Puddings, All
Laura Lynn (Ingle's) ◉
Puddings RTE Dairy, All
Mori-Nu
Mates Chocolate Pudding Mix
Mates Lemon Créme Pudding Mix
Mates Vanilla Pudding Mix
Safeway ⚊ ◉
Pudding (Cups & Instant)
Stop & Shop ⚊ ◉
Butterscotch Pudding Mix
Chocolate Fudge Pudding Snack Cups
Chocolate Instant Pudding & Pie Filling
Chocolate Pudding Snack Cups
Instant Low Calorie Vanilla Pudding & Pie Mix
Refrigerated Chocolate Pudding
Refrigerated Chocolate/Vanilla Pudding
Refrigerated Fat Free Chocolate Pudding
Refrigerated Fat Free Chocolate/Vanilla Pudding
Rice Pudding
Sugar Free Chocolate Instant Pudding Mix
Tapioca Pudding Mix
Vanilla Pudding Snack Cups
Wegman's ⚊ ◉ ()
Chocolate Pudding, 6 - 4oz snack cups
Chocolate Pudding, Fat Free, 6 - 4oz snack cups
Chocolate Vanilla Swirl Pudding, 6 - 4oz snack cups
Chocolate Vanilla Swirl Pudding - Fat Free, 6 - 4oz snack cups
Vanilla Pudding, 6 - 4 oz snack cups
Vanilla Pudding - Fat Free, 6 - 4 oz snack cups

Snacks & Convenience Foods

ZenSoy
Zensoy, All

RICE & CORN CAKES

Lundberg Family Farms
Eco-Farmed Rice Cakes - Apple Cinnamon
Eco-Farmed Rice Cakes - Brown Rice
Eco-Farmed Rice Cakes - Brown Rice (Salt Free)
Eco-Farmed Rice Cakes - Buttery Caramel
Eco-Farmed Rice Cakes - Honey Nut
Eco-Farmed Rice Cakes - Sesame Tamari
Eco-Farmed Rice Cakes - Toasted Sesame
Eco-Farmed Rice Cakes - Wild Rice
Organic Rice Cakes - Brown Rice
Organic Rice Cakes - Brown Rice Salt Free
Organic Rice Cakes - Caramel Corn
Organic Rice Cakes - Cinnamon Toast
Organic Rice Cakes - Koku Seaweed
Organic Rice Cakes - Mochi Sweet
Organic Rice Cakes - Popcorn
Organic Rice Cakes - Sesame Tamari
Organic Rice Cakes - Tamari Seaweed
Organic Rice Cakes - Wild Rice

Stop & Shop
Apple Cinnamon Rice Cakes
Corn Cakes - Caramel & Multigrain Unsalted
Rice Cakes - Caramel
Rice Cakes - Plain Salted & Unsalted
Rice Cakes - Sesame Unsalted
Rice Cakes - Sour Cream & Onion
Rice Cakes - White Cheddar

Winn-Dixie
Mini Rice Cakes, All
Unsalted Rice Cakes

SALSA & PICANTE SAUCE

Amy's Kitchen ()
Black Bean & Corn Salsa
Fire Roasted Vegetable Salsa
Medium Salsa
Mild Salsa
Spicy Chipotle Salsa

Bone Suckin' Sauce
Bone Suckin' Salsa - Hot
Bone Suckin' Salsa - Regular

Cedar's Mediterranean Foods
Salsa, All

Chi-Chi's
Fiesta Salsa

Garden Salsa
Natural Salsa
Original Salsa
Picante
Roasted Tomato Salsa

Drew's All Natural
Organic Chipotle Lime Salsa
Organic Double Fire Roasted Salsa
Organic Hot Salsa
Organic Medium Salsa
Organic Mild Salsa

EatSmart
Salsa Con Queso

Emeril's
Gaaahlic Lovers Medium Salsa
Kicked Up Chunky Hot Salsa
Original Recipe Medium Salsa
Southwest Style Medium Salsa

Fischer & Wieser
Salsa a La Charra
Salsa Verde Ranchera

Food You Feel Good About (Wegman's)
Hot Salsa, 16 oz
Medium Salsa, 24 & 68 oz
Medium Salsa, 16 oz
Mild Salsa, 24 oz
Mild Salsa, 16 oz
Santa Fe Style Salsa, 16 oz

Gold's
Salsa, All

Grand Selections (Hy-Vee)
Medium Black Bean & Corn Salsa, 24 oz
Mild Black Bean & Corn Salsa, 24 oz

Green Mountain Gringo
Salsas

Guiltless Gourmet
Salsas, All

Health Market (Hy-Vee)
Organic Medium Salsa, 16 oz
Organic Mild Salsa, 16 oz
Organic Pineapple Salsa, 16 oz

Herr's ()
Mild & Medium Chunky Salsa

Hy-Vee
Hot Picante Sauce, 16 oz
Hot Salsa, 16 oz
Medium Picante Sauce, 68 oz
Medium Picante Sauce, 16 oz
Medium Salsa, 68 oz
Medium Salsa, 16 oz

Mild Picante Sauce, 68 oz
Mild Picante Sauce, 16 oz
Mild Salsa, 68 oz
Mild Salsa, 16 oz

Laura Lynn (Ingle's) 👁
Salsa, Picante, All

Litehouse
Medium Salsa

Nature's Promise (Stop & Shop) 〆 👁
Chipotle Organic Salsa
Organic Salsa - Mild & Medium

Pace 👁
Organic Picante - Mild & Medium
Picante Sauces, All
Thick & Chunky Flavored Salsas, All
Thick & Chunky Salsas, All

Red Gold ⓘ
Salsa, All

Robert Rothschild Farm
Cilantro Lime Salsa
Ginger Peach Salsa
Mango Salsa
Raspberry Chipotle Salsa
Raspberry Fiery Salsa
Raspberry Garden Salsa
Raspberry Original Salsa
Roasted Green Chili Salsa

Safeway 〆 👁
Salsa Con Queso
Salsas (Deli Counter)

Santa Barbara Salsa
Santa Barbara Salsa, All

Select Brand (Safeway) 〆 👁
Salsa, All Select Varieties

Simply Enjoy (Stop & Shop) 〆 👁
Black Bean & Corn Salsa
Peach Mango Salsa
Pineapple Chipotle Salsa
Raspberry Chipotle
Tequila Lime Salsa

Stop & Shop 〆 👁
Salsa - Mild, Medium & Hot

TGI Friday's Salsa ☁
Medium Salsa, 16 oz Jar
Mild Salsa, 16 oz Jar

Timpone's Organic
Salsa Muy Rica

Tostitos () 👁
All Natural Chunky Salsa - Hot, Medium & Mild
All Natural Picante Sauce - Medium & Mild

Restaurant Style Salsa

Utz
Mt. Misery Mike's Salsa Jug
Sweet Salsa

Wegman's 〆 👁 ()
Hot Salsa - Organic, 16 oz
Mango Salsa - Organic, 16 oz
Medium Salsa - Organic, 16 oz
Mild Salsa - Organic, 16 oz

Winn-Dixie 👁
Salsa

Tortilla & Corn Chips

Baked! Tostitos () 👁
Scoops! Tortilla Chips

Chi-Chi's ☁ 👁
Chips, All

Doritos () 👁
Black Pepper Jack Cheese Flavored Tortilla Chips
Blazin' Buffalo Ranch Flavored Tortilla Chips
Cool Ranch Flavored Tortilla Chips
Fiery Habanero Flavored Tortilla Chips
Light Nacho Cheesier Flavored Tortilla Chips
Natural White Nacho Cheese Tortilla Chips
Ranchero Flavored Tortilla Chips
Reduced Fat Cool Ranch Flavored Tortilla Chips
Salsa Flavored Tortilla Chips
Salsa Verde Flavored Tortilla Chips
Smokin' Cheddar BBQ Flavored Tortilla Chips
Spicy Nacho Flavored Tortilla Chips
Taco Flavored Tortilla Chips
Toasted Corn Tortilla Chips
Wild White Nacho Flavored Tortilla Chips

Fritos () 👁
Flavor Twists Honey BBQ Flavored Corn Chips
Original Corn Chips
Scoops! Corn Chips

Green Mountain Gringo
Tortilla Strips

Guiltless Gourmet
Chips, All

Health Market (Hy-Vee) 〆 👁
Organic Blue Corn Tortilla Chips, 13.5 oz
Organic White Corn Tortilla Chips, 14 oz
Organic Yellow Corn Tortilla Chips, 14 oz

Herr's ()
BBQ Corn Chips
Bite Size Dippers Tortilla Chips
Jalapeno Tortilla Chips
Nachitas Tortilla Chips

Original Corn Chips
Restaurant Style Tortilla Chips

Laura Lynn (Ingle's) 👁

Mini Corn Tortilla Chips, 13.5 oz
Nacho Tortilla Chips, 13.5 oz
Ranch Tortilla Chips, 13.5 oz
Regular Corn Chips, 10 oz
White Corn Tortilla Chips, 13.5 oz

Michael Season's

Organic Corn Tortilla Chips - Blue ()
Organic Corn Tortilla Chips - White ()
Organic Corn Tortilla Chips - Yellow ()

R.W. Garcia

R.W. Garcia, All BUT Whole Grain Spicy

Safeway ✓ 👁

White Corn Tortilla Chips

Santitas () 👁

White Corn Restaurant Style Tortilla Chips
Yellow Corn Tortilla Chips

Snyder's of Hanover

Multi Grain Golden Flax Tortilla Chips
Multi Grain Jalapeno Red Tortilla Chips
Multi Grain Savory Blue Tortilla Chips
Restaurant Style Tortilla Chips
White Corn Tortilla Chips
Yellow Corn Tortilla Chips

Stop & Shop ✓ 👁

Nacho Tortilla Chips
White Restaurant Tortilla Chips - Regular & Rounds
Yellow Round Tortilla Chips

Tostitos () 👁

100% White Corn Restaurant Style Tortilla Chips
Bite Size Gold Tortilla Chips
Bite Size Rounds Tortilla Chips
Crispy Rounds Tortilla Chips
Light Restaurant Style Tortilla Chips
Natural Blue Corn Restaurant Style Tortilla Chips
Natural Yellow Corn Restaurant Style Tortilla Chips
Restaurant Style with a Hint of Lime Flavor Tortilla
  Chips
Scoops! Tortilla Chips

Utz

Baked Tortilla Chips
BBQ Corn Chips
Cheesier Nacho Tortilla Chips
Creamy Ranch Tortilla Chips
Regular Corn Chips
Restaurant Style Tortilla Chips
White Round Tortilla Chips

Wegman's ✓ 👁 ()

Corn Chips, 10.5 oz

Organic Blue Corn Tortilla Chips - All Natural, 16 oz
Organic White Corn Tortilla Chips - All Natural, 16
  oz
Organic Yellow Corn Tortilla Chips - All Natural, 16
  oz
Round Tortilla Bite-Size Chips - 100% White Corn,
  14.5 oz
Round Tortilla Chips, 14.5 oz
Round Tortilla Chips - 100% White Corn, 14.5 oz
Tortilla Chips, Authentic - 100% White Corn, 14.5 oz

Winn-Dixie 👁

Big Dipper Corn Chips
Bite Size Tortilla Chips - Round White
Cheddar Cheese Dip with Tortilla Chips
Corn Chips
Restaurant Style Corn Tortilla Chips
Tortilla Chips
Tortilla Chips with Hint of Lime - Original and Hot
  & Spicy

BABY FOOD & FORMULA

BABY FOOD

Beech-Nut 👁

First Advantage - Apple Delight
First Advantage - Bananas Supreme
First Advantage - Rice Cereal with Apples
First Advantage - Sweet Potato Souffle
Stage 1 Fruits - Applesauce, 2.5 oz
Stage 1 Fruits - Chiquita Bananas, 2.5 oz
Stage 1 Fruits - Peaches, 2.5 oz
Stage 1 Fruits - Pears, 2.5 oz
Stage 1 Instant Cereal - Rice Cereal
Stage 1 Meats - Beef & Beef Broth, 2.5 oz
Stage 1 Meats - Chicken & Chicken Broth, 2.5 oz
Stage 1 Meats - Lamb & Lamb Broth, 2.5 oz
Stage 1 Meats - Turkey & Turkey Broth, 2.5 oz
Stage 1 Meats - Veal & Veal Broth, 2.5 oz
Stage 1 Vegetables - Butternut Squash, 2.5 oz
Stage 1 Vegetables - Tender Golden Sweet Potatoes, 2.5 oz
Stage 1 Vegetables - Tender Sweet Carrots, 2.5 oz
Stage 1 Vegetables - Tender Sweet Peas, 2.5 oz
Stage 1 Vegetables - Tender Young Green Beans, 2.5 oz
Stage 2 Desserts - Dutch Apple Dessert, 4 oz
Stage 2 Desserts - Fruit Dessert, 4 oz
Stage 2 Desserts - Mango Dessert, 4 oz
Stage 2 Desserts - Vanilla Custard Pudding with Apples, 4 oz
Stage 2 Dinners - Apples & Chicken, 4 oz
Stage 2 Dinners - Chicken & Rice Dinner, 4 oz
Stage 2 Dinners - Chicken Noodle Dinner, 4 oz
Stage 2 Dinners - Homestyle Chicken Soup, 4 oz
Stage 2 Dinners - Macaroni & Beef with Vegetables, 4 oz
Stage 2 Dinners - Pineapple Glazed Ham, 4 oz
Stage 2 Dinners - Sweet Potatoes & Chicken, 4 oz
Stage 2 Dinners - Turkey Rice Dinner, 4 oz
Stage 2 Dinners - Vegetables & Beef, 4 oz
Stage 2 Dinners - Vegetables & Chicken, 4 oz
Stage 2 Dinners - Vegetables & Ham, 4 oz
Stage 2 Fruit Yogurts - Banana Apple Yogurt, 4 oz
Stage 2 Fruit Yogurts - Mixed Fruit Yogurt, 4 oz
Stage 2 Fruits - Apples & Bananas, 4 oz
Stage 2 Fruits - Apples & Blueberries, 4 oz
Stage 2 Fruits - Apples & Cherries, 4 oz
Stage 2 Fruits - Apples & Pears, 4 oz
Stage 2 Fruits - Apples, Mango & Kiwi, 4 oz
Stage 2 Fruits - Apples, Pears & Bananas, 4 oz
Stage 2 Fruits - Applesauce, 4 oz
Stage 2 Fruits - Apricots with Pears & Apples, 4 oz
Stage 2 Fruits - Chiquita Bananas, 4 oz
Stage 2 Fruits - Chiquita Bananas & Strawberries, 4 oz
Stage 2 Fruits - Chiquita Bananas with Pears & Apples, 4 oz
Stage 2 Fruits - Cinnamon Raisin Pears with Apples, 4 oz
Stage 2 Fruits - Peaches, 4 oz
Stage 2 Fruits - Peaches & Bananas, 4 oz
Stage 2 Fruits - Pears, 4 oz
Stage 2 Fruits - Pears & Pineapples, 4 oz
Stage 2 Fruits - Pears & Raspberries, 4 oz
Stage 2 Fruits - Plums with Apples & Pears, 4 oz
Stage 2 Fruits - Prunes with Pears, 4 oz
Stage 2 Hispanic Variety - Banana, Apple & Pineapple
Stage 2 Hispanic Variety - Carrot, Apple & Mango
Stage 2 Hispanic Variety - Chicken with Carrots & Pink Beans
Stage 2 Hispanic Variety - Chicken with Sweet Potatoes & Rice
Stage 2 Hispanic Variety - Corn with Black Beans & Rice
Stage 2 Hispanic Variety - Guava Nectar
Stage 2 Hispanic Variety - Mango Nectar
Stage 2 Hispanic Variety - Rice Cereal with Island Fruits
Stage 2 Hispanic Variety - Sweet Potatoes & Guava
Stage 2 Instant Cereals - Rice & Golden Delicious

Apples Cereal, 8 oz box

Stage 2 Jar Cereals - Rice Cereal & Apples with Cinnamon, 4 oz

Stage 2 Vegetables - Butternut Squash, 4 oz

Stage 2 Vegetables - Carrots & Peas, 4 oz

Stage 2 Vegetables - Corn & Sweet Potatoes, 4 oz

Stage 2 Vegetables - Country Garden Vegetables, 4 oz

Stage 2 Vegetables - Mixed Vegetables, 4 oz

Stage 2 Vegetables - Sweet Corn Casserole, 4 oz

Stage 2 Vegetables - Sweet Potatoes & Apples, 4 oz

Stage 2 Vegetables - Tender Golden Sweet Potatoes, 4 oz

Stage 2 Vegetables - Tender Sweet Carrots, 4 oz

Stage 2 Vegetables - Tender Sweet Peas, 4 oz

Stage 2 Vegetables - Tender Young Green Beans, 4 oz

Stage 3 Desserts - Banana Pudding, 6 oz

Stage 3 Desserts - Fruit Dessert, 6 oz

Stage 3 Dinners - Country Vegetables & Chicken, 6 oz

Stage 3 Dinners - Turkey Rice Dinner, 6 oz

Stage 3 Fruits - Apples & Bananas, 6 oz

Stage 3 Fruits - Apples & Cherries, 6 oz

Stage 3 Fruits - Applesauce, 6 oz

Stage 3 Fruits - Apricots with Pears & Apples, 6 oz

Stage 3 Fruits - Chiquita Bananas, 6 oz

Stage 3 Fruits - Chiquita Bananas & Berries, 6 oz

Stage 3 Fruits - Peaches, 6 oz

Stage 3 Fruits - Pears, 6 oz

Stage 3 Jar Cereals - Rice Cereal & Pears, 6 oz

Stage 3 Vegetables - Carrots & Peas, 6 oz

Stage 3 Vegetables - Green Beans, Corn & Rice, 6 oz

Stage 3 Vegetables - Sweet Potatoes, 6 oz

Table Time Dices - Apple Dices

Table Time Dices - Carrot Dices

Table Time Dices - Green Bean Dices

Table Time Dices - Peach Dices

Table Time Dices - Pear Dices

Table Time Meals - Turkey Stew with Rice, 6 oz

Table Time Meals - Vegetable Stew with Beef, 6 oz

Table Time Meals - Veggie Soup, 6 oz

Hy-Vee ✗ 👁

Stage 2 - Mother's Choice Apple Blueberry, 4 oz

BABY FORMULA

EnfaCare ⓘ
Infant Formulas & Pediatric Products, All

Enfamil ⓘ
Infant Formulas & Pediatric Products, All

Nutramigen Lipil ⓘ
Pediatric Products & Infant Formulas, All

PBM Products
Formulas, All

Pedialyte 👁 ⓘ
Pediatric Liquid Nutritional Products, All

PediaSure 👁 ⓘ
Pediatric Liquid Nutritional Products, All

Pregestimil ⓘ
Pediatric Products & Infant Formulas, All

Similac 👁 ⓘ
Infant Formula Products, All

BABY JUICE & OTHER DRINKS

Beech-Nut 👁
Apple Cherry Juice from Concentrate, 4 & 32 oz
Apple Cranberry Juice from Concentrate, 4 oz
Apple Juice from Concentrate, 4 & 32 oz
Mixed Fruit Juice from Concentrate, 4 & 32 oz
Pear Juice from Concentrate, 4 & 32 oz
Spring Water with Fluoride
White Grape Juice from Concentrate, 4 & 32 oz

Hy-Vee ✗ 👁
Mother's Choice Infant Water, 1 gal
Mother's Choice Pediatric Vanilla with Fiber Drink, 6 - 8 fl oz

Wegman's ✗ 👁 ()
Baby Water - Purified Water with Fluoride, 128 fl oz

Baby Food & Formula

BREAD, PASTA & SIDES

BREAD

Ener-G
Ener-G, All BUT Low Protein Products

Enjoy Life Foods 🍴
Enjoy Life Foods, All

Food for Life
Wheat & Gluten Free Raisin Pecan Bread
Wheat & Gluten Free Rice Almond Bread
Wheat & Gluten Free Rice Pecan Bread
Wheat & Gluten Free White Rice Bread
Wheat & Gluten Free Whole Grain Bhutanese Red
   Rice Bread
Wheat & Gluten Free Whole Grain Brown Rice
   Bread
Wheat & Gluten Free Whole Grain China Black Rice
   Bread
Wheat & Gluten Free Whole Grain Millet Bread
Yeast Free Wheat & Gluten Free Fruit & Seed Medley
   Bread
Yeast Free Wheat & Gluten Free Multi Grain Bread
Yeast Free Wheat & Gluten Free White Rice Bread
Yeast Free Wheat & Gluten Free Whole Grain Brown
   Rice Bread

Gillian's Foods
Gillian's Foods, All

Glutino
Glutino, All

Lydia's Organics 🍴
Lydia's Organics, All

PASTAS & NOODLES

Annie Chun's
Original Pad Thai Noodles
Original Rice Noodles

Annie's Homegrown
Gluten-Free & Wheat-Free Rice Pasta & Cheddar

Dynasty
Maifun Rice Stick Noodles, #03188
Saifun Bean Thread Noodles, #03194

Eden Foods
Bifun (Rice) Pasta, UPC# 024182206029
Harusame (Mung Bean) Pasta, UPC# 024182205022
Kuzu Pasta, UPC# 024182227949

Glutino
Glutino, All

Lundberg Family Farms
Gluten-Free Penne
Gluten-Free Rotini
Gluten-Free Spaghetti

Manischewitz
Passover Noodles

OrgraN
Orgran, All

Taste of Thai, A
Thin Rice Noodles
Wide Rice Noodles
Rice Noodles

Thai Kitchen
Stir- Fry Rice Noodles
Thin Rice Noodles

Tinkyada Rice Pasta
Tinkyada Rice Pasta, All

POTATO, INSTANT & OTHER MIXES

Barbara's Bakery ()
Mashed Potatoes

Hy-Vee ✗ ◉
Four Cheese Mashed Potatoes, 7.6 oz
Instant Mashed Potatoes, 2.75 oz
Instant Mashed Potatoes, 16 oz
Roasted Garlic Mashed Potatoes, 7.6 oz
Sour Cream & Chive Mashed Potatoes, 7.6 oz

Idahoan
Baby Reds Mashed
Butter & Herb Mashed
Buttery Homestyle Mashed
Cheesy AuGratin Potato Casserole (Pouch), Item 172
Four Cheese Mashed
Hash Browns
Naturally Garlic Flavored Mashed Potatoes
Naturally Mashed Potatoes (Flakes)
Naturally Scalloped Potato Casserole
Original Mashed Potatoes
Real Premium Mashed
Roasted Garlic Mashed
Scalloped Potato Casserole (Pouch), Item 174
Southwest Mashed

Laura Lynn (Ingle's) 👁
Herb & Garlic Mashed Potatoes, 7.2 oz
Mashed Potatoes, 2 & 26.7oz
Mashed Potatoes, 13.3 oz
Roasted Garlic Mashed Potatoes, 7.2 oz
Sour Cream & Chives Mashed Potatoes, 7.2 oz

Manischewitz
Chicken Flavor Instant Mashed Potatoes
Homestyle Potato Latke Mix
Mini Potato Knish Mix
Potato Kugel Mix
Potato Pancake Mix
Sweet Potato Pancake Mix

Safeway 𝄢 👁
Herb/Butter Instant Mashed Potatoes
Roasted Garlic Instant Mashed Potatoes

Select Brand (Safeway) 𝄢 👁
Potato Cups - Buttermilk Ranch ()
Potato Cups - Roasted Garlic ()
Potato Cups - Sour Cream Chive ()
Potato Cups - Three Cheese Broccoli ()

Streit's
Mashed Potatoes
Potato Kugel Mix

Winn-Dixie 👁
Instant Mashed Potatoes

Rice & Rice Mixes

Alter Eco Fair Trade
Jasmine Rice - Full Line

Annie Chun's
Rice Express Sprouted Brown Rice
Rice Express Sticky White Rice

Botan Calrose
Rice

Dynasty
Jasmine Rice

Fantastic Foods ()
Arborio Rice
Basmati Rice
Jasmine Rice

Food You Feel Good About (Wegman's) 𝄢 👁 ()
Basmati Rice, 35.2 oz
Boil-In-Bag Rice (Enriched), 14 oz
Brown Rice - Long Grain, 16 oz
Enriched Long, 5 lb
Enriched Long Grain White Rice, 16 oz
Instant Brown Rice, 14 oz
Instant Rice, 28 oz
Instant Rice, 14 oz
Jasmine Rice, 35.2 oz
Medium Grain - White Rice, 5 lb
Rice Medium Grain, 16 oz

Hy-Vee 𝄢 👁
Boil-In-Bag Rice, 14 oz
Enriched Extra Long Grain Rice, 5 lb
Enriched Extra Long Grain Rice, 10 lb
Enriched Long Grain Instant Rice, 42 oz
Enriched Long Grain Instant Rice, 28 oz
Extra Long Grain Rice, 32 oz
Instant Brown Rice, 14 oz
Natural Long Grain Brown Rice, 32 oz
Spanish Rice, 15 oz

Italian Classics (Wegman's) 𝄢 👁 ()
Arborio Rice, 35.2 oz

Laura Lynn (Ingle's) 👁
Boil N' Bag Rice
Flavored Rice, All
Instant Rice
Long Grain White Rice

Lotus Foods
Lotus Foods, All

Lundberg Family Farms
Rice, All Varieties
Rice Sensations - Ginger Miso
Rice Sensations - Moroccan Pilaf
Rice Sensations - Thai Coconut Ginger
Rice Sensations - Zesty Southwestern
RiceXpress - Chicken Herb
RiceXpress - Classic Beef
RiceXpress - Santa Fe Grill
Risotto - Butternut Squash
Risotto - Cheddar Broccoli
Risotto - Creamy Parmesan
Risotto - Garlic Primavera
Risotto - Italian Herb

Bread, Pasta & Sides

Risotto - Organic Alfredo
Risotto - Organic Florentine
Risotto - Organic Porcini Mushroom
Risotto - Organic Tuscan

Manischewitz
Lentil Pilaf Mix
Spanish Pilaf Mix

Midwest Country Fare (Hy-Vee) ⋌ ☉
Pre-Cooked Instant Rice, 28 oz

Nishiki
Rice

Nueva Cocina
Chicken & Rice
Mexican Rice
Paella

RiceSelect
Rice Select, All Rice BUT Shiitake Mushroom Rice,
    Teriyaki Fried Rice & Whole Grain Royal Blends

Safeway ⋌ ☉
Instant Rice
Risotto - Cheese ()
White Long Grain Rice

Select Brand (Safeway) ⋌ ☉
Basmati Rice

Stop & Shop ⋌ ☉
Instant Brown Rice
Organic Long Grain Rice - Brown & White

Taste of Thai, A
Coconut Ginger Rice
Yellow Curry Rice

Thai Kitchen
Jasmine Rice Mixes - Green Chili & Garlic
Jasmine Rice Mixes - Jasmine Rice
Jasmine Rice Mixes - Lemongrass & Ginger
Jasmine Rice Mixes - Roasted Garlic & Chili
Jasmine Rice Mixes - Spicy Thai Chili
Jasmine Rice Mixes - Sweet Chili & Onion
Jasmine Rice Mixes - Thai Yellow Curry

Uncle Ben's ☉
Boil-In-Bag Rice
Fast & Natural Whole Grain Instant Brown Rice
Instant Rice
Original Converted Brand Rice
Whole Grain Brown Rice

Wegman's ⋌ ☉ ()
Long Grain Rice, 10 lb

Winn-Dixie ☉
Plain Rice

TACO SHELLS

Casa Fiesta ☉
Taco Dinners, 08122 - 9.75 oz
Taco Shells, 08102 - 4.5 oz

Hy-Vee ⋌ ☉
Taco Shells, 18 count - 6.89 OZ
Taco Shells, 12 count - 4.6 oz

Safeway ⋌ ☉
Jumbo Taco Shells
White Corn Taco Shells

Winn-Dixie ☉
Corn Shells - White & Yellow

TORTILLAS & OTHER WRAPS

Food for Life
Wheat & Gluten Free Whole Grain Brown Rice
    Tortillas

Hy-Vee ⋌ ☉
White Corn Tortilla, 12 count - 9 oz

La Tortilla Factory ♟
Corn Tortillas, All
GF Dark Teff Wraps
GF Ivory Teff Wraps

Laura Lynn (Ingle's) ☉
White Corn Tortilla, 20 oz

Manny's ⚘ ☉
Corn Tortillas

Winn-Dixie ☉
Corn Tortilla - White & Yellow

WHOLE GRAINS

Alter Eco Fair Trade
Whole Grain Quinoa - GF Red & White

Bob's Red Mill ⓘ ♟
Amaranth Grain, Item# 1011
Flaxseed (Brown), Item# 1230
Hulled Millet, Item# 1295
Organic Buckwheat Berries, Item# 1096
Organic Buckwheat Groats, Item# 1092
Organic Buckwheat Kernels - Kasha, Item# 1094
Organic Flaxseed - Brown, Item# 6031
Organic Golden Flaxseed, Item# 6034
Organic Quinoa Grain, Item# 1447
Teff Grain, Item# 1533

Eden Foods
Quinoa, UPC# 024182021509

Ener-G
Ener-G, All BUT Low Protein Products

Bread, Pasta & Sides

FROZEN FOODS

BEANS

Food You Feel Good About (Wegman's) ✔ 👁 ()
Baby Lima Beans, 16 oz
Fordhook Lima Beans, 16 oz
Hy-Vee ✔ 👁
Baby Lima Beans, 16 oz
Nature's Promise (Stop & Shop) ✔ 👁
Organic Edamame in Pod
Stop & Shop ✔ 👁
Baby Lima Beans
Fordhook Lima Beans
Italian Beans
Wegman's ✔ 👁 ()
Micro Baby Lima Beans, 10 oz
Winn-Dixie 👁
Beans, All
Lima Beans

FISH & SEAFOOD PRODUCTS

Dr. Praeger's
Potato Crusted Fillet Fish Sticks
Potato Crusted Fish Fillets
Potato Crusted Fishies
Ian's Natural Foods
Wheat Free Gluten Free Recipe Battered Fish
Wheat Free Gluten Free Recipe Fish Sticks
Wegman's ✔ 👁 ()
Alaskan Halibut, 2 Fillets - 12 oz
Atlantic Salmon Fillets - Farm Raised (Club Pack), 32 oz
Orange Roughy, 2 Fillets - 12 oz
Sea Bass, 2 Fillets - 12 oz
Sockeye Salmon, 2 Fillets - 12 oz
Swordfish - Sashimi Grade, 2 Steaks - 12 oz
Tilapia Fillets - Farm Raised (Club Pack), 32 oz
Yellowfin Tuna - Sashimi Grade, 2 Steaks - 12 oz

FROZEN YOGURT

Edy's
Slow Churned Yogurt Blends - Black Cherry Vanilla Swirl
Slow Churned Yogurt Blends - Cappuccino Chip
Slow Churned Yogurt Blends - Caramel Praline Crunch
Slow Churned Yogurt Blends - Chocolate Vanilla Swirl
Slow Churned Yogurt Blends - Strawberry
Slow Churned Yogurt Blends - Vanilla
Hood
Chocolate Almond Praline Frozen Yogurt
Fat Free Double Raspberry Frozen Yogurt
Lucerne (Safeway) ✔ 👁
Fat Free Vanilla Frozen Yogurt
WholeSoy & Co.
Frozen Yogurt, All

FRUIT

Food You Feel Good About (Wegman's) ✔ 👁 ()
Sweet Cherries (Grade A), 16 oz
Hy-Vee ✔ 👁
Blueberries, 16 oz
Cherry Berry Blend, 16 oz
Red Raspberries, 12 oz
Sliced Strawberries, 16 oz
Whole Strawberries, 16 oz
Stop & Shop ✔ 👁
Berry Medley
Blackberries
Blueberries
Dark Sweet Cherries
Mango
Mixed Fruit
Peaches
Pineapple

Raspberries
Raspberries in Syrup
Sliced Strawberries
Sliced Strawberries in Sugar
Sliced Strawberries with Artificial Sweetener
Strawberries

Wegman's ⁄ ◉ ()
Frozen Fruit - Berry Medley, 16 oz
Frozen Fruit - Blackberries, 16 oz
Frozen Fruit - Blueberries, 16 & 48 oz
Frozen Fruit - Mixed Fruit, 16 & 40 oz
Frozen Fruit - Raspberries, 12 oz
Frozen Fruit - Raspberries with Sugar, 10 oz
Frozen Fruit - Sliced Peaches, 16 oz & 3 lb
Frozen Fruit - Sliced Strawberries with Sugar, 16 oz
Frozen Fruit - Sliced Strawberries, Light, (with Aspartame), 15 oz
Frozen Fruit - Strawberries, 16 & 40 oz
Tropical Fruit, 16 oz

Winn-Dixie ◉
Frozen Berry Medley
Frozen Blackberries
Frozen Blueberries
Frozen Dark Sweet Cherries
Frozen Mango Chunks
Frozen Mixed Fruit
Frozen Raspberries
Frozen Sliced Peaches
Frozen Strawberries

Wyman's
Wyman's, All

ICE CREAM

Blue Bunny
Chocolate Ice Cream
Strawberry Ice Cream
Vanilla Ice Cream

Edy's
Classic Limited Edition Flavors - Peppermint
Classic Limited Edition Flavors - Pumpkin
Edy's Loaded - Chocolate Peanut Butter Cup
Edy's Loaded - Nestle Butterfinger
Grand Ice Cream - Almond Praline
Grand Ice Cream - Butter Pecan
Grand Ice Cream - Cherry Chocolate Chip
Grand Ice Cream - Cherry Vanilla
Grand Ice Cream - Chocolate
Grand Ice Cream - Chocolate Chip
Grand Ice Cream - Coffee
Grand Ice Cream - Double Vanilla
Grand Ice Cream - Dulce De Leche
Grand Ice Cream - French Vanilla
Grand Ice Cream - Fudge Swirl
Grand Ice Cream - Fudge Tracks
Grand Ice Cream - Mint Chocolate Chip
Grand Ice Cream - Mocha Almond Fudge
Grand Ice Cream - Neapolitan
Grand Ice Cream - Nestle Turtle Sundae
Grand Ice Cream - Peanut Butter Cup
Grand Ice Cream - Real Strawberry
Grand Ice Cream - Rocky Road
Grand Ice Cream - Spumoni
Grand Ice Cream - Toffee Bar Crunch
Grand Ice Cream - Ultimate Caramel Cup
Grand Ice Cream - Vanilla
Grand Ice Cream - Vanilla Bean
Grand Ice Cream - Vanilla Chocolate
Slow Churned Light - Almond Praline
Slow Churned Light - Butter Pecan
Slow Churned Light - Caramel Delight
Slow Churned Light - Cherry Chocolate Chip
Slow Churned Light - Choc 'n Roll Caramel (American Idol)
Slow Churned Light - Chocolate
Slow Churned Light - Chocolate Chips!
Slow Churned Light - Chocolate Fudge Chunk
Slow Churned Light - Coffee
Slow Churned Light - Eggnog (Limited Edition Flavors)
Slow Churned Light - French Vanilla
Slow Churned Light - Fudge Tracks
Slow Churned Light - Mint Chocolate Chips!
Slow Churned Light - Mocha Almond Fudge
Slow Churned Light - Neapolitan
Slow Churned Light - Peanut Butter Cup
Slow Churned Light - Peppermint (Limited Edition Flavors)
Slow Churned Light - Pumpkin (Limited Edition Flavors)
Slow Churned Light - Raspberry Chip Royale
Slow Churned Light - Rocky Road
Slow Churned Light - Strawberry
Slow Churned Light - Take the Cake (American Idol)
Slow Churned Light - Triple Talent (American Idol)
Slow Churned Light - Vanilla
Slow Churned Light - Vanilla Bean
Slow Churned Light - Vanilla Chocolate
Slow Churned No Sugar Added Light - Butter Pecan
Slow Churned No Sugar Added Light - Caramel Chocolate Swirl
Slow Churned No Sugar Added Light - Chocolate
Slow Churned No Sugar Added Light - Chocolate Chip

Slow Churned No Sugar Added Light - Chocolate Fudge
Slow Churned No Sugar Added Light - Coffee
Slow Churned No Sugar Added Light - French Vanilla
Slow Churned No Sugar Added Light - Fudge Tracks
Slow Churned No Sugar Added Light - Mint Chocolate Chip
Slow Churned No Sugar Added Light - Mocha Almond Fudge
Slow Churned No Sugar Added Light - Neapolitan
Slow Churned No Sugar Added Light - Triple Chocolate
Slow Churned No Sugar Added Light - Vanilla
Slow Churned No Sugar Added Light - Vanilla Bean
Slow Churned No Sugar Added Light - Vanilla Chocolate

Guaranteed Value (Stop & Shop) ⁄ ◉

Chocolate Ice Cream
Chocolate Marshmallow
Fudge Royal Ice Cream
Neapolitan Ice Cream
Vanilla Ice Cream
Vanilla Orange Ice Cream

Hood

Almond Praline Delight Light
Bear Creek Caramel New England Creamery
Boston Vanilla Bean New England Creamery
Butter Pecan Light
Butter Toffee Crunch Light
Butterscotch Blast
Cape Cod Fudge Shop New England Creamery
Caribbean Coffee Royale Light
Chippedy Chocolaty
Chocolate
Classic Trio
Creamy Coffee
Creamy Vanilla Light
Fudge Twister
Golden Vanilla
Holiday EggNog
Light Butter Pecan New England Creamery
Light Chocolate Chip New England Creamery
Light French Silk New England Creamery
Light Mint Chocolate Chip New England Creamery
Light Under the Stars New England Creamery
Light Vanilla New England Creamery
Maine Blueberry & Sweet Cream New England Creamery
Maple Walnut
Martha's Vineyard Black Raspberry New England Creamery

Moosehead Lake Fudge New England Creamery
Mystic Lighthouse Mint New England Creamery
Natural Vanilla Bean
New England Homemade Vanilla New England Creamery
New England Lighthouse Coffee New England Creamery
North End Spumoni New England Creamery
Patchwork
Peppermint Stick
Raspberry Swirl Light
Red Sox, All Flavors
Strawberry
Vermont Maple Nut New England Creamery

Hy-Vee ⁄ ◉

Butter Crunch Ice Cream, 1/2 gal
Cherry Nut Ice Cream, 1/2 gal
Cherry Nut Light Ice Cream, 1/2 gal
Chocolate Chip Ice Cream, 4.5 qt
Chocolate Chip Ice Cream, 1/2 gal
Chocolate Chip Light Ice Cream, 1/2 gal
Chocolate Ice Cream, 4.5 qt
Chocolate Ice Cream, 1/2 gal
Chocolate Marshmallow Ice Cream, 1/2 gal
Chocolate/Vanilla Flavored Ice Cream, 4.5 qt
Dutch Chocolate Light Ice Cream, 1/2 gal
Fudge Marble Ice Cream, 1/2 gal
Mint Chip Ice Cream, 1/2 gal
Neapolitan Ice Cream, 4.5 qt
Neapolitan Ice Cream, 1/2 gal
Neapolitan Light Ice Cream, 1/2 gal
New York Vanilla Flavored Ice Cream, 1/2 gal
New York Vanilla Ice Cream, 4.5 qt
Orange Blossom Ice Cream & Sherbet, 4.5 qt
Peanut Butter Fudge Ice Cream, 1/2 gal
Peppermint Ice Cream, 1/2 gal
Strawberry Ice Cream, 1/2 gal
Vanilla Flavored Ice Cream, 4.5 qt
Vanilla Flavored Ice Cream, 1/2 gal
Vanilla Light Ice Cream, 1/2 gal

Italian Classics (Wegman's) ⁄ ◉ ()

All Natural Chocolate, 1/2 gal
All Natural Coffee Explosion, 1/2 gal
All Natural French Vanilla, 1/2 gal
All Natural Vanilla, 1/2 gal
All Natural Vanilla Fudge, 1/2 gal
Black Raspberry, 1/2 gal
Café Latte with Whipped Cream Flavored Ripple Coffee, qt
Chocolate, 1.75 qt
Chocolate Chip, 1.75 qt
Chocolate Marshmallow, 1.75 qt

Frozen Foods

Heavenly Hash, 1/2 gal
Low Fat Chocolate Indulgence, 1.75 qt
Neapolitan, 1.75 qt
Neapolitan - All Natural, 1/2 gal
Peanut Butter & Jelly Super Premium, pt
Peanut Butter Swirl, 1/2 gal
Strawberry, 1.75 qt
Tin Roof, 1/2 gal
Venetian Cappuccino Ice Cream, 1/2 gal

It's Soy Delicious ☺
Almond Pecan, pt
Awesome Chocolate, pt
Black Leopard, pt
Carob Peppermint, pt
Chocolate Almond, pt
Chocolate Peanut Butter, pt
Espresso, pt
Green Tea, pt
Mango Raspberry, pt
Pistachio Almond, pt
Raspberry, pt
Tiger Chai, pt
Vanilla, pt
Vanilla Fudge, pt

Midwest Country Fare (Hy-Vee) ✓ ◉
Chocolate Chip Ice Cream, 4 qt
Chocolate Ice Cream, 4 qt
Light Vanilla Ice Cream, 4 qt
Neapolitan Ice Cream, 4 qt
Vanilla Ice Cream, 4 qt

Organic So Delicious ☺
Dairy Free Quarts - Butter Pecan
Dairy Free Quarts - Chocolate Peanut Butter
Dairy Free Quarts - Chocolate Velvet
Dairy Free Quarts - Creamy Vanilla
Dairy Free Quarts - Dulce De Leche
Dairy Free Quarts - Mint Marble Fudge
Dairy Free Quarts - Mocha Fudge
Dairy Free Quarts - Neapolitan
Dairy Free Quarts - Peanut Butter
Dairy Free Quarts - Strawberry
Dairy Free Quarts - Twisted Vanilla Orange

Prestige (Winn-Dixie) ◉
Cherry Vanilla Ice Cream
Chocolate Almond Ice Cream
French Vanilla Ice Cream

Purely Decadent ☺
Dairy Free Pints - Cherry Nirvana
Dairy Free Pints - Chocolate Obsession
Dairy Free Pints - Mint Chocolate Chip
Dairy Free Pints - Mocha Almond Fudge

Dairy Free Pints - Peanut Butter Zig Zag
Dairy Free Pints - Praline Pecan
Dairy Free Pints - Purely Vanilla
Dairy Free Pints - Rocky Road
Dairy Free Pints - Swinging Anna Banana
Dairy Free Pints - Turtle Tracks
Dairy Free Pints - Vanilla Swiss Almond

Reed's
Ice Cream, All

Select Brand (Safeway) ✓ ◉
Chocolate Chunk Ice Cream
Dutch Chocolate Ice Cream
Fat Free Caramel Swirl Ice Cream
Fat Free No Sugar Added Vanilla Ice Cream
Light Peppermint Ice Cream
Mother Load Ice Cream

Skondra's (Hy-Vee) ✓ ◉
Caramel Pecan Lite Ice Cream, 1/2 gal

Stop & Shop ✓ ◉
Butterscotch Ripple Ice Cream
Chocolate Chip Ice Cream
Coffee Ice Cream
Country Club Ice Cream
Heavenly Hash Ice Cream
Natural Butter Pecan Ice Cream
Natural Chocolate Chip Ice Cream
Natural Chocolate Ice Cream
Natural Coffee Ice Cream
Natural French Vanilla Ice Cream
Natural Mint Chocolate Chip Ice Cream
Natural Mocha Almond Ice Cream
Natural Strawberry Ice Cream
Natural Vanilla Bean Ice Cream
Natural Vanilla Fudge Ripple Ice Cream
Neapolitan Ice Cream
Peppermint Stick Ice Cream
Strawberry Ice Cream
Vanilla Fudge Swirl Ice Cream
Vanilla Ice Cream

Wegman's ✓ ◉ ()
All Natural Mint Chocolate Chip, 1/2 gal
Chocolate Caramel Premium Ice Cream, pt
Chocolate Vanilla Ice Cream, 1.75 qt
Crème De Menthe Ice Cream, 1/2 gal
Egg Nog Flavored Ice Cream, 1/2 gal
French Roast Coffee Ice Cream, qt
French Vanilla Ice Cream, 1.75 qt
Hazelnut Chip Coffee Ice Cream, 32 oz
Low Fat Cappuccino Chip Ice Cream, 1/2 gal
Low Fat Mint Chip Ice Cream, 1/2 gal
Low Fat Praline Pecan Ice Cream, 1/2 gal

Frozen Foods

Low Fat Raspberry Truffle Ice Cream, 1.75 qt
Low Fat Vanilla Ice Cream, 1.75 qt
Maple Walnut Ice Cream, 1.75 qt
Peak of Perfection - Black Cherry Ice Cream, 1.75 qt
Peak of Perfection - Blueberry Ice Cream, 1.75 qt
Peak of Perfection - Mango Ice Cream, 1.75 qt
Peak of Perfection - Peach Ice Cream, 1/2 gal
Peak of Perfection - Strawberry Ice Cream, 1.75 qt
Peanut Butter Cup Ice Cream, 1/2 gal
Peanut Butter Cup Premium Ice Cream, pt
Peanut Butter Sundae Ice Cream, 1.75 qt
Pistachio Vanilla Swirl Ice Cream, 1.75 qt
Premium Vanilla Ice Cream, pt
Raspberry Cashew Swirl Ice Cream, 1/2 gal
Super Premium Ice Cream - Butter Pecan, pt
Super Premium Ice Cream - Cherry Armagnac, pt
Super Premium Ice Cream - Chocolate, pt
Super Premium Ice Cream - Coconut Mango, pt
Super Premium Ice Cream - Creamy Caramel, pt
Super Premium Ice Cream - Crème Brulee, pt
Super Premium Ice Cream - Dark Chocolate, pt
Super Premium Ice Cream - French Roast, pt
Super Premium Ice Cream - Hazelnut Chip, pt
Super Premium Ice Cream - Jamocha Almond Fudge, pt
Super Premium Ice Cream - Rum Raisin, pt
Triple Flip Vanilla Ice Cream, 1/2 gal
Vanilla Ice Cream, 1.75 qt
Vanilla Ice Cream with Orange Sherbet, 1.75 qt
Vanilla Raspberry Sorbet Ice Cream, 1.75 qt

Winn-Dixie 👁
Butter Pecan Ice Cream
Chocolate Ice Cream
Classic Chocolate Low Fat Ice Cream
Strawberry Ice Cream
Vanilla Ice Cream

JUICE

Food You Feel Good About (Wegman's) ∕ 👁 ()
Grapefruit Juice Concentrate, 12 oz
Orange Juice Concentrate, 6, 12 & 16 oz
Orange Juice Concentrate - Country Style, 12 oz
Orange Juice Concentrate - Pulp Free, 12 oz

Hy-Vee ∕ 👁
Apple Juice Frozen Concentrate, 12 fl oz
Fruit Punch Frozen Concentrate, 12 fl oz
Grape Juice Cocktail Frozen Concentrate, 12 fl oz
Grapefruit Juice Frozen Concentrate, 12 fl oz
Lemonade Frozen Concentrate, 12 fl oz
Limeade Frozen Concentrate, 12 fl oz
Orange Juice Frozen Concentrate, 16 fl oz

Orange Juice Frozen Concentrate, 12 fl oz
Orange Juice with Added Calcium, 12 fl oz
Pineapple Juice from Concentrate, 46 fl oz
Pink Lemonade Frozen Concentrate, 12 fl oz

Midwest Country Fare (Hy-Vee) ∕ 👁
Orange Juice Frozen Concentrate, 12 oz

Stop & Shop ∕ 👁
Frozen Concentrate 100% Grape Juice
Frozen Concentrate Apple Juice
Frozen Concentrate Cranberry Cocktail
Frozen Concentrate Fruit Punch
Frozen Concentrate Grape Cocktail
Frozen Concentrate Lemonade
Frozen Concentrate Limeade
Frozen Concentrate Orange Juice
Frozen Concentrate Pink Lemonade
Frozen Concentrate White Grape Cocktail
Frozen Concentrate Wildberry Punch

Wegman's ∕ 👁 ()
Frozen Concentrate Limeade, 12 oz
Lemonade Concentrate, 12 oz
Orange Juice Concentrate with Calcium, 12 oz
Pink Lemonade Concentrate, 12 oz

Welch's ⓘ
Welch's, All

Winn-Dixie 👁
Frozen Apple Juice
Frozen Grape Juice
Frozen Grape Juice Cocktail
Frozen Lemonade
Frozen Orange Juice
Frozen Pink Lemonade

MEAT

Applegate Farms 👁 ∕
Applegate Farms, All BUT Chicken Nuggets & Chicken Pot Pie

Bubba Burger
Bubba Burger, All

Empire Kosher
Frozen Chicken
Frozen Ground Turkey
Frozen Whole Turkey & Turkey Breasts
Individually Quick Frozen Chicken Parts

Honeysuckle White
Honeysuckle White, All BUT Asian Grill Marinated Turkey Strips, Cajun Fried Turkey, Frozen Turkey Burgers, Italian Style Meatballs & Teriyaki Turkey Breast Tenderloins

Frozen Foods

Jennie-O ☘ ◉
Frozen Ground Seasoned Turkey
Frozen Ground Turkey
Frozen Turkey Breast, Gravy packet NOT GF
Frozen Turkey Burgers

Manor House (Safeway) ✚ ◉
Chicken (4 lb Resealable Bags), All Varieties
Frozen Enhanced Turkey

Perdue
Individually Frozen - Chicken Breasts
Individually Frozen - Chicken Tenderloins
Individually Frozen - Chicken Wings

Philly Gourmet
100% Pure Beef Homestyle Patties
Pure Beef Sandwich Steaks

Wegman's ✚ ◉ ()
Beef Burgers - Fully Cooked, 8 - 4 oz burgers

Wellshire Farms
Frozen Beef Hamburgers, Item# 00210
Frozen Chicken Apple Patties, Item# 00415 - 12 oz
Frozen Chicken Apple Sausage Links, Item# 00410 - 10 oz
Frozen Country Sage Sausage Links, Item# 00320 - 10 oz
Frozen Country Sage Sausage Patties, Item# 00325 - 12 oz
Frozen Original Breakfast Sausage Links, Item# 00330 - 10 oz
Frozen Original Breakfast Sausage Patties, Item# 00335 - 12 oz
Frozen Sunrise Maple Sausage Links, Item# 00340 - 10 oz
Frozen Sunrise Maple Sausage Patties, Item# 00345 - 12 oz
Frozen Turkey Maple Patties, Item# 00295 - 12 oz
Frozen Turkey Maple Sausage Links, Item# 00290 - 10 oz

Winn-Dixie ◉
Boneless Skinless Chicken Breasts
Chicken Wings
Frozen Boneless Skinless Chicken Tenderloins
Frozen Chicken Breasts with Rib Meat
Frozen Chicken Wings

NOVELTIES

Edy's
Cherry, Grape & Tropical Variety Pack
Fruit Bars - Creamy Coconut
Fruit Bars - Grape
Fruit Bars - Lemonade
Fruit Bars - Lime
Fruit Bars - Lime, Strawberry & Wildberry Variety Pack
Fruit Bars - No Sugar Added Black Cherry, Strawberry Kiwi & Mixed Berry Variety Pack
Fruit Bars - No Sugar Added Raspberry, Strawberry & Tangerine Variety Pack
Fruit Bars - Orange & Cream
Fruit Bars - Strawberry
Fruit Bars - Strawberry-Banana Smoothie
Fruit Bars - Tangerine
Fruit Bars - Tropical Smoothie
Slow Churned Light Ice Cream - Vanilla Almond (No Sugar Added) Ice Cream Bars

Food You Feel Good About (Wegman's) ✚ ◉ ()
Juice Bars Variety Pack - Orange, Lime & Raspberry, 12 - 2.5 fl oz bars

Hood
Hendries Citrus Stix
Hendries Kids Karnival Stix
Hendries Kids Stix
Hendries Mix Stix
Hendries NSA Citrus 'n Berry
Hendries Pop Stix
Hoodsie Cups
Hoodsie Pops - 6 Flavor Assortment Twin Pops
Hoodsie Sundae Cups
Ice Cream Bar
Orange Cream Bar
Rocket

Hy-Vee ✚ ◉
Assorted Twin Pops, 50 fl oz
Chocolate & Strawberry Sundae Cups, 36 fl oz
Fat Free No Sugar Added Fudge Bars, 21 fl oz
Freedom Pops, 21 fl oz
Fudge Bars, 50 fl oz
Fudge Bars, 21 fl oz
Galaxy Reduced Fat Ice Cream Bars, 50 fl oz
Pops - Cherry, Orange & Grape, 21 fl oz
Reduced Fat Galaxy Bars, 24 fl oz

Lucerne (Safeway) ✚ ◉
Fudge Ice Cream Bars
Orange Ice Cream Bars
Root Beer Float Ice Cream Bars
Toffee Brittle Ice Cream Bars
Vanilla Ice Cream Bars
Vanilla Sundae Ice Cream Cups
Vanilla/Sherbet Ice Cream Bars

Nestlé Ice Cream ◉
Bars - Husky
Bars - Nestlé Butterfinger

Frozen Foods

Bars - Nestlé Butterfinger Loaded
Bars - Rolo
Frozen Pops - Nestlé Itzakadoozie
Frozen Pops - Nestlé Scooby-Doo! Mystery Pops
(Strawberry Suspicion, Orange Zoinks, Berry
Jinkies & Mystery)
Frozen Pops - Nestlé Shrek Sludge Fudge
Frozen Pops - Nestlé Shrek Swamp Pops
Frozen Pops - Nestlé Superman Sticks
Frozen Pops - Nestlé Triple Blast
Push-Up - Sherbet Orange
Push-Up - Sherbet Rainbow (Cherry, Orange, Grape
& Lemon)
Shrek Push-Up Fruity Sherbet Swirls

Organic So Delicious ⚇
Dairy Free 3-pk Novelties - Creamy Fudge Bar
Dairy Free 3-pk Novelties - Creamy Orange Bar
Dairy Free 3-pk Novelties - Creamy Raspberry Bar
Dairy Free Novelties - Creamy Fudge Bar
Dairy Free Novelties - Creamy Vanilla Bar
Dairy Free Novelties - Vanilla & Almond Bar

PhillySwirl
PhillySwirl, All

Purely Decadent ⚇
Dairy Free Novelties - Purely Vanilla Bar
Dairy Free Novelties - Vanilla Almond Bar

Select Brand (Safeway) ✔ ◉
Caramel Caribou Ice Cream Bars

So Delicious ⚇
Sugar Free Novelty Multipacks - Fudge Bar
Sugar Free Novelty Multipacks - Vanilla Bar

Sweet Nothings ⚇
Fudge Bar
Mango Raspberry Bar

Wegman's ✔ ◉ ()
Assorted Fruity Pops - Cherry, Orange, & Grape, 12
& 24 pops
Assorted Fruity Pops (Sugar Free) - Cherry, Orange
& Grape, 12 pops
Cherry with Dark Chocolate Ice Cream Bars, 6 - 3.0
fl oz bars
Fudge Bars, 12 - 2.5 oz
Fudge Bars - No Sugar Added, 10 - 2.5 fl oz bars
Ice Cream Bars, 12 - 2.5 oz
Ice Cream Cups, 12 - 3 oz
Ice Pops (Twin Stick), 12 bars
Peanut Butter Candy Sundae Cups
Peanut Butter Cup Sundae Cups
Vanilla & Dark Chocolate Premium Ice Cream Bars,
6 - 3 oz bars

Welch's ⓘ
Welch's, All

Winn-Dixie ◉
12 Assorted Pops
Banana Pops
Crème Bars
Red White & Blue Pops

PIZZA & PIZZA CRUSTS

Amy's Kitchen ()
Rice Crust Cheese Pizza
Rice Crust Spinach Pizza

Glutino
Glutino, All

POTATOES

Alexia Foods ()
Potato Products, All

Hy-Vee ✔ ◉
Country Style Hash Brown Potatoes, 30 oz
Crinkle Cut Fries, 80 oz
Crinkle Cut Fries, 32 oz
Criss Cut Potatoes, 32 oz
Steak Fries, 28 oz

Ian's Natural Foods
Wheat Free Gluten Free Recipe Alphatots
Wheat Free Gluten Free Recipe Supertots

Ingles Markets ◉
Frozen Potatoes, All BUT Seasoned Fries

Ore-Ida ☖
Cottage Fries, UPC# 1312000377 - 32 oz
Country Style Hashbrowns, UPC# 1312000833 - 30
oz
Country Style Hashbrowns, UPC# 1312000862 - 6 lb
Country Style Hashbrowns, UPC# 1312000654 - 6 lb
Crunch Time Classics Crinkle Cut, UPC#
1312000810 - 24 oz
Crunch Time Classics Straight Cut, UPC#
1312000809 - 24 oz
Deep Fries Crinkle Cuts, UPC# 1312000845 - 24 oz
Extra Crispy Fast Food Fries, UPC# 1312001417 - 26
oz
French Fries, UPC# 1312000647 - 8 lb
Golden Crinkles, UPC# 1312000291 - 5 lb
Golden Crinkles, UPC# 1312008572 - 8 lb
Golden Crinkles, UPC# 1312000286 - 32 oz
Golden Crinkles, UPC# 1312008564 - 8 lb
Golden Fries, UPC# 1312000258 - 32 oz
Golden Fries, UPC# 1312008565 - 8 lb

Golden Fries, UPC# 1312000278 - 5 lb
Golden Patties, UPC# 1312000080 - 9 ct
Hash Browns, UPC# 1312000854 - 5 lb
Pixie Crinkles, UPC# 1312000296 - 26 oz
Potato Wedges with Skins, UPC# 1312001012 - 24 oz
Potatoes O'Brien, UPC# 1312000469 - 28 oz
Shoestrings, UPC# 1312000828 - 28 oz
Shoestrings, UPC# 1312000829 - 40 oz
Shoestrings, UPC# 1312000801 - 5 lb
Snackin' Fries, UPC# 1312000198 - 105 oz
Southern Style Hash Browns, UPC# 1312000392 - 32 oz
Steak Fries, UPC# 1312001190 - 375 lb
Tater Tots, All Varieties, UPC# 13120xxxxx

Safeway 𝄭 ◉
Crinkle Cut Potatoes
Crispy Fries
French Fried Potatoes
Hash Browns - Country Style, Shredded & Southern Style
O'Brien Potatoes
Potato Sticks
Restaurant Style Crinkle Cut Potatoes
Shoestring Potatoes
Steak Cut Potatoes
Twice Baked Potatoes

Select Brand (Safeway) 𝄭 ◉
Roasted Rosemary Wedges

Stop & Shop 𝄭 ◉
Butter Twice Baked Potatoes
Cheddar Cheese Twice Baked Potatoes
Crinkle Cut French Fries
Crispy Fries
Extra Crispy Crinkle Cut Fries
Frozen Natural Wedges
Latkes
Puffs with Onions
Shoestring Fries
Shredded Hash Browns
Sour Cream & Chive Twice Baked Potatoes
Southwestern Style Hash Browns
Steak Fries
Straight Cut French Fries

Wegman's 𝄭 ◉ ()
Country Style Hash Browns, 30 oz
Crinkle Cut, 5 lb
Crinkle Cut, 32 oz
Hash Browns, 32 oz
Hash Browns O'Brien, 28 oz
Shoestring Potatoes, 28 oz
Steak Cut, Grade A Thick Sliced Potatoes, 28 oz
Straight Cut, 32 oz

Tater Puffs, 32 oz
Tater Puffs (Club Pack), 80 oz
Tater Rounds, 30 oz

Winn-Dixie ◉
Country Style Hash Browns
Crinkle Cut Fries
French Fries
O'Brien Potatoes
Potato Crowns
Shoestring Fries
Southern Style Hash Browns
Steak Fries

PREPARED MEALS & SIDES

Amy's Kitchen ()
Asian Noodle Stir-Fry
Baked Ziti Bowl
Baked Ziti Kids Meal
Black Bean Enchilada Whole Meal
Black Bean Vegetable Enchilada
Brown Rice & Vegetable Bowl
Brown Rice & Vegetable Bowl - Light in Sodium
Brown Rice Bowl with Black-Eyed Peas & Veggies
Cheese Enchilada
Cheese Enchilada Whole Meal
Garden Vegetable Lasagna
Indian Mattar Paneer
Indian Mattar Tofu
Indian Palak Paneer
Indian Paneer Tikka
Indian Vegetable Korma
Mexican Casserole Bowl
Mexican Tamale Pie
Rice Mac & Cheese
Santa Fe Enchilada Bowl
Shepherd's Pie
Teriyaki Bowl
Thai Stir-Fry
Tofu Rancheros
Tofu Scramble
Tortilla Casserole & Black Beans Bowl

Bell & Evans () 占
Gluten Free Chicken Breast Nuggets
Gluten Free Chicken Breast Tenders

Cedarlane Natural Foods
Five Layer Mexican Dip
Three Layer Enchilada Pie
Tofu Enchilada Meal

Delimex ☺
3-Cheese Taquitos, UPC# 1769600214 - 25 count.
Beef Deli Bulk Pack Tamales, UPC# 1769600556

Frozen Foods

Beef Taquitos, UPC# 1769600180 - 60 count.

Beef Taquitos (Mexico Import), UPC# 1769600481 - 36 count.

Beef Tamales, UPC# 1769600024 - 6 count.

Beef Tamales, UPC# 1769600018 - 12 count.

Beef Taquitos, UPC# 1769600095 - 12 count.

Beef Taquitos, UPC# 1769600048 - 36 count.

Beef Taquitos, UPC# 1769600028 - 25 count.

Beef/Deli-Pak Taquitos, UPC# 1769600500

Cheese Deli Bulk Pack Tamales, UPC# 1769600554

Chicken & Cheese Tamales, UPC# 1769600019 - 12 count.

Chicken Deli Bulk Pack Tamales, UPC# 1769600555

Chicken Taquitos, UPC# 1769600096 - 12 count.

Chicken Taquitos, UPC# 1769600012 - 36 count.

Chicken Taquitos, UPC# 1769600029 - 25 count.

Taquitos - Mini Beef Snacker Tray with Salsa, UPC# 1769600505 - 40 count.

Empire Kosher
Fully Cooked Barbecue Chicken (Fresh or Frozen)
Fully Cooked Barbecue Turkey (Fresh or Frozen)

Glutino
Glutino, All

Homestyle Meals
Frozen Fully Cooked Baby Back Ribs, Item# 00501

Ian's Natural Foods
Wheat Free Gluten Free Recipe - Chicken Nuggets
Wheat Free Gluten Free Recipe - Chicken Patties
Wheat Free Gluten Free Recipe - Popcorn Turkey Corndogs

Nate's
Black Bean & Soy Cheese Taquitos

Rice Expressions
Rice Products, All

Simply Enjoy (Stop & Shop) ✗ ◉
Butter Chicken
Pad Thai with Chicken
Tikka Masala

Stop & Shop ✗ ◉
Buffalo Style Wings
Honey BBQ Wings
Spinach, Artichoke & Cheese Dip

Tabatchnick Fine Foods
Black Bean
Broccoli Cheese
Cabbage
Corn Chowder
Cream of Broccoli
Cream of Mushroom
Cream of Spinach
Creamed Spinach

Lentil
New England Potato
Pea
Pea - No Salt
Potato
Rock Island
Salmon Chowder
Southwest Bean
Tomato Rice
Vegetarian Chili
Wild Rice
Yankee Bean

Wegman's ✗ ◉ ()
Asian Stir-Fry, 16 oz
Barbecue Pork Spareribs, 26.4 oz

Wellshire Kids
Frozen Dino Shaped Chicken Bites, Item# 00300 - 10 oz
Uncured Beef Corn Dogs, Item# 00370

Winn-Dixie ◉
Cajun Gumbo Mix
Stir Fry Mix

SHERBET & SORBET

Edy's
Berry Rainbow Sherbet
Key Lime Sherbet
Orange Cream Sherbet
Raspberry Sherbet
Strawberry Sherbet
Swiss Orange Sherbet
Tropical Rainbow Sherbet

Gaga's SherBetter
Gaga's SherBetter, All

Guaranteed Value (Stop & Shop) ✗ ◉
Rainbow Sherbet

Hood
Sherbet, All

Hy-Vee ✗ ◉
Lime Sherbet, 1/2 gal
Orange Blossom Ice Cream & Sherbet, 4.5 qt
Orange Sherbet, 1/2 gal
Pineapple Sherbet, 1/2 gal
Rainbow Sherbet, 1/2 gal
Raspberry Sherbet, 1/2 gal

Safeway ✗ ◉
Raspberry Sorbet
Sherbet - Key Lime & Lemon Crunch

Select Brand (Safeway) ✗ ◉
Chocolate Sorbet

Frozen Foods

VEGETABLES

Food You Feel Good About (Wegman's) ✗ ◉ ()
Brussels Sprouts, 16 oz
Carrots, Potatoes, Celery & Onions, 16 oz
Crinkle Cut Carrots, 20 oz
Cut Leaf Spinach, 16 oz
Far East Stir-Fry Vegetables, 20 oz
Green Beans - Broccoli, Onions & Mushrooms, 16 oz
Green Beans - French Style, 16 oz
Green Beans - Whole, 16 oz
Mixed Vegetables, 16 oz
Sugar Snap Peas, 16 oz
Sweet Petite Peas, 16 oz
Sweet Whole Kernel Corn Bread & Butter, 16 oz

Grand Selections (Hy-Vee) ✗ ◉
Frozen Caribbean Blend Vegetables, 32 oz
Frozen Normandy Blend Vegetables, 32 oz
Frozen Petite Green Peas, 16 oz
Frozen Petite Whole Carrots, 16 oz
Frozen Riviera Blend Vegetables, 32 oz
Frozen Sugar Snap Peas, 12 oz
Frozen Super Sweet Cut Corn, 16 oz
Frozen White Shoepeg Corn, 16 oz
Frozen Whole Green Beans, 16 oz

Hy-Vee ✗ ◉
Broccoli Cuts, 16 oz
Broccoli Florets, 16 oz
Brussels Sprouts, 16 oz
California Blend, 16 oz
California Mix, 32 oz
Cauliflower Florets, 16 oz
Chopped Broccoli, 16 oz
Chopped Broccoli, 10 oz
Chopped Spinach, 10 oz
Crinkle Cut Carrots, 16 oz
Cut Golden Corn, 32 oz
Cut Golden Corn, 16 oz
Cut Green Beans, 16 oz
French Cut Green Beans, 16 oz
Italian Blend, 6 oz
Leaf Spinach, 16 oz
Leaf Spinach, 10 oz
Mini Corn on the Cob, 12 count
Mixed Vegetables, 32 oz
Mixed Vegetables, 16 oz
Oriental Vegetables, 16 oz
Sweet Peas, 32 oz
Sweet Peas, 16 oz
Winter Mix, 16 oz

Ingles Markets ◉
2# Frozen Vegetables, All BUT Breaded Okra, Hushpuppies & Onion Rings

Italian Classics (Wegman's) ✗ ◉ ()
Artichoke Hearts - Halves & Quarters, 12 oz

Midwest Country Fare (Hy-Vee) ✗ ◉
Frozen Broccoli Cuts, 16 oz
Frozen Brussels Sprouts, 16 oz
Frozen California Blend, 16 oz
Frozen Cauliflower, 16 oz
Frozen Chopped Broccoli, 16 oz
Frozen Cut Corn, 16 oz
Frozen Cut Green Beans, 16 oz
Frozen Green Peas, 16 oz
Frozen Mixed Vegetables, 16 oz

Nature's Promise (Stop & Shop) ✗ ◉
Organic Asparagus Spears
Organic Broccoli Mini Spears
Organic Corn - Cut Corn & Corn on the Cob
Organic Cut Leaf Spinach
Organic Mixed Vegetables
Organic Peas
Organic Whole & Cut Green Beans

Stop & Shop ✗ ◉
Asparagus - Spears, Tips & Cuts
Broccoli - Chopped, Cuts & Spears
Broccoli & Cauliflower
Brussels Sprouts
Cauliflower
Chopped Green Pepper
Collard Greens
Cooked Squash
Corn - Cut, on the Cob & Supersweet Corn on the Cob
Corn & Butter
Corn & Peas
Country Blend
Cut Wax Beans
Green Beans - Cut, French, with Garlic, Italian & Whole
Green Beans & Wax Beans
Japanese Stir Fry Blend
Kale
Latino Blend
Mixed Vegetables
Mustard Greens
Peas & Diced Carrots
Ranchero Blend
Rutabagas
Spinach - Chopped & Leaf
Stew Vegetables

Frozen Foods

Sweet Peas
Whole Okra
Zucchini

Wegman's ⋒ 👁 ()
Baby Carrots, 16 oz
Broccoli Cuts, 16 oz
Broccoli Cuts & Cauliflower Florets, 16 oz
Broccoli Cuts, Cauliflower Florets & Carrots, 16 oz
Broccoli Spears, 16 oz
Broccoli Spears, 10 oz
Brussels Sprouts, 10 oz
Brussels Sprouts in Butter Sauce, 10 oz
Cauliflower Florets, 16 oz
Chopped Spinach, 10 oz
Corn on the Cob, 4
Green Beans, 9 oz
Green Beans - Cut, 16 & 40 oz
Green Beans - Italian, 16 oz
Mixed Vegetables, 40 oz
Peas, 40 oz
Peas, 20 oz
Peas with Pearl Onions, 16 oz
Pepper & Onion Mix, 16 oz
Petite Peas in Butter Sauce, 10 oz
Santa Fe Mix, 16 oz
Southern Mix, 16 oz
Spinach in Cream Sauce, 9 oz
Spring Mix, 16 oz
Stir Fry Vegetables - Hong Kong, 20 oz
Whole Kernel Corn, 20 oz
Whole Kernel Corn in Butter Sauce, 10 oz

Winn-Dixie 👁
Broccoli
Brussel Sprouts
California Blend
Carrots
Cauliflower
Corn
Diced Onions
Frozen Corn
Green Beans
Green Peppers
Greens
Mixed Vegetables
Okra - Non-Breaded
Peas, All
Spinach
Vegetable Soup Mix
Winter Mix

VEGGIE BURGERS

Amy's Kitchen ()
Bistro Burger

Gardenburger
Black Bean Chipotle Burger (In New Tan Box NOT Blue Box)
Breakfast Sausage (In New Tan Box NOT Blue Box)
Flame Grill Hamburger (In New Tan Box NOT Blue Box)

Nature's Promise (Stop & Shop) ⋒ 👁
Garlic & Cheese Veggie Burger
Soy Vegetable Burger
Vegan Soy Vegetable Burger

WAFFLES & FRENCH TOAST

Ian's Natural Foods
Wheat Free Gluten Free Recipe - French Toast Sticks

LifeStream () ⓘ
Buckwheat Wildberry Waffles
Mesa Sunrise Waffles

Van's International Foods
Wheat Free Waffles, All

Frozen Foods

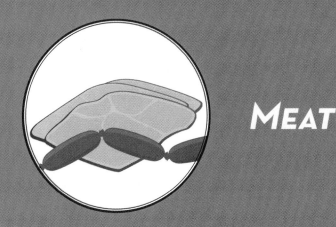

MEAT

BACON

Applegate Farms 👁 ✎
Applegate Farms, All BUT Chicken Nuggets & Chicken Pot Pie

Bar-S
Bar-S, All BUT Chuck Wagon Brand Franks & Corn Dogs

Beelers
Beelers, All BUT Calzones & Frozen Entrees

Butcher's Cut (Safeway) ✎ 👁
Bacon, All Varieties from EST 13331

Cloverdale Foods
Bacon, All

Coleman Natural
Bacon

Ejays So. Smokehouse
Applewood Smoked Bacon, Item# 61149
Arkansas Bacon, Item# 61193
Canadian Style Bacon, Item# 61180
Mesquite Smoked Jalapeno Pork Bacon, Item# 61146
Mesquite Smoked Pork Bacon, Item# 61144

Garrett County Farms
Bacon, Item# 01159 - 12 oz

Hormel ☼ 👁
Bacon Bits & Pieces
Black Label - Bacon
Canadian Style Bacon
Fully Cooked Bacon
Microwave Bacon
Natural Choice - Uncured Bacon
Natural Choice - Uncured Lower Sodium Bacon
Pillow Pack - Canadian Bacon

Hy-Vee ✎ 👁
Fully Cooked Bacon, 2.3 oz

Jennie-O ☼ 👁
Extra Lean Turkey Bacon
Turkey Bacon

Laura Lynn (Ingle's) 👁
Bacon Chips, 4.1 oz

Old Smokehouse ☼ 👁
Bacon

Range Brand ☼ 👁
Bacon

Red Label ☼ 👁
Bacon

Stop & Shop ✎ 👁
Center Cut Sliced Bacon
Lower Sodium Bacon
Maple Flavored Bacon
Regular Sliced Bacon

Value Brand ☼ 👁
Sliced Bacon

Wellshire Farms
Classic Sliced Dry Rubbed Bacon, Item# 01158 - 12 oz
Classic Sliced Turkey Bacon, Item# 01165 - 12 oz
Dry Rubbed Center Cut Bacon, Item# 01149 - 18 oz
Range Sliced Dry Rubbed Bacon, Item# 01157 - 12 oz
Range Sliced Peppered Bacon, Item# 01140 - 12 oz
Sliced Applewood Smoked Maple Bacon, Item# 01151 - 8 oz
Sliced Beef Bacon, Item# 01170 - 12 oz
Sliced Canadian Style Bacon, Item# 01180 - 8 oz
Sliced Pancetta Bacon, Item# 01190 - 8 oz
Sliced Peppered Turkey Bacon, Item# 01161 - 12 oz

Winn-Dixie 👁
Hickory Sweet Brown Sugar Bacon
Hickory Sweet Country Style Thick Sliced Bacon
Hickory Sweet Lower Sodium Sliced Bacon

BEEF

Applegate Farms 👁 ✎
Applegate Farms, All BUT Chicken Nuggets & Chicken Pot Pie

Boar's Head 👁 ⓘ
 Meats, All

Butcher's Cut (Safeway) ⚡ 👁
 Beef Burgers
 Corned Beef
 Corned Beef Brisket

Homestyle Meals
 Bulk Beef BBQ Cooked, Item# 00455
 Shredded Beef in BBQ Sauce, Item# 00460

Hormel 🐾 👁
 Always Tender - Non-Flavored Fresh Beef
 Always Tender - Peppercorn Flavored Fresh Beef
 Deli Sliced Cooked Corned Beef Pre-Packaged
  Refrigerated Lunch Meats
 Deli Sliced Cooked Pastrami Pre-Packaged
  Refrigerated Lunch Meats
 Deli Sliced Seasoned Roast Beef Pre-Packaged
  Refrigerated Lunch Meats
 Fully-Cooked Entrées - Beef Roast Au Jus
 Fully-Cooked Entrees - SW Shredded Beef
 Natural Choice - Roast Beef Pre-Packaged
  Refrigerated Lunch Meats

Hy-Vee ⚡ 👁
 Quarter Pounders, 48 oz
 Thin Sliced Beef, 2 oz
 Thin Sliced Corned Beef, 2 oz
 Thin Sliced Pastrami, 2 oz

Lloyd's 🐾 👁
 Beef Ribs with Original BBQ Sauce

Nature's Promise (Stop & Shop) ⚡ 👁
 Deli Meats, All

Primo Taglio (Safeway) ⚡ 👁
 Cooked Corned Beef

Safeway ⚡ 👁
 Corned Beef (Deli Counter)

Wellshire Farms
 Sliced Beef Pastrami Round, Item# 09155 - 8 oz
 Sliced Corned Beef Round, Item# 09145 - 8 oz
 Sliced Top Round Roast Beef, Item# 09135 - 8 oz

Winn-Dixie 👁
 Fresh Beef, All Cuts BUT Beef Barciole
 Fresh Ground Beef, All Types

BOLOGNA

Applegate Farms 👁 ⚡
 Applegate Farms, All BUT Chicken Nuggets &
  Chicken Pot Pie

Bar-S
 Bar-S, All BUT Chuck Wagon Brand Franks & Corn
  Dogs

Boar's Head 👁 ⓘ
 Meats, All

Empire Kosher
 Chicken Bologna - Slices
 Turkey Bologna (Slices)
 Turkey Bologna Roll

Hy-Vee ⚡ 👁
 Beef Bologna, 8 oz
 Bologna, 8 oz
 Bologna, 16 oz
 Garlic Bologna, 16 oz
 German Brand Bologna, 16 oz
 Thick Sliced Bologna, 16 oz
 Thin Sliced Bologna, 16 oz
 Turkey Bologna, 16 oz

Johnsonville
 JVL Smoked/Cooked - Beef Ring Bologna
 JVL Smoked/Cooked - Original Ring Bologna

Nature's Promise (Stop & Shop) ⚡ 👁
 Deli Meats, All

Perdue
 Deli Turkey Bologna

Wellshire Farms
 Sliced Old Fashioned Deli Style Beef Bologna, Item#
  09175 - 8 oz
 Sliced Turkey Bologna, Item# 08175 - 8 oz

Winn-Dixie 👁
 Beef Bologna
 Chicken/Pork Bologna
 Square Sliced Bologna
 Thick Sliced Bologna

CHICKEN

Applegate Farms 👁 ⚡
 Applegate Farms, All BUT Chicken Nuggets &
  Chicken Pot Pie

Boar's Head 👁 ⓘ
 Meats, All

Butcher's Cut (Safeway) ⚡ 👁
 Boneless Skinless Chicken Breast

Carl Buddig 🐾
 Meat Products, All

Empire Kosher
 Chicken Burgers
 Filled Chicken Breasts with Broccoli Filling
 Filled Chicken Breasts with Mixed Vegetable Filling
 Fresh Chill Pack Chicken & Turkey
 Fresh Rotisserie Chicken
 Fully Cooked Barbecue Chicken (Fresh or Frozen)
 Ground Chicken

Homestyle Meals
- Bulk Chicken BBQ Cooked, Item# 00445
- Shredded Chicken in BBQ Sauce, Item# 00440 - 18 oz

Hormel 🍖 👁
- Always Tender - Italian Flavored Fresh Chicken
- Always Tender - Lemon-Pepper Flavored Fresh Chicken
- Always Tender - Roast Flavored Fresh Chicken
- Natural Choice - Grilled Chicken Strips Pre-Packaged Refrigerated Lunch Meats
- Natural Choice - Oven Roasted Chicken Strips Pre-Packaged Refrigerated Lunch Meats

Hy-Vee ✗ 👁
- Thin Sliced Chicken, 2.5 oz

Jennie-O 🍖 👁
- Turkey Store - Buffalo Style Deli Chicken Breast (Deli Item)
- Turkey Store - Mesquite Smoked Deli Chicken Breast (Deli Item)
- Turkey Store - Oven Roasted Deli Chicken Breast (Deli Item)

Laura Lynn (Ingle's) 👁
- Boneless Skinless Chicken Breast, 64 oz

Nature's Promise (Stop & Shop) ✗ 👁
- Deli Meats, All
- Fresh Meat, Poultry

Perdue
- Buffalo Chicken Wings Hot N Spicy Seasoned
- Carving - Chicken Breast, Oven Roasted
- Ground Breast of Chicken
- Ground Chicken
- Ground Chicken Burgers
- Perfect Portions - Boneless Skinless Chicken Breasts
- Perfect Portions - Boneless Skinless Chicken Breasts, Italian Style
- Perfect Portions - Boneless Skinless Chicken Breasts, Tomato Basil
- Rotisserie Chicken - Barbecue
- Rotisserie Chicken - Italian
- Rotisserie Chicken - Lemon Pepper
- Rotisserie Chicken - Oven Roasted
- Rotisserie Chicken - Toasted Garlic
- Rotisserie Chicken - Tuscany Herb Roasted
- Short Cuts - Carved Chicken Breast Grilled Italian Style
- Short Cuts - Carved Chicken Breast Grilled Lemon Pepper
- Short Cuts - Carved Chicken Breast Grilled Southwestern Style
- Short Cuts - Carved Chicken Breast Honey Roasted
- Short Cuts - Carved Chicken Breast Original Roasted
- Sliced Chicken Breast - Oil Fried

Primo Taglio (Safeway) ✗ 👁
- Chicken Breast (Oven Roasted) Browned in Hot Cottonseed Oil

Safeway ✗ 👁
- Deli Roasted Chicken (Deli Counter)

Wellshire Farms
- Sliced Oven Roasted Chicken Breast, Item# 08101 - 8 oz

Wellshire Kids
- Refrigerated Dino Shaped Chicken Bites, Item# 00301 - 10 oz

Winn-Dixie 👁
- Fresh Chicken, All Cuts & Types
- Luncheon Meat
- Roasting Chicken with Southern Garden Herb Seasoning

HAM & PORK

Applegate Farms 👁 ✗
- Applegate Farms, All BUT Chicken Nuggets & Chicken Pot Pie

Bar-S
- Bar-S, All BUT Chuck Wagon Brand Franks & Corn Dogs

Beelers
- Beelers, All BUT Calzones & Frozen Entrees

Boar's Head 👁 ⓘ
- Meats, All

Butcher's Cut (Safeway) ✗ 👁
- Shank Cut Ham
- Spiral Sliced Ham, Glaze Packet is NOT GF

Carl Buddig 🍖
- Meat Products, All

Cloverdale Foods
- Hams, All

Cure 81 🍖 👁
- Bone-In Ham
- Boneless Ham
- Old Fashioned Spiral Ham

Ejays So. Smokehouse
- Black Forest Ham Steak, Item# 64042
- Honey Ham Steak, Item# 64043

Homestyle Meals
- Bulk Pork BBQ Cooked, Item# 00451
- Pork Baby Back Ribs with BBQ Sauce, Item# 00500 - 31 oz
- Shredded Pork in BBQ Sauce, Item# 00450 - 18 oz

Meat

Hormel ☖ ◉

Always Tender - Adobo Pork Cubes Flavored Fresh Pork
Always Tender - Apple Bourbon Flavored Fresh Pork
Always Tender - Citrus Flavored Fresh Pork
Always Tender - Fajita Pork Strips Flavored Fresh Pork
Always Tender - Honey-Mustard Flavored Fresh Pork
Always Tender - Lemon-Garlic Flavored Fresh Pork
Always Tender - Mesquite Flavored Fresh Pork
Always Tender - Mojo Criollo Flavored Fresh Pork
Always Tender - Non-Flavored Fresh Pork
Always Tender - Onion-Garlic Flavored Fresh Pork
Always Tender - Original Flavored Fresh Pork
Always Tender - Peppercorn Flavored Fresh Pork
Always Tender - Raspberry Chipotle Flavored Fresh Pork
Always Tender - Sun-Dried Tomato Flavored Fresh Pork
Deli Sliced Black Forest Ham Pre-Packaged Refrigerated Lunch Meats
Deli Sliced Cooked Ham Pre-Packaged Refrigerated Lunch Meats
Deli Sliced Double Smoked Ham Pre-Packaged Refrigerated Lunch Meats
Deli Sliced Honey Ham Pre-Packaged Refrigerated Lunch Meats
Deli Sliced Prosciutto Ham Pre-Packaged Refrigerated Lunch Meats
Diced Ham Pre-Packaged Refrigerated Lunch Meats
Fully-Cooked Entrées - Glazed Ham with Maple & Brown Sugar
Fully-Cooked Entrées - Pork Roast Au Jus
Fully-Cooked Entrees - SW Pork Carnitas
Julienne Ham Pre-Packaged Refrigerated Lunch Meats
Natural Choice - Cooked Deli Ham Pre-Packaged Refrigerated Lunch Meats
Natural Choice - Honey Deli Ham Pre-Packaged Refrigerated Lunch Meats
Natural Choice - Smoked Deli Ham Pre-Packaged Refrigerated Lunch Meats
Party Tray - Pork Rib Tips in Barbecue Sauce
Spiced Ham Pre-Packaged Refrigerated Lunch Meats

Hy-Vee ⁄ ◉

96% Sliced Cooked Ham, 16 oz
Brown Sugar Spiral Sliced Ham
Chopped Ham, 8 oz
Chopped Ham, 16 oz
Cooked Ham, 8 oz
Deli Thin Slices Honey Ham, 10 oz
Deli Thin Slices Smoked Ham, 10 oz

Ham & Cheese Loaf, 8 oz
Ham & Cheese Loaf, 16 oz
Honey & Spice Spiral Sliced Ham
Thin Sliced Ham, 2.5 oz
Thin Sliced Honey Ham, 2.5 oz

Jennie-O ☖ ◉

Refrigerated Honey Cured Turkey Ham
Refrigerated Turkey Ham

Lloyd's ☖ ◉

Pork Ribs with Original BBQ Sauce

Nature's Promise (Stop & Shop) ⁄ ◉

Deli Meats, All
Fresh Meat, Pork

Perdue

Carving Turkey Ham - Honey Smoked
Deli Pick Ups - Sliced Turkey Ham, Honey Smoked
Deli Turkey Ham - Hickory Smoked
Slicing - Turkey Ham

Primo Taglio (Safeway) ⁄ ◉

Black Forest Ham with Natural Juices, Coated with Caramel Color
Maple Ham (Old Fashioned) with Natural Juices
Prosciutto Dry Cured Ham

Select Brand (Safeway) ⁄ ◉

St. Louis Style Smoke House Signature Ribs

Stop & Shop ⁄ ◉

Cooked Ham - 97% Fat Free
Cooked Ham with Natural Juices - 98% Fat Free
Danish Brand Ham with Natural Juices - 97% Fat Free

Wegman's ⁄ ◉ ()

Cooked Ham - Thin Sliced with Natural Juices, 10 oz
Smoked Ham - Thin Sliced with Natural Juices, 10 oz
Smoked Honey Ham - Thin Sliced with Natural Juices, 10 oz

Wellshire Farms

Black Forest Boneless Ham Nugget, Item# 04045
Black Forest Deli Ham, Item# 04145
Old Fashioned Boneless Half Ham, Item# 04148
Old Fashioned Boneless Whole Ham, Item# 04149
Salt Cured Ham Café Slices, Item# 05145 - 6 oz
Semi Boneless Half Ham, Item# 04031
Sliced Black Forest Ham, Item# 04186 - 8 oz
Sliced Ham Capicola, Item# 04196
Sliced Tavern Ham, Item# 04191 - 8 oz
Sliced Turkey Ham, Item# 08185 - 8 oz
Sliced Virginia Brand Ham, Item# 04180 - 8 oz
Sunday Breakfast Ham, Item# 04041 - 8 oz
Turkey Ham Buffet Half Ham, Item# 08045
Turkey Ham Steak, Item# 08041 - 8 oz
Virginia Brand Boneless Ham Steak, Item# 04040 - 8

oz
Virginia Brand Buffet Ham, Item# 4141

Winn-Dixie 👁
Chopped Ham
Cubed Ham - Honey & Smoked
Fresh Pork, All Cuts
Ham & Cheese Loaf
Honey Smoked Ham
Virginia Cooked Ham

HOT DOGS & FRANKS

Applegate Farms 👁 ⁄
Applegate Farms, All BUT Chicken Nuggets &
Chicken Pot Pie
Bar-S
Bar-S, All BUT Chuck Wagon Brand Franks & Corn
Dogs
Boar's Head 👁 ⓘ
Meats, All
Butcher's Cut (Safeway) ⁄ 👁
Jumbo Franks (including Chicken & Pork)
Cloverdale Foods
Franks, All
Empire Kosher
Chicken Franks
Turkey Franks
Food You Feel Good About (Wegman's) ⁄ 👁 ()
Uncured Beef Hot Dogs - Skinless, 16 oz
Han's All Natural
Beef Hot Dogs - Cooked, 12 oz
Chicken Hot Dogs - Cooked, 12 oz
Jennie-O ☀ 👁
Turkey Franks
Johnsonville
JVL Smoked/Cooked (Links) - Natural Casing
Wieners
JVL Smoked/Cooked (Links) - Stadium Style Beef
Franks
Old Wisconsin
Old Wisconsin, All BUT Beef Jerky
Sabrett
Frankfurters, All
Wegman's ⁄ 👁 ()
Beef Hot Dogs - Skinless, 8 count - 16 oz
Hot Dogs - Natural Casing Red, 16 oz
Hot Dogs - Natural Casing White, 16 oz
Hot Dogs - Red Skinless, 8 count - 16 oz
Hot Dogs (Combo Pack), 8 count - 16 oz
Lite Red Hot Dogs - Skinless, 8 count - 16 oz

Uncured Hot Dogs - Skinless, 8 count - 16 oz
Wellshire Farms
Cheese Frank, Item# 09016 - 16 oz
Chicken Hot Dogs, Item# 09010 - 12 oz
NY Style Big Beef Franks, Item# 09017 - 16 oz
Old Fashioned Beef Frank, Item# - 09022 - 16 oz
Original Deli Frank, Item# - 09015 - 16 oz
Premium Beef Frank, Item# - 09020 - 16 oz
Turkey Franks, Item# 09000 - 12 oz
Winn-Dixie 👁
Beef Hot Dogs
Meat Hot Dogs
Wranglers ☀ 👁
Franks

SALAMI, PEPPERONI & OTHER CURED MEATS

Applegate Farms 👁 ⁄
Applegate Farms, All BUT Chicken Nuggets &
Chicken Pot Pie
Columbus Salame
Columbus Salame, All
Empire Kosher
Turkey Salami (Slices)
Turkey Salami Roll
Hormel ☀ 👁
Hard Salami Snack Size Meats & Cheese
Homeland - Hard Salami Pre-Packaged Refrigerated
Lunch Meats
Italian Dry Salami Snack Size Meats & Cheese
Pepperoni
Pillow Pack - Dried Beef
Pillow Pack - Hard Salami
Pillow Pack - Pepperoni
Pillow Pack - Turkey Pepperoni
Hy-Vee ⁄ 👁
Cooked Salami, 8 oz
Cooked Salami, 16 oz
Pepperoni, 8 oz
Pepperoni, 3.5 oz
Old Wisconsin
Old Wisconsin, All BUT Beef Jerky
Perdue
Deli Turkey Salami
Primo Naturale
Chub Hard Salami, Item# 00750 - 10 oz
Chub Salami with Black Pepper, Item# 00703 - 10 oz
Chub Salami with Herbs, Item# 00702
Chub Salami with Wine, Item# 00701 - 10 oz
Dried Pepperoni, Item# 00730 - 10 oz
Sliced Coppa Salami, Item# 00765 - 6 oz

Sliced Dried Pepperoni, Item# 00735 - 6 oz

Sliced Hard Salami, Item# 00755 - 6 oz

Sliced Original Salami with Wine, Item# 00745 - 6 oz

Sliced Premium Genoa Salami, Item# 00711

Sliced Salami with Black Pepper, Item# 00713 - 6 oz

Sliced Salami with Herbs, Item# 00712 - 6 oz

Primo Taglio (Safeway) ↗ ◉

Cervelat Salami

Genoa Salami

Salami (Peppered) Coated with Gelatin & Black Pepper

Safeway ↗ ◉

Genoa Salami (Deli Counter)

Hard Salami (Deli Counter)

Wegman's ↗ ◉ ()

Pepperoni - Italian Style (Sliced), 6 oz

Wellshire Farms

Sliced Beef Pepperoni, Item# 00615 - 8 oz

Sliced Cooked Salami, Item# 04176

Sliced Old Fashioned Deli Style Beef Salami, Item# 09165 - 8 oz

Winn-Dixie ◉

Cotto Salami

SAUSAGE

Applegate Farms ◉ ↗

Applegate Farms, All BUT Chicken Nuggets & Chicken Pot Pie

Bar-S

Bar-S, All BUT Chuck Wagon Brand Franks & Corn Dogs

Beelers

Beelers, All BUT Calzones & Frozen Entrees

Boar's Head ◉ ⓘ

Meats, All

Butcher's Cut (Safeway) ↗ ◉

Italian Sausage - Regular & Mild

Smoked Sausage

Cloverdale Foods

Sausages, All

Coleman Natural

Chicken Andouille - Cooked, 12 oz

Chicken Andouille - Raw

Chicken Apple - Cooked, 12 oz

Chicken Apple - Raw

Chicken Apple & Maple Breakfast Links - Raw

Chicken Basil & Sun Dried Tomato - Cooked, 12 oz

Chicken Basil & Sun Dried Tomato - Raw

Chicken Bratwurst - Cooked, 12 oz

Chicken Bratwurst - Raw

Chicken Breakfast Links - Cooked, 12 oz

Chicken Chipotle - Cooked, 12 oz

Chicken Chipotle - Raw

Chicken Chorizo - Cooked, 12 oz

Chicken Garlic & Cheese - Cooked, 12 oz

Chicken Garlic & Cheese - Raw

Chicken Ginger Plum - Raw

Chicken Italian Mild - Cooked, 12 oz

Chicken Italian Mild - Raw

Chicken Italian Spicy - Cooked, 12 oz

Chicken Italian Spicy - Raw

Chicken Spicy Thai - Raw

Chicken Spinach & Feta - Cooked, 12 oz

Chicken Spinach & Feta - Raw

Chicken Sweet Basil - Raw

Chicken Tequila Black Bean & Lime - Cooked, 12 oz

Chicken Tequila Black Bean & Lime - Raw

Lamb Mediterranean - Raw

Lamb Mint Garlic - Raw

Polish Kielbasa Ring - Cooked, 12 oz

Pork Andouille - Raw

Pork Apple & Cherry - Raw

Pork Bratwurst - Raw

Pork Breakfast Links - Raw

Pork Chorizo - Raw

Pork Italian Mild - Raw

Pork Italian Spicy - Raw

Pork Roasted Red Pepper & Provolone - Raw

Turkey Italian Mild - Raw

Turkey Spinach & Feta - Raw

Di Lusso 🐾 ◉

Beef Summer Sausage

Ejays So. Smokehouse

German Sausage, Item# 66022

Smoke Jalapeno Sausage, Item# 66021

Smoked Kielbasa, Item# 66020

Empire Kosher

Chicken Sausage Mushroom & Garlic

Chicken Sausage Sun Dried Tomato Basil

Chicken Sausage Sweet Apple & Cinnamon

Global Gourmet

Andouille Chicken Sausage, Item# 02950

Apple Oven Roasted Chicken Sausage, Item# 02910

Chipotle Pepper Chicken Sausage, Item# 02960

Feta Cheese & Fresh Spinach Chicken Sausage, Item# 02940

Fontina Cheese & Roasted Garlic Chicken Sausage, Item# 02930

Spicy Italian Chicken Sausage, Item# 02990

Sun Dried Tomato Chicken Sausage, Item# 02920

Meat

Han's All Natural

Chicken Andouille - Cooked, 12 oz
Chicken Andouille - Raw
Chicken Apple - Cooked, 12 oz
Chicken Apple - Raw
Chicken Apple & Maple Breakfast Links - Raw
Chicken Bratwurst - Cooked, 12 oz
Chicken Bratwurst - Raw
Chicken Breakfast Links - Cooked, 12 oz
Chicken Chipotle - Cooked, 12 oz
Chicken Chipotle - Raw
Chicken Chorizo - Cooked, 12 oz
Chicken Garlic & Cheese - Cooked, 12 oz
Chicken Italian Mild - Cooked, 12 oz
Chicken Italian Mild - Raw
Chicken Italian Spicy - Cooked, 12 oz
Chicken Italian Spicy - Raw
Chicken Mushroom Asiago - Cooked, 12 oz
Chicken Mushroom Asiago - Raw
Chicken SD Tomato Basil - Cooked, 12 oz
Chicken SD Tomato Basil - Raw
Chicken Spicy Thai - Raw
Chicken Spinach & Feta - Cooked, 12 oz
Chicken Spinach & Feta - Raw
Chicken Sweet Basil - Raw
Chicken Tequila Black Bean - Cooked, 12 oz
Chicken Tequila Black Bean - Raw
Lamb Mediterranean - Raw
Lamb Mint Garlic - Raw
Polish Kielbasa Ring - Cooked, 12 oz
Pork Andouille - Raw
Pork Apple & Cherry - Raw
Pork Bratwurst - Raw
Pork Breakfast Links - Raw
Pork Chorizo - Raw
Pork Italian Mild - Raw
Pork Italian Spicy - Raw
Pork Parsley & Cheese Rope - Raw
Pork Smoked Jalapeno Cheddar - Cooked, 12 oz
Turkey Breakfast Links - Raw
Turkey Italian Mild - Raw
Turkey Italian Spicy - Raw
Turkey Spinach & Feta - Raw

Honeysuckle White

Honeysuckle White, All BUT Asian Grill Marinated Turkey Strips, Cajun Fried Turkey, Frozen Turkey Burgers, Italian Style Meatballs & Teriyaki Turkey Breast Tenderloins

Hormel ☷ ◉

Crumbled Sausage
Smokies
Summer Sausage Snack Size Meats & Cheese

Hy-Vee ↗ ◉

Bratwurst, 19.5 oz
Bratwurst - Grill Pack, 40 oz
Sausage Links, 12 oz
Sausage Patties, 12 oz

Jennie-O ☷ ◉

Breakfast Lover's - Turkey Sausage
Extra Lean Smoked Kielbasa Turkey Sausage
Extra Lean Smoked Turkey Sausage
Turkey Store - Cheddar Turkey Bratwurst Fresh Dinner Sausage
Turkey Store - Hot Italian Fresh Dinner Sausage
Turkey Store - Lean Turkey Bratwurst Fresh Dinner Sausage
Turkey Store - Maple Links Fresh Breakfast Sausage
Turkey Store - Mild Links Fresh Breakfast Sausage
Turkey Store - Mild Patties Fresh Breakfast Sausage
Turkey Store - Sweet Italian Fresh Dinner Sausage

Johnsonville

JVL Breakfast Sausage - (Hot) Premium Pork Sausage
JVL Breakfast Sausage - Homestyle Patties
JVL Breakfast Sausage (Links) - Heat & Serve Maple Syrup
JVL Breakfast Sausage (Links) - Heat & Serve Original
JVL Breakfast Sausage (Links) - Original Breakfast
JVL Breakfast Sausage (Links) - Vermont Maple Syrup
JVL Breakfast Sausage (Original) - Premium Pork Sausage
JVL Breakfast Sausage (Patties) - Original Breakfast Sausage
JVL Breakfast Sausage (Patties) - Vermont Maple Syrup
JVL Fresh Grilling - Bratwurst Patties
JVL Fresh Grilling - Hot Italian Ground Sausage
JVL Fresh Grilling - Mild Italian Ground Sausage
JVL Fresh Grilling (Links) - Cheddar Bratwurst
JVL Fresh Grilling (Links) - Chorizo
JVL Fresh Grilling (Links) - Hot 'N Spicy Bratwurst
JVL Fresh Grilling (Links) - Irish O'Garlic
JVL Fresh Grilling (Links) - Mild/Hot/Sweet Italian
JVL Fresh Grilling (Links) - Original Bratwurst
JVL Fresh Grilling (Links) - Party Pack (Mild), 3 lb
JVL Fresh Grilling (Links) - Party Pack (Original), 3 lb
JVL Smoked/Cooked - Beef Hot Links
JVL Smoked/Cooked - Little Smokies
JVL Smoked/Cooked - Smoked Hot Links
JVL Smoked/Cooked (Links) - Beddar with Cheddar
JVL Smoked/Cooked (Links) - Heat & Serve Brat
JVL Smoked/Cooked (Links) - Heat & Serve Italian

JVL Smoked/Cooked (Links) - New Orleans Style
Smoked Sausage

JVL Smoked/Cooked (Links) - Smoked Beef
Bratwurst

JVL Smoked/Cooked (Links) - Smoked Bratwurst

JVL Smoked/Cooked (Links) - Smoked Polish
Sausage

JVL Smoked/Cooked (Links) - Stadium Style Brats

JVL Summer Sausage (Links) - Beef, 34 oz

JVL Summer Sausage (Links) - Beef, 12 oz

JVL Summer Sausage (Links) - Garlic, 24 oz

JVL Summer Sausage (Links) - Garlic, 12 oz

JVL Summer Sausage (Links) - Old World Summer,
32 oz

JVL Summer Sausage (Links) - Original, 24 oz

JVL Summer Sausage (Links) - Original, 12 oz

Perri (Links) - Hot Italian

Perri (Links) - Sweet Italian

Perri (Links) - Sweet Italian, 3 lb

Perri (Patties) - Sweet Italian

Little Sizzlers
Sausage Links & Patties

Nature's Promise (Stop & Shop)
Italian Spicy Pork Sausage

Mild Italian Chicken Sausage

Red Pepper & Provolone Pork Sausage

Spiced Apple Chicken Sausage

Spinach & Feta Chicken Sausage

Sun Dried Tomato & Basil Chicken Sausage

Old Wisconsin
Old Wisconsin, All BUT Beef Jerky

Perdue
Seasoned Fresh Lean Turkey Sausage - Hot Italian

Seasoned Fresh Lean Turkey Sausage - Sweet Italian

Primo Naturale
Dried Hot Chorizo, Item# 00722

Sliced Dried Chorizo, Item# 00741

Sliced Hot Chorizo, Item# 00742

Sliced Sopressata, Item# 00726 - 6 oz

Sopressata, Item# 00725 - 10 oz

Stick Dried Chorizo, Item# 00721

Sweet Abruzzi Sausage, Item# 00720 - 10 oz

Primo Taglio (Safeway)
Mortadella - Black Pepper Added

Sopressata

Select Brand (Safeway)
Beef Hot Link

Beef Smoked Sausage

Cajun Style Link

Chicken Andouille Sausage

Chicken Apple Sausage

Italian Pork Sausage

Italian Sausage

Parmesan Basil Sausage

Polish Sausage

Turkey Chicken Sun Dried Tomato Sausage

Wellshire Farms
Aged Cheddar Bratwurst, Item# 06070 - 12 oz

Bratwursts Hot Links New Orleans Style Smoked,
Item# 06065

Mild Italian Style Turkey Dinner Link Sausage, Item#
08200 - 12 oz

Morning Maple Turkey Breakfast Link Sausage,
Item# 08220 - 12 oz

Original Bratwurst, Item# 06050 - 12 oz

Polska Kielbasa, Item# 06020 - 12 oz

Pork Andouille Sausage, Item# 06010 - 12 oz

Pork Chorizo Sausage, Item# 06030 - 12 oz

Pork Linguica Sausage, Item# 06040 - 12 oz

Pork Sausage with Green Peppers & Onions, Item#
06085 - 12 oz

Pork Sausage with Jalapeno & Aged Cheddar, Item#
06090 - 12 oz

Roasted Garlic & Parsley Turkey Dinner Link
Sausage, Item# 08210 - 12 oz

Sliced Mortadella, Item# 04166

Smoked Bratwurst, Item# 06051 - 12 oz

Smoked Pork Kielbasa Links, Item# 06025 - 12 oz

Spicy Hot Style Bratwurst, Item# 06060 - 12 oz

Turkey Andouille Sausage, Item# - 08310 - 12 oz

Turkey Dinner Sausage Links Jalapeno Herb, Item#
08230

Turkey Kielbasa, Item# 08300 - 12 oz

Winn-Dixie
Beef Skinless Smoked Sausage

Chorizo Sausage

Hot Italian Sausage

Hot Italian Turkey Sausage

Hot Skinless Smoked Sausage

Mild Italian Sausage

Mild Italian Turkey Sausage

Polish Sausage

Polska Kielbasa Skinless Smoked Sausage

Sausage - Andouille, Cajun, Chicken & Apple and
Sweet Red Pepper

Sausage Rolls - Hot, Medium & Mild

Smoked Skinless Sausage

SEAFOOD

Captains Choice (Safeway)
Cod Fillets

Cooked Tail on Shrimp

Kasilof
Kasilof, All

Winn-Dixie 👁
Fresh Shrimp, All BUT Breaded Items & Items with Cocktail Sauce

TOFU & TEMPEH

Azumaya
Extra Firm Tofu, UPC# 7432600013
Extra Firm Tofu Chinese Style, UPC# 7432600032
Firm Tofu, UPC# 7432600012
Firm Tofu Japanese Style, UPC# 7432600033
Lite Extra Firm Tofu, UPC# 7432600019
Lite Silken Tofu, UPC# 7432600018
Silken Tofu, UPC# 7432600014
Silken Tofu Kinugoshi, UPC# 7432600011
Zesty Garlic, UPC# 7432600030

Eden Foods
Dried Tofu, UPC# 024182357011

Food You Feel Good About (Wegman's) ✗ 👁 ()
Tofu, 16 oz

Lightlife
Organic Flax Tempeh
Organic Garden Vegetable Tempeh
Organic Soy Tempeh
Organic Wild Rice Tempeh
Tofu Pups

More than Tofu
Seasoned Tofu, All

Mori-Nu
Chinese Spice Seasoned Tofu
Japanese Miso Seasoned Tofu
Organic Silken Tofu
Silken Extra Firm Tofu
Silken Firm Tofu
Silken Lite Extra Firm Tofu
Silken Lite Firm Tofu
Silken Soft Tofu

Nasoya
Extra Firm Tofu, UPC# 2548400012
Firm Tofu, UPC# 2548400010
Garlic & Onion Tofu, UPC# 2548400061
Lite Firm Tofu, UPC# 2548400021
Lite Silken Tofu, UPC# 2548400020
Silken Tofu, UPC# 2548400013
Soft Tofu, UPC# 2548400011
Super Firm Cubed, UPC# 2548400029

Stop & Shop ✗ 👁
Tofu - Firm & Extra Firm

Turtle Island Foods
Five Grain Tempeh
Indonesian Tempeh
Soy Tempeh
Veggie Edamame Tempeh

Vitasoy
Firm Tofu, UPC# 6195400023
Regular Tofu, UPC# 6195400022
Silken Tofu, UPC# 6195400021

Wegman's ✗ 👁 ()
X-Firm Tofu, 16 oz

TURKEY

Applegate Farms 👁 ✗
Applegate Farms, All BUT Chicken Nuggets & Chicken Pot Pie

Bar-S
Bar-S, All BUT Chuck Wagon Brand Franks & Corn Dogs

Boar's Head 👁 ⓘ
Meats, All

Butcher's Cut (Safeway) ✗ 👁
Ground Turkey
Oven Roasted Turkey Breast - 98% Fat Free & Regular

Carl Buddig 🖐
Meat Products, All

Empire Kosher
Fresh Chill Pack Chicken & Turkey
Fresh Ground Turkey
Fully Cooked Barbecue Turkey (Fresh or Frozen)
Preferred - Signature Edition Smoked Turkey Breast, Skinless
Preferred - Signature Edition Turkey Breast Pastrami, Skinless
Preferred - Signature Edition Turkey Pastrami, Skinless
Premiere - Signature Edition All Natural Turkey Breast Skinless
Premiere - Signature Edition All Natural Turkey Breast with Skin
Signature Edition - Oven Prepared Turkey Breast
Signature Edition - Smoked Turkey Breast
Smoked Turkey Breast - Slices
Turkey Breast (Slices)
Turkey Burgers
Turkey Pastrami (Slices)
White Turkey Roll

Honeysuckle White

Honeysuckle White, All BUT Asian Grill Marinated Turkey Strips, Cajun Fried Turkey, Frozen Turkey Burgers, Italian Style Meatballs & Teriyaki Turkey Breast Tenderloins

Hormel ☻ 👁

Deli Sliced Oven Roasted Turkey Breast Pre-Packaged Refrigerated Lunch Meats

Deli Sliced Smoked Turkey Breast Pre-Packaged Refrigerated Lunch Meats

Julienne Turkey Pre-Packaged Refrigerated Lunch Meats

Natural Choice - Honey Deli Turkey Pre-Packaged Refrigerated Lunch Meats

Natural Choice - Oven Roasted Deli Turkey Pre-Packaged Refrigerated Lunch Meats

Natural Choice - Smoked Deli Turkey Pre-Packaged Refrigerated Lunch Meats

Hy-Vee ✁ 👁

Deli Thin Slices Honey Roasted Turkey Breast, 10 oz

Deli Thin Slices Oven Roasted Turkey Breast, 10 oz

Oven Roasted White Turkey, 16 oz

Smoked White Turkey, 16 oz

Thin Sliced Honey Turkey, 2.5 oz

Thin Sliced Turkey, 2.5 oz

Turkey - Natural & Moisture Enhanced

Jennie-O ☻ 👁

Apple Cinnamon Turkey Breast (Deli Item)

Cajun-Style Refrigerated Qtr Turkey Breasts

Cracked Pepper Refrigerated Qtr Turkey Breasts

Festive Tender Cured Turkey

Garlic Peppered Turkey Breast (Deli Item)

Grand Champion - Hickory Smoked Turkey Breast (Deli Item)

Grand Champion - Homestyle Pan Roasted Turkey Breast (Deli Item)

Grand Champion - Honey Cured Turkey Breast (Deli Item)

Grand Champion - Mesquite Smoked Turkey Breast (Deli Item)

Grand Champion - Oven Roasted Turkey Breast (Deli Item)

Grand Champion - Tender Browned Turkey Breast (Deli Item)

Hickory Smoked Refrigerated Qtr Turkey Breasts

Honey Cured Refrigerated Qtr Turkey Breasts

Honey Maple Turkey Breast (Deli Item)

Honey Mesquite Turkey Breast (Deli Item)

Hot Red Peppered Turkey Breast (Deli Item)

Italian Style Turkey Breast (Deli Item)

Maple Spiced Turkey Breast (Deli Item)

Mesquite Smoked Turkey Breast (Deli Item)

Natural Choice - Oven Roasted Turkey Breast (Deli Item)

Natural Choice - Peppered Turkey Breast (Deli Item)

Natural Choice - Tender Browned Turkey Breast (Deli Item)

Oven Roasted Refrigerated Qtr Turkey Breasts

Oven Roasted Turkey Breast (Deli Item)

Peppered Turkey Breast (Deli Item)

Prime Young Turkey - Fresh or Frozen, Gravy packet NOT GF

Refrigerated Dark Turkey Pastrami

Smoked Peppered Turkey Breast (Deli Item)

Smoked Turkey Breast (Deli Item)

Smoked Turkey Wings & Drumsticks

Sun-Dried Tomato Refrigerated Qtr Turkey Breasts

Tender Browned Turkey Breast (Deli Item)

Tomato Basil Turkey Breast (Deli Item)

Turkey Store - Barbecue Turkey Thighs

Turkey Store - Cracked Pepper Hickory Smoked Turkey Breast (Deli Item)

Turkey Store - Extra Lean Fresh Ground Turkey

Turkey Store - Fresh Lean Turkey Patties

Turkey Store - Garlic & Herb Oven Ready Turkey

Turkey Store - Garlic Pesto Hickory Smoked Turkey Breast (Deli Item)

Turkey Store - Hickory Smoked Turkey Breast (Deli Item)

Turkey Store - Homestyle Oven Ready Turkey

Turkey Store - Honey Cured Hickory Smoked Turkey Breast (Deli Item)

Turkey Store - Honey Cured Smoked Turkey Breast (Deli Item)

Turkey Store - Italian Fresh Ground Turkey

Turkey Store - Lean Fresh Ground Turkey

Turkey Store - Lemon-Garlic Flavored Tenderloins

Turkey Store - Mesquite Smoked Turkey Breast (Deli Item)

Turkey Store - Oven Ready Turkey Breast, Gravy packet NOT GF

Turkey Store - Oven Roasted Turkey Breast (Deli Item)

Turkey Store - Seasoned Pepper Flavored Tenderloins

Turkey Store - Sun Dried Tomato Hickory Smoked Turkey Breast (Deli Item)

Turkey Store - Tenderloins Fresh Tray

Turkey Store - Tequila Lime Flavored Tenderloins

Turkey Store Fresh Tray - Breast Slices

Turkey Store Fresh Tray - Breast Strips

Turkey Store So Easy - BBQ Glazed Breast Filets

Turkey Store So Easy - Broccoli & Cheese Stuffed Breasts

Turkey Store So Easy - Honey Glazed Breast Filets

Turkey Store So Easy - Pepper Cheese & Rice Stuffed
  Breasts
Turkey Store So Easy - Slow Roasted Turkey Breast
Turkey Store So Easy - Swiss Cheese & Ham Stuffed
  Breasts

Nature's Promise (Stop & Shop) ✔ 👁
Deli Meats, All
Fresh Meat, Poultry

Norbest
Norbest, All BUT Items with Gravy Packets

Norwestern ☤ 👁
Hickory Smoked Deli Turkey (Deli Item)
Oven Roasted Deli Turkey (Deli Item)
Turkey Pastrami Deli Turkey (Deli Item)

Perdue
Carving - Turkey Breast, Hickory Smoked
Carving - Turkey Breast, Honey Smoked
Carving - Turkey Breast, Mesquite Smoked
Carving - Turkey Breast, Oven Roasted
Carving - Whole Turkey
Carving Classics - Pan Roasted Turkey Breast,
  Cracked Pepper
Carving Classics - Turkey Breast Pan Roasted
Carving Classics - Turkey Breast Pan Roasted, Honey
  Smoked
Deli Dark Turkey Pastrami - Hickory Smoked
Deli Pick Ups - Sliced Turkey Breast, Golden
  Browned
Deli Pick Ups - Sliced Turkey Breast, Honey Smoked
Deli Pick Ups - Sliced Turkey Breast, Mesquite
  Smoked
Deli Pick Ups - Sliced Turkey Breast, Oven Roasted
Deli Pick Ups - Sliced Turkey Breast, Smoked
Deli Turkey Breast - Oil Browned
Fresh Ground Breast of Turkey
Fresh Lean Ground Turkey
Ground Turkey Burgers
Healthsense - Turkey Breast Oven Roasted - Fat Free,
  Reduced Sodium
Rotisserie Turkey Breast
Short Cuts - Carved Turkey Breast Oven Roasted
Tender & Tasty Products
Whole Turkeys Seasoned with Broth

Safeway ✔ 👁
Roasted Turkey Breast (Deli Counter)

Stop & Shop ✔ 👁
Oven Roasted Turkey Breast - Fat Free
Smoked Turkey Breast

Wegman's ✔ 👁 ()
Oven Roasted Turkey Breast - Thin Sliced, 10 oz
Smoked Honey Turkey Breast - Thin Sliced, 10 oz

Smoked Turkey Breast - Thin Sliced, 10 oz

Wellshire Farms
All Natural Pan Roasted Turkey Breast, Item# 08011
All Natural Smoked Turkey Breast, Item# 08016
Sliced Oven Roasted Turkey Breast, Item# 08110 - 8
  oz
Sliced Smoked Turkey Breast, Item# 08115 - 8 oz
Turkey Breast Oven Roasted, Item# 08030

Winn-Dixie 👁
Fresh Turkey

MISCELLANEOUS

Hy-Vee ✔ 👁
Old Fashioned Loaf, 16 oz
Pickle Loaf, 8 oz
Pickle Loaf, 16 oz
Spiced Luncheon Loaf, 16 oz

Wellshire Farms
Pork Liverwurst, Item# 06110
Turkey Liverwurst, Item# 06130

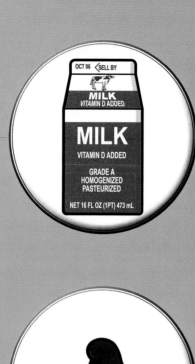

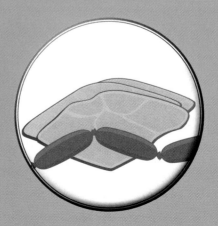

Section 3:
Company Contact Information

Symbols Defined

⚱ **No reply** to our inquiries was received.

⊘ **No gluten-free list** was provided by the brand, manufacturer or company representative in their replies. Please note: Many companies that do not provide a GF list have "full disclosure" labeling policies. Please read the Company Notes for each brand to determine whether their products may be suitable for you.

✕ **All items are NOT gluten-free,** according to the brand, manufacturer or company representative.

Don't forget to read Section 1, particularly Chapters 3 and 4 for more information on the information presented in this guide and how to use it.
Happy Shopping!

100 Grand ⊘
5/3/2007 ⊙ See *Nestlé*.

3 Musketeers ⊘
www.3musketeers.com
4/9/2007 ⊙ (800) 551-0698
Company Notes: The ingredient statement on the wrapper is the "best source" of information. ⊙ See *MasterFoods USA*.

365 Every Day Value ⊘
4/22/2007 ⊙ See *Whole Foods*.

365 Organic ⊘
4/22/2007 ⊙ See *Whole Foods*.

5th Avenue ⊘
3/20/2007 ⊙ See *Hershey Company, The*.

7UP
www.7up.com
3/12/2007 ⊙ (866) 787-7632
See *Cadbury Schweppes (Beverages)*.

8th Continent ⊘
www.8thcontinent.com
3/19/2007 ⊙ (800) 247-6458
See *General Mills*.

A & E Cheese
4/9/2007 ⊙ See *Wellshire Farms*.

A & W
www.aandwrootbeer.com
3/12/2007 ⊙ See *Cadbury Schweppes (Beverages)*.

A.1. ⊘
3/19/2007 ⊙ See *Kraft*.

Abbott's Ross Products Division
www.ross.com
4/9/2007 ⊙ (800) 227-5767
Company Notes: Visit their online "Product Handbook." Always read labels for the most current information. The decision to use their products is the consumer or medical professional's responsibility.

Acadia ⊘
5/9/2007 ⊙ See *World Harbors*.

Ac'cent
4/19/2007 ⊙ See *B&G Foods*.

ACH
www.achfood.com
3/16/2007 ⊙ (800) 691-1106

ACT II ⊘
www.actii.com
(800) 736-2212
See *ConAgra Foods*.

Adagio Teas
www.adagio.com
3/14/2007

Additions ⊘
5/3/2007 ⊙ See *Nestlé*.

Adirondack Beverages
www.adirondackbeverages.com
5/2/2007 ⊙ Company Notes: The modified food starch used is made from corn.

After Eight Biscuits & Mints ⊘
5/3/2007 ⊙ See *Nestlé*.

Aidell's Sausage Company ⊘
www.aidells.com
4/11/2007 ⊙ (877) 243-3557
Company Notes: The soy sauce used in some sausages can contain hydrolyzed vegetable protein derived from wheat. Flavors that contain soy sauce are Fresh Lamb & Rosemary Sausage, Smoked and Fresh Thai Sausage and Teriyaki Meatballs. Products are made in a non-dedicated plant. The plant procedure is to "thoroughly clean everything with hot water and sanitizers" after each batch run. Aidell recommends that very sensitive persons exclude Aidell products from their diet.

Air Crisps ⊘
3/19/2007 ⊙ See *Kraft*.

Airforce Nutrisoda
www.nutrisoda.com
4/11/2007 ⊙ (612) 746-2770

Al Dente Pasta Company ✗
www.aldentepasta.com
4/9/2007 ⊙ (800) 536-7278

Albers Corn Meal And Grits ⊘
5/3/2007 ⊙ (800) 432-9371
See *Nestlé*.

Alexia Foods
www.alexiafoods.com
4/10/2007 ⊙ (718) 609-5665
Company Notes: Potato products are GF. Their products are produced on dedicated lines, but they are processed in a facility where wheat-containing products are also made. Equipment is cleaned in between production runs "in accordance with organic and kosher guidelines," though, they cannot guarantee there is no cross-contamination.

All Whites
3/14/2007 ⊙ See *Better'n Eggs*.

Almond Joy ⊘
3/20/2007 ⊙ See *Hershey Company, The*.

Alouette
www.alouettecheese.com
4/9/2007 ⊙ (800) 322-2743

Alpine Lace ⊘
www.alpinelace.com
3/15/2007 ⊙ (800) 328-9680
Company Notes: They note that the FDA and USDA have not defined what GF is, then go on to state that all Alpine Lace cheese ingredients are GF "to the best of our knowledge."

Alta Dena ⊘
3/15/2007 ⊙ See *Dean Foods*.

Alta Springs (Winn-Dixie)
4/25/2007 ⊙ See *Winn-Dixie*.

Alter Eco Fair Trade
www.altereco-usa.com
4/9/2007 ⊙ (415) 701-1212

Altoids ⊘
www.altoids.com
3/16/2007 ⊙ See *Wrigley*.

American Heritage ⊘
4/23/2007 ⊙ See *Schreiber Foods*.

Amy's Kitchen
www.amyskitchen.com
5/7/2007 ⊙ (707) 578-7270
Company Notes: Products are made in a plant that also handles wheat.

Andes
3/15/2007 ⊙ See *Tootsie Roll Industries*.

Andy Capp's ⊘
(800) 382-5775
See *ConAgra Foods*.

Andy's Seasoning ✗
www.andysseasoning.com
4/11/2007 ⊙ (800) 305-3004
Company Notes: The seasoning salt does not contain wheat as an ingredient, but is manufactured in a facility that produces wheat-based products. The batter and breaders contain wheat.

Angostura ⊘
5/9/2007 ⊙ See *World Harbors*.

Annie Chun's
www.anniechuns.com
4/11/2007 ⊙ (415) 479-8272

Annie's Homegrown
www.annies.com
4/9/2007 ⊙ (800) 288-1089

Annie's Naturals
www.consorzio.com
4/9/2007 ⊙ (800) 288-1089
Company Notes: Dressings and marinades are produced on equipment that also processes wheat; oils are made in a facility where wheat is present. However, "great precaution is taken" to prevent cross-contamination.

Apple & Eve
www.appleandeve.com
4/9/2007 ⊙ (800) 969-8018

Apple Leaf
4/20/2007 ⊙ See *Knouse Foods*.

Apple Time
4/20/2007 ⊙ See *Knouse Foods*.

Applegate Farms
www.applegatefarms.com
4/12/2007 ⊙ (866) 587-5858
Company Notes: Information on
ingredients, nutrition and
allergens is available for all
products on their website. Use
the information as a guide
only. The most current information will be on the package
label.

Aqua (Wegman's)
5/8/2007 ⊙ See *Wegman's*.

Argo
www.argostarch.com
3/16/2007 ⊙ (866) 373-2300

**Arico Natural Food Com-
pany**
www.aricofoods.com
4/9/2007 ⊙ (866) 982-7426

AriZona
www.arizonabev.com
3/14/2007 ⊙ (800) 832-3775

Arm & Hammer
www.armandhammer.com
5/4/2007 ⊙ (800) 524-1328

Armour ⊘
www.pinnaclefoodscorp.com
3/19/2007 ⊙ (888) 267-4752

Arrowhead Mills ⊘
www.arrowheadmills.com
4/11/2007 ⊙ Company Notes: No
GF list is available. The best
way to check for gluten is to
read the label. If gluten is an
ingredient, it will be listed
separately. It will not be listed
under "natural flavors" or
"spices." "Major and minor
ingredients" and "all processing procedures and equip-
ment" are "closely scrutinized."
All potential allergen issues,
as determined by the Hain
Celestial Group, are declared
on the label. Their manufacturing facilities follow allergen
control programs, including
"staff training, segregation of
allergen ingredients, production scheduling, and thorough
cleaning and sanitation." ⊙ See
Hain Celestial.

Astor (Winn-Dixie)
4/25/2007 ⊙ See *Winn-Dixie*.

Athenos ⊘
3/19/2007 ⊙ See *Kraft*.

Atkins Advantage ⬢
www.atkins.com
(800) 628-5467

Attune ✘
www.attunefoods.com
4/9/2007 ⊙ (800) 641-4508
Company Notes: Attune wellness
bars are wheat-free but not GF.

Aunt Jemima
www.auntjemima.com
3/12/2007 ⊙ (800) 432-3102
See *Quaker Oats Company,
The*.

Axelrod
www.axelrod.com
3/15/2007 ⊙ (800) 637-0019

Azumaya
4/10/2007 ⊙ See *Vitasoy*.

B&G Foods
www.bgfoods.com
4/19/2007

B&M Baked Beans
4/19/2007 ⊙ See *B&G Foods*.

Baby Ruth
5/5/2007 ⊙ See *Nestlé Chocolate and Confections*.

BACI ⊘
www.nestleeuropeanchocolate.com
5/3/2007 ⊙ See *Nestlé*.

Back to Nature ⊘
3/19/2007 ⊙ See *Kraft*.

Baked! Cheetos
4/12/2007 ⊙ See *Frito Lay*.

Baked! Lay's
4/12/2007 ⊙ See *Frito Lay*.

Baked! Ruffles
4/12/2007 ⊙ See *Frito Lay*.

Baked! Tostitos
4/12/2007 ⊙ See *Frito Lay*.

Baken-Ets
4/12/2007 ⊙ See *Frito Lay*.

Baker's ⊘
3/19/2007 ⊙ See *Kraft*.

Bakipan
www.bakipan.com
3/19/2007 ⊙ Company Notes: No
ingredients containing gluten
are present in the manufacturing facility.

Balance ⊘
3/19/2007 ⊙ See *Kraft*.

Balance CarbWell ⊘
3/19/2007 ⊙ See *Kraft*.

**Baldwin Richardson
Foods Co.**
www.brfoods.com
3/22/2007 ⊙ (815) 464-9994

Ball Park ⬢
www.ballparkfranks.com
(800) 925-3326

Banquet ⊘
(800) 257-5191
See *ConAgra Foods*.

Barbara's Bakery
www.barbarasbakery.com
3/16/2007 ⊙ (707) 765-2273
Company Notes: Products may
be produced at facilities that
also process gluten-containing
ingredients for other products.

Barber's ⊘
3/15/2007 ⊙ See *Dean Foods*.

Barbe's ⊘
3/15/2007 ⊙ See *Dean Foods*.

Barengo
www.barengovinegar.com
3/9/2007 ⊙ (800) 323-4358

Barilla ✘
www.barillaus.com
3/20/2007 ⊙ (800) 922-7455

Barnum's Animals ⊘
3/19/2007 ⊙ See *Kraft*.

Barq's
www.barqs.com
4/21/2007 ⊙ See *Coca-Cola
Company, The*.

Bar-S
www.bar-s.com
5/7/2007 ⊙ Company Notes: Their
source of modified food starch
is corn.

Bay Valley Foods ⊘
www.bayvalleyfoods.com
5/7/2007 ⊙ (800) 236-1119
Company Notes: The creamers do
not have gluten-containing
ingredients, but they are not
guaranteed GF because of the
possibility of cross-contamination and because the formula
may change.

Bear Naked ✘
www.bearnakedgranola.com
3/15/2007 ⊙ (866) 374-4442
Company Notes: All products contain oats. Peak protein, apple
cinnamon and banana nut also
contain barley malt.

Bearitos ⊘
www.littlebearfoods.com
5/21/2007 ⊙ See *Hain Celestial*.

Beech-Nut
www.beechnut.com
4/26/2007 ⊙ (800) 233-2468
Company Notes: Always read
ingredient statements, as
the product may have been
produced before or after the
time period covered by the GF
list. The GF list is as of January
2007.

Beelers
www.beelerspurepork.com
3/15/2007 ⊙ (712) 546-4402

Before & After Candy
www.beforeandaftercandy.com
4/9/2007 ⊙ (866) 468-6468

Bel Brands U.S.A. ⊘
4/11/2007 ⊙ (800) 558-3500
Company Notes: No products are
guaranteed to be GF because
neither they nor their suppliers perform gluten tests.
Ingredient statements will
include any added gluten or
wheat flour.

BelGioioso Cheese
www.belgioioso.com
4/24/2007 ⊚ (877) 863-2123
Triumph Notes: The GF list was
dated revised 3/26/07

Bell & Evans
www.bellandevans.com
5/13/2007 ⊚ (717) 865-6626
Company Notes: GF products are
in a labeled black box. GF and
non-GF items are produced
in a common facility. Steps to
prevent cross-contamination
include segregation and
sanitization protocols. All new
hires are trained in handling
allergenic ingredients. Ingredients containing allergens, like
gluten, are tagged and sepa-
rated from other ingredients
and packaging materials. In
case of a spill, only specifically
identified cleaning materials
are used to clean up allergenic
ingredients. GF items are
produced at the beginning of
a shift and after all processing
equipment has been cleaned
and sanitized. Also, each new
shift for GF production starts
with fresh oil.

Bellybar ✗
www.nutrabella.com
4/10/2007 ⊚ (800) 952-3559
Company Notes: All Bellybars contain oats and are not GF.

Ben & Jerry's Homemade Ice Cream ⊘
www.benjerry.com
5/3/2007 ⊚ (800) 418-3275
See *Unilever.*

Benecol
www.benecol.com
4/2/2007 ⊚ (888) 236-3265

Berkeley Farms ⊘
3/15/2007 ⊚ See *Dean Foods.*

Bertolli ⊘
www.bertolli.us
5/3/2007 ⊚ (800) 908-9789
Company Notes: The source of
its modified food starch is
corn. For a variety of reasons,
including the fact that product

formulations may change,
always read the label's ingredient list. ⊚ See *Unilever.*

Best Foods ⊘
www.bestfoods.com
5/3/2007 ⊚ (800) 418-3275
See *Unilever.*

Better Cheddars ⊘
3/19/2007 ⊚ See *Kraft.*

Better'n Eggs
www.betterneggs.com
3/4/2007 ⊚ (877) 727-3884

Betty Crocker ⊘
www.bettycrocker.com
3/19/2007 ⊚ (800) 446-1898
See *General Mills.*

Big Red
3/16/2007 ⊚ See *Wrigley.*

Bigelow
www.bigelowtea.com
3/14/2007 ⊚ (888) 244-3569
Company Notes: Blueberry Harvest
Herb Tea, Chamomile Mango
Herb Tea, Cinnamon Spice
Herb Tea (formerly Sinfully
Cinnamon Herb Tea) and
Take-A-Break Loose Tea con-
tain barley malt, though test
results showed no detectable
gluten. All other teas are GF.

Birds Eye Foods ⊘
www.birdseyefoods.com
5/7/2007 ⊚ (800) 563-1786
Company Notes: Refer to ingredient statements.

Biscos ⊘
3/19/2007 ⊚ See *Kraft.*

Bisquick ⊘
www.bisquick.com
3/19/2007 ⊚ (800) 446-1898
See *General Mills.*

Bit-O-Honey
5/5/2007 ⊚ See *Nestlé Chocolate and Confections.*

Blow Pops
3/15/2007 ⊚ See *Tootsie Roll
Industries.*

Blue Bonnet ⊘
www.bluebonnet.com
(800) 988-7808
See *ConAgra Foods.*

Blue Boy ⊘
4/19/2007 ⊚ See *Seneca Foods.*

Blue Bunny
www.bluebunny.com
3/15/2007 ⊚ (800) 331-0830

Blue Diamond Growers
www.bluediamond.com
4/10/2007 ⊚ (916) 442-0771
Company Notes: The crackers
are made in a facility that
produces wheat products. In
order to reduce the chance of
cross-contamination, production lines are "aggressively"
cleaned. In addition, routine
testing is done to adhere to
the less than 20 ppm CODEX
standard. "Most" almond
products are GF, except for
the BOLD Wasabi & Soy and
Jordan Almonds. ⊚ Triumph Notes:
We have also seen the CODEX
standard for gluten written as
200 ppm.

Boar's Head
www.boarshead.com
5/13/2007 ⊚ (800) 352-6277
Company Notes: Always read
ingredient statements. And,
check labels on entrées and
sandwiches prepared by the
store, as they may have gravies
and sauces that contain gluten.

Bob's Candies ⊘
3/22/2007 ⊚ See *Farley's &
Sathers Candy Company.*

Bob's Red Mill
www.bobsredmill.com
3/14/2007 ⊚ (800) 349-2173
Company Notes: Not all GF
products are sourced from
the United States, but they are
all packaged in their Oregon
facility. GF products are batch
tested "and promoted as
Gluten-Free according to the
ELISA Gluten Assay Test."

Boca ✗
www.bocaburger.com
5/13/2007 ⊚ Company Notes: All
BOCA products contain wheat
gluten. Always read ingredient
statements.

Bolthouse Farms
www.bolthouse.com
3/15/2007

Bone Suckin' Sauce
www.bonesuckin.com
5/13/2007 ⊚ (800) 446-0947
Company Notes: New labels for GF
products state "Gluten Free"
on the top right of the label for
the 4, 5, 6.2 and 16 oz. products and the back of the 1/2
gallon and gallon products.

Bookbinder's Foods ⊘
www.bookbindersfoods.com
3/21/2007 ⊚ See *Silver Spring.*

Boost ⊘
www.boost.com
4/21/2007 ⊚ (800) 247-7893
Company Notes: Except for Boost
Chocolate Malt, Boost products "may be suitable for a
gluten free diet." ⊚ Triumph Notes:
Boost does not definitively
state their product is GF.

Borden ⊘
www.elsie.com
4/19/2007 ⊚ (888) 337-2407
Company Notes: Their cheeses do
not contain gluten-containing
ingredients.

Bossa Nova
www.bossausa.com
4/21/2007 ⊚ (310) 566-7851
Company Notes: All Bossa Nova's
products are GF, including
ingredients listed as "natural
ingredients."

Boston Tea
www.bostontea.com
4/25/2007 ⊚ (201) 440-3004

Boston's ⊘
www.bostonssnacks.com
5/21/2007 ⊚ See *Hain Celestial.*

Botan Calrose
4/10/2007 ⊚ See *JFC International.*

BottleCaps
5/5/2007 ⊚ See *Nestlé Chocolate and Confections.*

Boylan Bottling Co.
www.boylanbottling.com
4/10/2007 ⊚ (800) 289-7978

Brach's Confections ✗
www.brachs.com
3/16/2007 ⊚ (800) 283-6303
Company Notes: They do not consider any of their products GF, as the FDA has not established any guidelines on GF.

Bragg
www.bragg.com
5/1/2007 ⊚ (800) 446-1990

Breadshop ⊘
5/21/2007 ⊚ See *Hain Celestial.*

Breakstone's ⊘
3/19/2007 ⊚ See *Kraft.*

BreathSavers ⊘
3/20/2007 ⊚ See *Hershey Company, The.*

Brer Rabbit
4/19/2007 ⊚ See *B&G Foods.*

Breyers ⊘
www.breyers.com
5/3/2007 ⊚ (920) 499-5151
See *Unilever.*

Brianna's
www.briannassaladdressing.com
4/9/2007 ⊚ (979) 836-5978
Company Notes: The items on the GF list are compiled to the best of their knowledge.

Brown Cow
www.browncowfarm.com
3/14/2007 ⊚ (888) 429-5459
Company Notes: The plain yogurts (nonfat, low fat, and whole milk) are GF. However, while no gluten is added to other yogurts, there may be trace amounts that come from processing fruits and flavors with a grain alcohol.

Brown 'N Serve ⊘
(888) 267-4752
See *ConAgra Foods.*

Brown Rice Snaps
4/10/2007 ⊚ See *Edward & Sons.*

Brown's Dairy ⊘
3/15/2007 ⊚ See *Dean Foods.*

Bruce Foods
www.brucefoods.com
4/9/2007 ⊚ (800) 299-9082
Company Notes: They have a program for "management and labeling of allergens." Always read ingredient lists. The GF list contains examples of their many GF products.

Bruce's Yams
4/9/2007 ⊚ See *Bruce Foods.*

Brummel & Brown
www.brummelandbrown.com
5/3/2007 ⊚ (800) 735-3554

Bubba Burger
www.bubba-burger.com
4/9/2007 ⊚ (877) 879-2822

Bubble Yum ⊘
3/20/2007 ⊚ See *Hershey Company, The.*

Bubblicious
www.theultimatebubble.com
3/19/2007 ⊚ See *Cadbury Adams.*

Bufalo ⊘
3/2/2007 ⊚ See *Hormel Foods.*

Bugles ⊘
3/19/2007 ⊚ See *General Mills.*

Buitoni ⊘
www.buitoni.com
5/3/2007 ⊚ (800) 727-0050
See *Nestlé.*

Bull's-Eye ⊘
3/19/2007 ⊚ See *Kraft.*

Bumble Bee
www.bumblebee.com
5/7/2007 ⊚ (800) 800-8572

BumbleBar
www.bumblebar.com
4/9/2007 ⊚ (888) 453-3369

Bush's Best
www.bushbeans.com
3/14/2007 ⊚ Company Notes: The product line is growing and new products that contain gluten may be added. Therefore, always read ingredient labels.

Butcher's Cut (Safeway)
5/9/2007 ⊚ See *Safeway.*

Butter Kernel ⊘
3/16/2007 ⊚ See *Faribault Foods.*

Butterball ⊘
www.butterball.com
4/30/2007 ⊚ (800) 288-8372

Butterfinger
5/5/2007 ⊚ See *Nestlé Chocolate and Confections.*

Cabot Creamery
www.cabotcheese.com
3/15/2007 ⊚ (888) 792-2268
Company Notes: All ingredients, including anti-caking agents, are researched and verified to be GF. All starches are derived from corn, distillates are grain-free, and conveyor "dressings" are cornstarch.

Cacao Reserve ⊘
3/20/2007 ⊚ See *Hershey Company, The.*

Cadbury (Chocolates) ⊘
3/20/2007 ⊚ See *Hershey Company, The.*

Cadbury Adams
www.ctai.ca
3/19/2007 ⊚ (866) 782-3267
Company Notes: Cadbury identifies all known instances of gluten on product labels. Products are continually assessed to update labels and listed allergens.

Cadbury Schweppes (Beverages)
www.brandspeoplelove.com
3/12/2007 ⊚ (800) 696-5891

Company Notes: They have a food allergen management policy. Their policy is to label wheat, rye, barley, triticale, spelt, kamut, oats and other allergens. They "continually" assess their products and update supplier information; therefore, the labels reflect the presence of listed allergens.

Cadbury Schweppes (Candy) ⊘
www.brandspeoplelove.com
5/3/2007 ⊚ (800) 565-6317
Company Notes: They have an "internal food allergen management policy," which covers gluten. They "continuously" assess their products and "update supplier information" to make sure labels accurately list the presence of gluten.

Café Creme ⊘
3/19/2007 ⊚ See *Kraft.*

Cains
www.cainsfoods.com
3/15/2007 ⊚ (800) 225-0601

Cajun King
4/9/2007 ⊚ See *Bruce Foods.*

California Pizza Kitchen ⊘
3/19/2007 ⊚ See *Kraft.*

Calumet ⊘
3/19/2007 ⊚ See *Kraft.*

Cameo ⊘
3/19/2007 ⊚ See *Kraft.*

Campbell's
www.campbellsoup.com
4/10/2007 ⊚ (800) 257-8443
Company Notes: Always read ingredient lists on the product label, as changes may occur. They make every effort to keep the GF list up-to-date, but some GF products may not be included.

Canada Dry
www.canadadry.com
3/12/2007 ⊚ See *Cadbury Schweppes (Beverages).*

Cantaré Foods
www.cantarefoods.com
5/4/2007 ⊙ (858) 578-8490

Cap'n Crunch ✗
www.capncrunch.com
3/12/2007 ⊙ (800) 234-6281
See *Quaker Oats Company, The.*

Capri Sun ⊘
3/19/2007 ⊙ See *Kraft.*

Captains Choice (Safeway)
5/9/2007 ⊙ See *Safeway.*

Cara Mia
www.caramiaproducts.com
4/10/2007

Caramel Apple Pops
3/15/2007 ⊙ See *Tootsie Roll Industries.*

Carapelli
3/2/2007 ⊙ See *Hormel Foods.*

CarbWell ⊘
3/19/2007 ⊙ See *Kraft.*

Cardini's ⊘
3/7/2007 ⊙ See *Marzetti.*

Carl Buddig
www.buddig.com
5/14/2007 ⊙ (888) 633-5684
Triumph Notes: They claim all their meat products are GF and free of wheat, oats and barley. However, they do not mention rye.

Carlos V ⊘
5/3/2007 ⊙ See *Nestlé.*

Carnation Instant Breakfast
www.carnationinstantbreakfast.com
3/15/2007 ⊙ Company Notes: The flavorings used in Carnation Instant Breakfast Ready to Drink contain barley malt syrup. All sources of gluten are disclosed by adding a label statement about the use of barley. The amount of gluten is less than 1 part per million and they write that it is not likely to "cause an intolerance," but that individuals should discuss this with a physician if there are any concerns about consuming this product. The Carnation Instant Breakfast Junior is not GF. ⊙ See *Nestlé.*

Carole's Soycrunch
www.soycrunch.com
5/6/2007 ⊙ (516) 487-4211

Caroline's
3/15/2007 ⊙ See *Cains.*

Casa Fiesta
4/9/2007 ⊙ See *Bruce Foods.*

Casbah ⊘
www.casbahnaturalfoods.com
5/21/2007 ⊙ See *Hain Celestial.*

Cascade Fresh
www.cascadefresh.com
3/14/2007 ⊙ (800) 511-0057
Company Notes: They do not use preservatives, artificial sweeteners, color, flavors or additives. Tapioca and pectin are used as stabilizers.

Cascadian Farm ⊘
www.cascadianfarm.com
3/19/2007 ⊙ (800) 624-4123
See *General Mills.*

Cattlemen's Barbecue
www.cattlemensbbqsauce.com
4/20/2007 ⊙ (800) 841-1256
Company Notes: The Cattlemen's Gold formula has wheat as part of one of the ingredients, but it is "completely digested during the manufacturing process" resulting in the "complete elimination of gluten." ⊙ See *Reckitt Benckiser.*

Cedarlane Natural Foods
www.cedarlanefoods.com
3/15/2007 ⊙ (310) 886-7722

Cedar's Mediterranean Foods
www.cedarsfoods.com
4/9/2007 ⊙ (978) 372-8010

Celestial Seasonings ⊘
www.celestialseasonings.com
5/21/2007 ⊙ See *Hain Celestial.*

Cella's
3/15/2007 ⊙ See *Tootsie Roll Industries.*

Ceres
www.ceresjuices.com
3/14/2007 ⊙ (800) 778-6498

Certo ⊘
3/19/2007 ⊙ See *Kraft.*

Charleston Chew
3/15/2007 ⊙ See *Tootsie Roll Industries.*

Charms
3/15/2007 ⊙ See *Tootsie Roll Industries.*

Cheerios ⊘
www.cheerios.com
3/19/2007 ⊙ See *General Mills.*

Cheese Nips ⊘
3/19/2007 ⊙ See *Kraft.*

Cheetos
4/12/2007 ⊙ See *Frito Lay.*

Cheez Whiz ⊘
3/19/2007 ⊙ See *Kraft.*

Chef Boyardee ⊘
www.chefboyardee.com
4/7/2007 ⊙ (800) 544-5680
See *ConAgra Foods.*

Chef Creations ⊘
www.chefcreations.com
4/10/2007 ⊙ (888) 757-2433

Chef-Mate ⊘
5/3/2007 ⊙ (800) 288-8682
See *Nestlé.*

Chek (Winn-Dixie)
4/25/2007 ⊙ See *Winn-Dixie.*

Cherrybrook Kitchen
www.cherrybrookkitchen.com
4/9/2007 ⊙ (781) 272-0400

Chester's
4/12/2007 ⊙ See *Frito Lay.*

Chex ⊘
www.chex.com
3/19/2007 ⊙ (800) 328-1144
See *General Mills.*

Chi-Chi's
www.chichissalsa.com
3/2/2007 ⊙ See *Hormel Foods.*

Chicken Helper ⊘
www.chickenhelper.com
3/19/2007 ⊙ (800) 446-1898
See *General Mills.*

Chicken of the Sea
www.chickenofthesea.com
3/15/2007 ⊙ (800) 456-1511

Chiclets
www.chiclets.com
3/19/2007 ⊙ See *Cadbury Adams.*

Child's Play
3/15/2007 ⊙ See *Tootsie Roll Industries.*

China Cola
4/9/2007 ⊙ See *Reed's.*

Chips Ahoy! ⊘
3/19/2007 ⊙ See *Kraft.*

Chocolove ⊘
www.chocolove.com
4/9/2007 ⊙ (303) 786-7888
Company Notes: No items are guaranteed to be GF. Chocolove chocolate bars are formulated without "intentional addition" of gluten containing products. The vanilla extract is "sprayed on" maltodextrin. The maltodextrin or starch is "believed," but not guaranteed, to be made from corn.

Cholula Hot Sauce
www.cholulastore.com
4/25/2007 ⊙ (866) 608-4877

Chuckles ⊘
3/22/2007 ⊙ See *Farley's & Sathers Candy Company.*

Chunky ⊘
5/3/2007 ⊙ See *Nestlé.*

Churny ⊘
3/19/2007 ⊙ See *Kraft.*

Clabber Girl
www.bakewithlove.com
5/13/2007 ⊙ (812) 232-9446

Clamato ✗
www.clamato.com
3/16/2007 ⊙ (800) 426-4891

Clark Bar
3/6/2007 ⊙ See *Necco*.

Classico
www.classico.com
3/21/2007 ⊙ (888) 337-2420
See *Heinz*.

Claussen ⊘
3/19/2007 ⊙ See *Kraft*.

Clearfield Deli ⊘
4/23/2007 ⊙ See *Schreiber Foods*.

Clearly Prestige (Winn-Dixie)
4/25/2007 ⊙ See *Winn-Dixie*.

Clif Bar ✗
www.clifbar.com
3/20/2007 ⊙ (800) 254-3227
Company Notes: Their bars contain gluten from oats. The ingredients in Clif Nectar are GF, but there may be a "trace" of gluten due to the manufacturing process.

Clorets
3/19/2007 ⊙ See *Cadbury Adams*.

Cloverdale Foods
www.cloverdalefoods.com
3/14/2007

Coca-Cola Company, The
www.coca-cola.com
4/21/2007 ⊙ (800) 438-2653
Company Notes: After Coca-Cola listed their GF products, they wrote that all other products not listed meet the Codex definition of GF, which is less than 200 ppm. The exact amount of gluten "in all these products" is "very low" or maybe zero. However, since "minor" ingredients may be manufactured from plants that gluten-sensitive individuals may react to, they will not categorically state those products are GF. They advise "extremely gluten-sensitive" individuals to discuss consumption of their product with their health care providers.

Coffee-Mate
www.coffee-mate.com
5/3/2007 ⊙ See *Nescafé*.

Coke
4/21/2007 ⊙ See *Coca-Cola Company, The*.

Coleman Natural
www.colemannatural.com
4/18/2007 ⊙ (800) 442-8666

College Inn
www.collegeinn.com
3/22/2007 ⊙ See *Del Monte*.

Colombo ⊘
www.colomboyogurt.com
3/19/2007 ⊙ See *General Mills*.

Columbus Salame
www.columbussalame.com
5/3/2007

Comet Cups ⊘
3/19/2007 ⊙ See *Kraft*.

Comstock/Wilderness
www.birdseyefoods.com
3/15/2007 ⊙ (800) 270-2743
Company Notes: "Most" packages have a clearly labeled allergen statement. Carefully read this statement and the ingredient list.

ConAgra Foods ⊘
www.conagrafoods.com
3/27/2007 ⊙ (877) 266-2472
Company Notes: The flour used in the products is often wheat flour. Fermented and distilled products, such as vinegar, may be derived from wheat. Consult your physician to see if you need to avoid them. No GF list is available. Contact them with questions about ingredients in specific products. Always read ingredient statements on labels, as formula and ingredients may change.

Concord Foods
www.concordfoods.com
5/1/2007 ⊙ (508) 580-1700

Connoisseur ⊘
www.connoisseurcheese.com
4/11/2007 ⊙ See *Bel Brands U.S.A.*

Contadina
www.contadina.com
3/22/2007 ⊙ (888) 668-2847
See *Del Monte*.

Cool Whip ⊘
3/19/2007 ⊙ See *Kraft*.

Cooper ⊘
4/23/2007 ⊙ See *Schreiber Foods*.

Corn Nuts ⊘
3/19/2007 ⊙ See *Kraft*.

Costco ⊘
www.costco.com
5/8/2007 ⊙ (800) 774-2678

Country Crock ⊘
www.countrycrock.com
5/3/2007 ⊙ (800) 579-3663
See *Unilever*.

Country Delite ⊘
3/15/2007 ⊙ See *Dean Foods*.

Country Fresh ⊘
3/15/2007 ⊙ See *Dean Foods*.

Country Time ⊘
3/19/2007 ⊙ See *Kraft*.

Country Time (Cadbury Schweppes/Ready-to-Drink)
3/12/2007 ⊙ See *Cadbury Schweppes (Beverages)*.

Cracker Barrel ⊘
3/19/2007 ⊙ See *Kraft*.

Cracker Jack
www.crackerjack.com
4/12/2007 ⊙ See *Frito Lay*.

Craisins
3/5/2007 ⊙ See *Ocean Spray*.

Creamland ⊘
3/15/2007 ⊙ See *Dean Foods*.

Crisco
www.crisco.com
5/21/2007 ⊙ (800) 766-7309
See *Smucker's*.

Crofter's Food
www.croftersorganic.com
4/9/2007 ⊙ (705) 746-6301

Crosby's Molasses
www.crosbys.com
5/2/2007 ⊙ (506) 634-7515

Crowley Foods
www.crowleyfoods.com
3/15/2007 ⊙ (800) 247-6269

Crown Pilot ⊘
3/19/2007 ⊙ See *Kraft*.

Crows
3/15/2007 ⊙ See *Tootsie Roll Industries*.

Crucial ⊘
5/3/2007 ⊙ See *Nestlé*.

Crunch 'n Munch ⊘
(800) 376-1919
See *ConAgra Foods*.

Crunchies
www.crunchiesfood.com
4/9/2007 ⊙ (805) 565-4625

Crunchmaster ⊘
www.crunchmaster.com
3/14/2007 ⊙ See *TH Foods*.

Crush
3/12/2007 ⊙ See *Cadbury Schweppes (Beverages)*.

Crystal Light ⊘
3/19/2007 ⊙ See *Kraft*.

Cucina Antica
www.cucina-antica.com
4/10/2007 ⊙ (914) 244-9700

Cure 81
3/2/2007 ⊙ See *Hormel Foods*.

Da Vinci Foods ✗
www.davincifoods.com
4/10/2007 ⊙ (514) 769-1234

Dad's ⊘
3/19/2007 ⊙ See *Kraft*.

Daniel's Bar-B-Q
www.danielsbbq.com
5/2/2007 ⊙ (913) 369-2440

Dannon
www.dannon.com
3/15/2007 ⊙ (877) 326-6668

Company Notes: Except for the items listed, all other yogurts and yogurt drinks are not "gluten safe" because the "natural flavor systems" may have ingredients added to "stabilize the flavor" that are derived from gluten.

DariFree
www.vancesfoods.com
4/20/2007 ◉ (800) 497-4834

Dasani
4/21/2007 ◉ See *Coca-Cola Company, The.*

David ⃠
www.davidseeds.com
(800) 799-2800
See *ConAgra Foods.*

Davis Baking Powder
5/13/2007 ◉ See *Clabber Girl.*

Dean Foods ⃠
www.deanfoods.com
3/15/2007 ◉ (800) 395-7004
Company Notes: They do not maintain a list of GF products. The "best strategy" is to read ingredient labels.

Dean's ⃠
3/15/2007 ◉ See *Dean Foods.*

DeBoles ⃠
www.deboles.com
4/11/2007 ◉ (800) 434-4246
Company Notes: No GF list is available. The best way to check for gluten is to read the label. The label always declares gluten containing ingredients. If gluten is an ingredient, it will be listed separately, not under "natural flavors" or "spices." Items labeled "gluten free" or "Made with gluten free ingredients" are tested and formulated to have a gluten level below the detectable limit of 10 ppm.

DeCecco ✗
www.dececcousa.com
4/11/2007

Deep South (Winn-Dixie)
4/25/2007 ◉ See *Winn-Dixie.*

Del Monte
www.delmonte.com
3/22/2007 ◉ (800) 543-3090
Company Notes: The GF list is compiled "to the best of our knowledge." It may not be complete and may change, as there may be new products or changes in formulae. Always read ingredient labels for the most current information.

Delimex
3/21/2007 ◉ See *Heinz.*

Dennison's ⃠
(800) 544-5680
See *ConAgra Foods.*

Dentyne
www.dentyne.com
3/19/2007 ◉ See *Cadbury Adams.*

Di Lusso
3/2/2007 ◉ See *Hormel Foods.*

Diamond A ⃠
4/19/2007 ◉ See *Seneca Foods.*

Diet Coke
4/21/2007 ◉ See *Coca-Cola Company, The.*

Diet Rite
3/12/2007 ◉ See *Cadbury Schweppes (Beverages).*

Dietz & Watson ⃠
www.dietzandwatson.com
4/20/2007 ◉ (800) 333-1974
Company Notes: "Nearly all" meats are GF except the following: Bockwurst, Chicken Cordon Bleu, Chicken Florentine, Chicken Portabella, Fat Free Beef Franks, Gourmet Lite Franks, Gourmet Lite Beef Franks, Rotisserie Style Chicken and Scrapple.

DiGiorno ⃠
3/19/2007 ◉ See *Kraft.*

Dinty Moore
3/2/2007 ◉ See *Hormel Foods.*

Dixie Crystal
4/9/2007 ◉ See *Imperial Sugar.*

Dole ⚓
www.dole.com
(800) 232-8888

Domino
www.dominosugar.com
3/15/2007 ◉ **Company Notes:** None of their sugars contain gluten. The anti-caking agent in the powdered sugar is corn starch. Except for corn starch and cane sugar, no other ingredients, additives or preservatives are used in their products.

Doña María ⃠
3/2/2007 ◉ See *Hormel Foods.*

Doo Dad ⃠
3/19/2007 ◉ See *Kraft.*

Doritos
4/12/2007 ◉ See *Frito Lay.*

Dots
3/15/2007 ◉ See *Tootsie Roll Industries.*

Doublemint
3/16/2007 ◉ See *Wrigley.*

Dove
www.dovechocolate.com
3/27/2007 ◉ (800) 551-0704
See *MasterFoods USA.*

Dr. Kracker ✗
www.drkracker.com
5/7/2007 ◉ (214) 503-1971

Dr. McDougall's Right Foods
www.rightfoods.com
3/14/2007 ◉ (650) 583-4993

Dr. Pepper
www.drpepper.com
3/15/2007 ◉ (888) 377-3773
See *Cadbury Schweppes (Beverages).*

Dr. Praeger's
www.drpraegers.com
4/19/2007

Dream Whip ⃠
3/19/2007 ◉ See *Kraft.*

Drew's All Natural
www.chefdrew.com
4/9/2007 ◉ (800) 228-2980

Duncan Hines ✗
www.duncanhines.com
6/28/2007 ◉ (800) 362-9834
Company Notes: No items are guaranteed to be GF at this time. Always read labels.

Durkee
www.spiceadvice.com
3/16/2007 ◉ (800) 247-5251

Dynasty
4/10/2007 ◉ See *JFC International.*

D-Zerta ⃠
3/19/2007 ◉ See *Kraft.*

Earth's Best ⃠
www.earthsbest.com
5/21/2007 ◉ See *Hain Celestial.*

Easy Cheese ⃠
3/19/2007 ◉ See *Kraft.*

EatSmart
www.eatsmartsnacks.com
3/21/2007 ◉ See *Snyder's of Hanover.*

Eckrich ⃠
www.eckrichbrand.com
(800) 325-7424
See *ConAgra Foods.*

Eclipse
3/16/2007 ◉ See *Wrigley.*

Eden Foods
www.edenfoods.com
3/15/2007 ◉ (888) 424-3336
Company Notes: The GF list was marked updated on 3/1/06.

EdenSoy
3/15/2007 ◉ See *Eden Foods.*

Edward & Sons
www.edwardandsons.com
4/10/2007 ◉ (805) 684-8500
Company Notes: Finished products are randomly tested for gluten by an independent laboratory. Tests are sensitive up to 10 ppm.

Edy's
www.edys.com
3/19/2007 ◉ (888) 590-3397
Company Notes: As a "general rule," the ice cream itself is GF

and if gluten is present, it's in added bakery products like cookies or cake. The modified food starch is derived from a vegetable source and is GF. ⊚ Triumph Notes: The GF list was dated 2/22/07.

Egg Beaters ⊘
www.eggbeaters.com
(800) 988-7808
See *ConAgra Foods.*

Eggo
www.leggomyeggo.com
5/7/2007 ⊚ (800) 962-1413

Ejays So. Smokehouse
4/9/2007 ⊚ See *Wellshire Farms.*

El Cafetal (Winn-Dixie)
4/25/2007 ⊚ See *Winn-Dixie.*

El Torito
3/2/2007 ⊚ See *Hormel Foods.*

Emeril's
4/19/2007 ⊚ See *B&G Foods.*

Empire Kosher
www.empirekosher.com
5/2/2007 ⊚ (717) 436-7055

Endangered Species Chocolate
www.chocolatebar.com
4/9/2007 ⊚ (800) 293-0160
Company Notes: All products are free of gluten ingredients.

Ener-G
www.ener-g.com
4/9/2007 ⊚ (800) 331-5222

EnfaCare
3/14/2007 ⊚ See *Mead Johnson.*

Enfamil
www.enfamil.com
3/14/2007 ⊚ See *Mead Johnson.*

Enjoy Life Foods
www.enjoylifefoods.com
3/16/2007 ⊚ (888) 503-6569
Company Notes: All products are manufactured in a dedicated GF bakery.

Enlighten (Safeway)
5/9/2007 ⊚ See *Safeway.*

Ensure
www.ensure.com
4/9/2007 ⊚ (800) 986-8501

Enviga
4/21/2007 ⊚ See *Coca-Cola Company, The.*

EnviroKidz
4/9/2007 ⊚ See *Nature's Path.*

Equal
www.equal.com
3/16/2007 ⊚ (888) 848-6911
Company Notes: The bulking agent, dextrose with malto-dextrin, is derived from corn.

Equal Exchange
www.equalexchange.com
4/10/2007 ⊚ (774) 776-7400
Company Notes: The hot cocoa has an allergen statement that notes that it's manufactured on equipment that processes wheat. However, they note the equipment is cleaned between each process.

Erewhon
5/15/2007 ⊚ See *U.S. Mills.*

Estee ⊘
www.esteefoods.com
5/21/2007 ⊚ See *Hain Celestial.*

Ethnic Gourmet ⊘
www.ethnicgourmet.com
5/21/2007 ⊚ See *Hain Celestial.*

Ever Fresh ⊘
3/19/2007 ⊚ See *Kraft.*

Extra
3/16/2007 ⊚ See *Wrigley.*

Faa ⊘
5/3/2007 ⊚ See *Nestlé.*

Fair Field Farm Kitchens ✗
www.fairfieldfarmkitchens.com
4/19/2007 ⊚ (877) 400-5997
Company Notes: They do not consider any of their GF products acceptable to Celiacs because their products are made in a facility that makes wheat products.

Familia ✗
www.bio-familia.com
4/10/2007

Family Favorites ⊘
3/19/2007 ⊚ See *Kraft.*

Famous Chocolate Wafers ⊘
3/19/2007 ⊚ See *Kraft.*

Fantastic Foods
www.fantasticfoods.com
4/9/2007 ⊚ (800) 288-1089
Company Notes: All products are made on equipment that also processes wheat. However, "great precaution is taken" to separate gluten-containing items from those without. After gluten-containing items are made on the equipment, the equipment is opened, cleaned and then inspected by Quality Assurance. All GF products are sent for laboratory analysis to the University of Nebraska's Food Allergy Research and Resource program.

Faribault Foods ⊘
www.faribaultfoods.com
3/16/2007 ⊚ (877) 331-9805
Company Notes: No GF list is available due to the large number of products. Contact the company directly for questions about specific products.

Farley's & Sathers Candy Company ⊘
www.farleysandsathers.com
3/22/2007 ⊚ (888) 247-9855
Company Notes: No GF list is available due to "constant changes in manufacturing and packaging." Items are not specifically labeled for gluten.

Festal ⊘
4/19/2007 ⊚ See *Seneca Foods.*

Fiddle Faddle
3/19/2007 ⊚ See *Lincoln Snacks.*

Filippo Berio
www.filippoberio.com
3/14/2007 ⊚ **Company Notes:** The

plant does not process anything on the same equipment that contains gluten.

Finlandia Cheese
www.finlandiacheese.com
3/15/2007 ⊚ (973) 316-6699

Fischer & Wieser
www.jelly.com
4/9/2007 ⊚ (800) 880-8526

Fisher Nuts
www.fishernuts.com
4/9/2007 ⊚ (800) 874-8734

Fla Vor Ice ⊘
4/20/2007 ⊚ See *Jel Sert.*

Flavor Aid ⊘
4/20/2007 ⊚ See *Jel Sert.*

Flavor Crisps ⊘
3/19/2007 ⊚ See *Kraft.*

Fleischmann's Yeast
www.breadworld.com
3/16/2007

Florida's Natural
www.floridasnatural.com
3/15/2007 ⊚ (888) 657-6600

Fluffy Stuff Cotton Candy
3/15/2007 ⊚ See *Tootsie Roll Industries.*

Folgers
www.folgers.com
3/16/2007 ⊚ (800) 937-9745
See *Procter & Gamble.*

Follow Your Heart
www.followyourheart.com
5/3/2007 ⊚ (818) 725-2820

Food for Life
www.foodforlife.com
3/14/2007 ⊚ (800) 797-5090

Food Lion ⊘
www.foodlion.com
5/8/2007 ⊚ (800) 210-9569
Company Notes: They do not provide a GF list because their product line is updated often and product selection can change quickly and vary in different areas.

Food You Feel Good About (Wegman's)
5/8/2007 ⊙ See *Wegman's*.

Food-Tek
www.foodtek.com
4/9/2007 ⊙ (800) 648-8114

Foremost ⊘
3/15/2007 ⊙ See *Dean Foods*.

Four Monks
www.fourmonks.com
3/9/2007 ⊙ (800) 323-4358

Frankly Natural Bakers
www.franklynatural.com
5/2/2007 ⊙ (800) 727-7229

Frank's RedHot
www.franksredhot.com
4/20/2007 ⊙ See *Reckitt Benckiser*.

FreeBird Chicken ⊘
www.freebirdchicken.com
5/21/2007 ⊙ See *Hain Celestial*.

Freedent
3/16/2007 ⊙ See *Wrigley*.

French's
www.frenchsmustard.com
4/20/2007 ⊙ Company Notes: The caramel color in the Worcestershire Sauce is GF. ⊙ See *Reckitt Benckiser*.

Fresca
www.fresca.com
4/21/2007 ⊙ See *Coca-Cola Company, The*.

Friendly's Ice Cream ⚓
www.friendlys.com
(800) 966-9970

Friendship Dairies
www.friendshipdairies.com
3/15/2007

Frito Lay
www.fritolay.com
4/12/2007 ⊙ (800) 352-4477
Company Notes: Products are produced on the same line as gluten-containing products. Lines are washed between batches, though a "slight residue" may remain. "Extremely sensitive" people may be affected.

However, Lay's Stax are made on GF lines. For accurate and current information, always read labels, as ingredients can change. ⊙ Triumph Notes: The GF list was dated 4/3/07.

Fritos
4/12/2007 ⊙ See *Frito Lay*.

Frizzante (Wegman's)
5/8/2007 ⊙ See *Wegman's*.

Frontier Natural Products Co-op ⊘
www.frontiercoop.com
4/9/2007 ⊙ (800) 669-3275
Company Notes: No GF statement is available because their facility and lines have not been verified GF. However, they do follow "strict Good Manufacturing Practices" to reduce the risk of cross contamination. Their products are not tested for gluten.

Frooties
3/15/2007 ⊙ See *Tootsie Roll Industries*.

Fruit by the Foot ⊘
3/19/2007 ⊙ See *General Mills*.

Fruit Gushers ⊘
3/19/2007 ⊙ See *General Mills*.

Fruit Rolls
3/15/2007 ⊙ See *Tootsie Roll Industries*.

Fruit Roll-Ups ⊘
3/19/2007 ⊙ See *General Mills*.

Fruit Shapes ⊘
3/19/2007 ⊙ See *General Mills*.

Fruit Smoothie Pops
3/15/2007 ⊙ See *Tootsie Roll Industries*.

Fruit Stripe ⊘
3/22/2007 ⊙ See *Farley's & Sathers Candy Company*.

Fruit₂0 ⊘
3/19/2007 ⊙ See *Kraft*.

Fruitwater
5/2/2007 ⊙ See *Glacéau*.

Funyuns
4/12/2007 ⊙ See *Frito Lay*.

Furmano's ⊘
www.furmanfoods.com
4/6/2007 ⊙ (877) 877-6032

Fuze
www.fuzebev.com
4/9/2007 ⊙ (201) 461-6640
Company Notes: Products may be made at facilities or on production lines that make gluten-containing products.

Gaga's SherBetter
www.gogagas.com
4/11/2007 ⊙ (401) 921-1377

Galaxy Nutritional Foods
www.galaxyfoods.com
3/15/2007 ⊙ (800) 441-9419

Gandy's ⊘
3/15/2007 ⊙ See *Dean Foods*.

Garden of Eatin' ⊘
www.gardenofeatin.com
4/11/2007 ⊙ (800) 434-4246
Company Notes: The label always declares gluten-containing ingredients and all potential allergen issues. "Major and minor ingredients" and "all processing procedures and equipment" are "closely scrutinized." Their manufacturing facilities follow allergen control programs, including "staff training, segregation of allergen ingredients, production scheduling, and thorough cleaning and sanitation."

Gardenburger
www.gardenburger.com
3/15/2007 ⊙ (800) 459-7079

Gardetto's ⊘
3/19/2007 ⊙ See *General Mills*.

Garelick Farms ⊘
3/15/2007 ⊙ See *Dean Foods*.

Garner
4/9/2007 ⊙ (888) 875-3111

Garrett County Farms
4/9/2007 ⊙ See *Wellshire Farms*.

Gatorade
www.gatorade.com
4/25/2007 ⊙ (800) 884-2867

Gebhardt ⊘
(877) 528-0745
See *ConAgra Foods*.

General Foods International ⊘
3/19/2007 ⊙ See *Kraft*.

General Mills ⊘
www.generalmills.com
3/19/2007 ⊙ (800) 248-7310
Company Notes: Always check the ingredient label for accurate and current information. If the ingredient label does not list Wheat, Rye, Barley, Oats or gluten-containing ingredients sourced from these grains, the product is GF. Even if the source of gluten is part of another ingredient, for example, flavoring or spice, the source of gluten will be listed on the label.

Genisoy ⊘
www.genisoy.com
4/10/2007 ⊙ (866) 606-3829
Company Notes: Their products are not produced on dedicated GF lines and some products are testing higher than the 20 ppm, which is the proposed FDA limit. Therefore, they do not currently have a GF list.

Gerber ⊘
www.gerber.com
4/20/2007 ⊙ (800) 443-7237
Company Notes: Always consult your baby's doctor about foods that are appropriate for a GF diet. Formulation may change at any time, therefore, a list may become outdated. Always read ingredient statements on labels.

Gevalia ⊘
3/19/2007 ⊙ See *Kraft*.

Ghirardelli ⊘
www.ghirardelli.com
3/2/2007 ⊙ (800) 877-9338
Company Notes: Most products are manufactured in a GF facility.

If applicable, cross-contamination warnings are printed on the packaging. Classic White Chips may contain trace amounts of "flour gluten."

Gilardi Foods ⃠
(800) 722-1344
See *ConAgra Foods.*

Gillian's Foods
www.gilliansfoods.com
4/9/2007 ⊚ (781) 586-0086

Ginger People ⃠
www.gingerpeople.com
4/18/2007 ⊚ (800) 551-5284
Company Notes: Except for Ginger Lime Marinade & Cooking Sauce, Ginger Peanut Dipping & Cooking Sauce, Ginger Sesame Vinaigrette & Marinade, Ginger Jerk Marinade & Cooking Sauce and Ginger Shortbread, "most" of their products are GF.

Glacéau
www.glaceau.com
5/2/2007 ⊚ (877) 452-2328

Global Gourmet
4/9/2007 ⊚ See *Wellshire Farms.*

Glucerna
www.glucerna.com
4/9/2007 ⊚ (800) 227-5767
Company Notes: The Lemon Crunch and Caramel Nut Glucerna Snack bars do not have gluten-containing ingredients, but they are made on lines that handle other gluten-containing items. The plant has cleaning procedures between each batch to reduce cross-contamination.

Gluten-Free Pantry, The
www.glutenfree.com
6/11/2007 ⊚ (800) 291-8386

Glutino
www.glutino.com
4/10/2007 ⊚ (800) 363-3438

Gobstoppers
5/5/2007 ⊚ See *Nestlé Chocolate and Confections.*

Gold Medal ⃠
www.gmflour.com
3/19/2007 ⊚ (800) 446-1898
See *General Mills.*

Gold's
www.goldshorseradish.com
4/25/2007 ⊚ (516) 483-5600

Goobers
5/5/2007 ⊚ See *Nestlé Chocolate and Confections.*

Good & Plenty ⃠
3/20/2007 ⊚ See *Hershey Company, The.*

Good Humor ⃠
www.icecreamusa.com
5/3/2007 ⊚ (920) 499-5151
See *Unilever.*

Good Seasons ⃠
3/19/2007 ⊚ See *Kraft.*

Good Start Infant Formulas ⃠
www.verybestbaby.com
5/3/2007 ⊚ See *Nestlé.*

Gorton's ⃠
www.gortons.com
4/10/2007 ⊚ (800) 222-6846
Company Notes: No GF list is provided as product formulations may change, as well as other factors. Always read label's ingredient listing. Ingredients with gluten will always be "listed separately" on labels.

Grand Selections (Hy-Vee)
5/8/2007 ⊚ See *Hy-Vee.*

Grandma's Molasses
4/19/2007 ⊚ See *B&G Foods.*

Green & Black's Organic ⃠
www.greenandblacks.com
3/5/2007

Green Giant ⃠
www.greengiant.com
3/19/2007 ⊚ (800) 446-1898
See *General Mills.*

Green Mountain Coffee
www.greenmountaincoffee.com
3/2/2007 ⊚ (888) 879-4627

Green Mountain Gringo
www.greenmountaingringo.com
4/9/2007 ⊚ (888) 875-3111

Grey Poupon ⃠
3/19/2007 ⊚ See *Kraft.*

Guaranteed Value (Stop & Shop)
5/8/2007 ⊚ See *Stop & Shop.*

Guiltless Gourmet
www.guiltlessgourmet.com
3/6/2007

Guittard
www.guittard.com
5/13/2007 ⊚ (800) 468-2462
Company Notes: Their products and "processing" are GF.

Gulden's ⃠
(800) 544-5680
See *ConAgra Foods.*

Gwaltney ⃠
www.gwaltneyfoods.com
4/10/2007 ⊚ Company Notes: "Most" items are GF. Avoid BBQ sauces and entrees with gravy.

Häagen-Dazs ⃠
www.haagen-dazs.com
3/19/2007 ⊚ (800) 767-0120
See *General Mills.*

Hain Celestial ⃠
www.hain-celestial.com
5/21/2007 ⊚ (800) 434-4246
Company Notes: No GF list is available. Their labeling always declares gluten-containing ingredients. If an ingredient contains gluten, it will be listed separately and "not under 'natural flavors' or 'spices.'" "Major and minor" ingredients, all processing procedures and all processing equipment are "closely scrutinized" and potential issues pertaining to allergens are declared on labels. Their manufacturing facilities follow "allergen control programs," including training, segregation of allergens, scheduling, cleaning and sanitation.

Hain Pure Foods ⃠
www.hainpurefoods.com
5/21/2007 ⊚ See *Hain Celestial.*

Hain Pure Snax ⃠
www.hainpuresnax.com
5/21/2007 ⊚ See *Hain Celestial.*

Hamburger Helper ⃠
www.hamburgerhelper.com
3/19/2007 ⊚ (800) 328-1144
See *General Mills.*

Handi-Snacks ⃠
3/19/2007 ⊚ See *Kraft.*

Hannaford ⃠
www.hannaford.com
5/7/2007 ⊚ (800) 213-9040
Company Notes: No GF list is available for store brand products as they have many manufacturers that can change at any time. Also, product formulations are subject to change. They encourage customers to call with questions about specific products. Have a UPC number and product name handy when calling.

Han's All Natural
www.hansallnatural.com
4/25/2007 ⊚ (800) 442-8666

Hansen's
www.hansens.com
3/2/2007 ⊚ (800) 426-7367

HARIBO ⃠
www.haribo.com
3/2/2007 ⊚ (800) 638-2327
Company Notes: They write that "most" products are GF, except for Allsorts, Black Licorice Wheels, Fruity Pasta, Pico-Balla, Pontefract Cakes, Red Licorice Wheels, and Sour S'ghetti.

Harris Teeter ⃠
www.harristeeter.com
5/9/2007 ⊚ (800) 432-6111
Company Notes: No GF list is available. They recommend reading ingredient statements. Contact them with questions about specific items, though

since they use different suppliers, the GF status can change with no warning.

Harry's Premium Snacks ⊘
www.harryssnacks.com
5/21/2007 ⊚ See *Hain Celestial.*

Harvest Crisps ⊘
3/19/2007 ⊚ See *Kraft.*

Harvest Moon ⊘
3/19/2007 ⊚ See *Kraft.*

Haviland
3/6/2007 ⊚ See *Necco.*

Hawaiian Punch
www.hawaiianpunch.com
3/16/2007 ⊚ Company Notes: They have a food allergen management policy. Their policy is to label wheat, rye, barley, triticale, spelt, kamut, oats and other allergens. They "continually" assess their products and update supplier information; therefore, the labels reflect the presence of listed allergens. ⊚ See *Cadbury Schweppes (Beverages).*

Health Market (Hy-Vee)
5/8/2007 ⊚ See *Hy-Vee.*

Health Valley ⊘
www.healthvalley.com
5/21/2007 ⊚ See *Hain Celestial.*

Healthy Advantage (Safeway)
5/9/2007 ⊚ See *Safeway.*

Healthy Choice ⊘
www.healthychoice.com
(800) 323-9980
See *ConAgra Foods.*

Heath ⊘
3/20/2007 ⊚ See *Hershey Company, The.*

Hebrew National ⊘
www.hebrewnational.com
(866) 432-6281
See *ConAgra Foods.*

Heide ⊘
3/22/2007 ⊚ See *Farley's & Sathers Candy Company.*

Heini's
www.heinis.com
4/9/2007 ⊚ (800) 253-6636

Heinz
www.heinz.com
3/21/2007 ⊚ (800) 255-5750
Company Notes: If a product is not on their GF list, it is not GF.

Hellmann's
www.mayo.com
3/15/2007 ⊚ (800) 418-3275
Company Notes: The starch base in the Light and Low Fat mayonnaise type dressings is made from modified corn starch. The vinegar in Hellmann's mayonnaise is distilled and GF. Product formulations can change, so always read the label's ingredient list. Ingredients that contain gluten will always be listed on the label.

Heluva Good
www.heluvagood.com
3/15/2007 ⊚ See *Crowley Foods.*

Herb-Ox Bouillon
3/2/2007 ⊚ See *Hormel Foods.*

Herdez ⊘
3/2/2007 ⊚ See *Hormel Foods.*

Herr's
www.herrs.com
3/6/2007 ⊚ (610) 932-9330
Company Notes: There are no "designated processing lines or areas," so there is a chance that "small amounts" of gluten will be left behind. Machinery is wiped and/or washed out between products. Information is subject to change without notice.

Hershey Company, The ⊘
www.hersheys.com
3/20/2007 ⊚ (800) 468-1714
Company Notes: Check the ingredient label. The label provides accurate and current information on all product ingredients. Ingredient lists may change.

Hershey's Milk ⊘
3/15/2007 ⊚ See *Dean Foods.*

HGD Foods
www.hgdfoods.com
4/19/2007 ⊚ (210) 650-3105

Hickory Farms ⊘
www.hickoryfarms.com
5/7/2007 ⊚ (800) 442-5671

Hidden Valley ⊘
www.hiddenvalley.com
3/2/2007 ⊚ (800) 537-2823
Company Notes: Check the label on the product. If it contains wheat, it will be listed. ⊚ Triumph Notes: Their correspondence did not include any information on rye, barley or oats.

Hillshire Farms ⚓
www.hillshirefarm.com
(800) 925-3326

Hint Mint
www.hintmint.com
4/9/2007 ⊚ (800) 991-6468

Hires
3/12/2007 ⊚ See *Cadbury Schweppes (Beverages).*

Hodgson Mill
www.hodgsonmill.com
4/9/2007 ⊚ (800) 525-0177

Hoffman's ⊘
3/19/2007 ⊚ See *Kraft.*

Hollywood ⊘
www.hollywoodoils.com
5/21/2007 ⊚ See *Hain Celestial.*

Homestyle Meals
4/9/2007 ⊚ See *Wellshire Farms.*

Honest Tea
www.honesttea.com
5/7/2007 ⊚ (800) 865-4736

Honey Maid ⊘
3/19/2007 ⊚ See *Kraft.*

Honeysuckle White
www.honeysucklewhite.com
3/4/2007

Hood
www.hphood.com
3/5/2007

Horizon Organics ⊘
www.horizonorganic.com
3/15/2007 ⊚ (888) 494-3020
See *Dean Foods.*

Hormel Foods
www.hormel.com
3/2/2007 ⊚ (800) 523-4635
Company Notes: The GF list is a "general guideline" and lists products with formulae that do not contain gluten. Always read the label's ingredient list. Certain products listed as GF may contain vinegar. Hormel believes these vinegars to be GF, but Hormel requests that you make your own determination as to suitability for your diet.

Hot Tamales
www.hottamales.com
3/5/2007 ⊚ See *Just Born.*

House Of Tsang
3/2/2007 ⊚ See *Hormel Foods.*

Hungry Jack ⊘
www.hungryjack.com
3/2/2007 ⊚ (888) 767-7494
Company Notes: A review is currently being conducted with suppliers to determine which products are GF. Results will be posted on the Smucker's website over the next several months.

Hungry Man ⊘
www.swansonmeals.com
3/19/2007 ⊚ See *Pinnacle Foods Corp.*

Hunt's ⊘
www.hunts.com
(800) 858-6372
See *ConAgra Foods.*

Hunt's Snack Pack ⊘
www.snackpack.com
(800) 457-4178
See *ConAgra Foods.*

Hy-Vee
www.hy-vee.com
5/8/2007 ⊙ (800) 289-8343
Company Notes: Items on the GF list are GF to the best of their knowledge. They make no representation or warranty regarding the GF list or its accuracy or "fitness of any product for any particular purpose." The list should not be a substitute for independent confirmation and examination of ingredients, which may vary from time to time. ⊙ Triumph Notes: The list was dated 11/28/2006. Visit www.hy-vee.com/default.asp?p=health for the most up-to-date version.

I Can't Believe It's Not Butter ⊘
www.tasteyoulove.com
5/3/2007 ⊙ (800) 735-5554
See *Unilever*.

I.M. Healthy
www.soynutbutter.com
4/9/2007 ⊙ (800) 288-1012
Company Notes: Production plants are GF.

Ian's Natural Foods
www.iansnaturalfoods.com
3/5/2007

IBC
www.ibcrootbeer.com
3/3/2007 ⊙ (800) 570-6620

Ice Breakers ⊘
3/20/2007 ⊙ See *Hershey Company, The*.

Idahoan
www.idahoan.com
3/5/2007 ⊙ (800) 635-6100
Company Notes: No gluten containing products are used in processing, packaging containers or package surfaces.

Illy Caffé
www.illyusa.net
4/27/2007 ⊙ (877) 469-4559

Imagine ⊘
www.imaginefoods.com
5/21/2007 ⊙ See *Hain Celestial*.

Immaculate Baking Co. ✘
www.immaculatebaking.com
5/7/2007 ⊙ (828) 696-1655

Imperial Sugar
www.imperialsugar.com
4/9/2007 ⊙ (800) 727-8427

Ingles Markets
www.ingles-markets.com
5/8/2007 ⊙ (828) 669-2941
Company Notes: The GF list represents information from the manufacturer of their private label goods. Always read ingredient labels. Ingles is not responsible or liable for changes in products or their ingredients.

International Delight
www.internationaldelight.com
5/13/2007 ⊙ (800) 441-3321

Italian Classics (Wegman's)
5/8/2007 ⊙ See *Wegman's*.

It's Soy Delicious
4/9/2007 ⊙ See *Turtle Mountain*.

Izze Beverage Company
www.izze.com
3/9/2007 ⊙ (303) 327-5515

Jack Daniel's EZ Marinader
www.jackdanielssauces.com
3/21/2007 ⊙ (800) 577-2823
See *Heinz*.

Jack's ⊘
3/19/2007 ⊙ See *Kraft*.

Jays ⊘
www.jaysfoods.com
4/10/2007 ⊙ (800) 621-6152
Company Notes: The plant does not have a dedicated GF area or equipment.

Jel Sert ⊘
www.jelsert.com
4/20/2007 ⊙ (800) 323-2592
Triumph Notes: They provided a wheat-free list, but not a GF list.

Jell-O ⊘
www.jello.com
3/19/2007 ⊙ See *Kraft*.

Jelly Belly
www.jellybelly.com
3/20/2007 ⊙ (800) 522-3267

Jennie-O
3/2/2007 ⊙ Company Notes: Always request the ingredient list from deli manager. Gluten is not listed under "flavoring" on labels. ⊙ See *Hormel Foods*.

Jet-Puffed ⊘
3/19/2007 ⊙ See *Kraft*.

JFC International
www.jfc.com
4/10/2007 ⊙ (800) 633-1004
Company Notes: JFC has over 8,000 products and cannot list all GF items on its GF list. JFC suggests contacting them with questions about specific products.

Jiffy Pop ⊘
(800) 379-1177
See *ConAgra Foods*.

Jimmy Dean ⚓
www.jimmydean.com
(800) 925-3326

Joan of Arc
4/19/2007 ⊙ See *B&G Foods*.

Jŏcalat
3/5/2007 ⊙ See *Lärabar*.

Johnsonville
www.johnsonville.com
3/6/2007 ⊙ (888) 556-2728
Company Notes: The list is current as of 1/9/07. Visit the website or call to confirm that this is the most recent list.

Jolly Rancher ⊘
3/20/2007 ⊙ See *Hershey Company, The*.

Jolly Time
www.jollytime.com
3/15/2007 ⊙ (712) 239-1232

Jones Dairy Farm ⊘
www.jonesdairyfarm.com
5/3/2007 ⊙ (800) 563-1004

Company Notes: All products except "flavored" items such as maple are GF.

Juicy Fruit
3/16/2007 ⊙ See *Wrigley*.

Junior Caramels
3/15/2007 ⊙ See *Tootsie Roll Industries*.

Junior Mints
3/15/2007 ⊙ See *Tootsie Roll Industries*.

Just Born
www.justborn.com
3/5/2007 ⊙ (800) 445-5787
Company Notes: To the best of their knowledge, all the candies are GF. The only exception is the Peeps Inside a Crispy Milk Chocolate Egg, which may contain traces of gluten in the crispy egg. The modified food starch used in jelly beans is corn starch.

K.C. Masterpiece
www.kcmasterpiece.com
3/16/2007

KA-ME ⊘
www.kame.com
3/9/2007 ⊙ (201) 843-8900
Company Notes: "Many" of their products are "gluten free by nature of their ingredients," but are not marketed as GF because the manufacturer cannot guarantee there is no cross-contamination.

Karo
www.karosyrup.com
3/16/2007 ⊙ (866) 430-5276

Kashi
www.kashi.com
5/9/2007 ⊙ (858) 274-8870
Company Notes: Most Kashi products are based on their signature 7 whole grains and sesame blend, which includes grains with gluten, and there are no current plans to develop a GF blend.

Kasilof
www.kasilof.com
4/9/2007 ⊙ (800) 322-7552

Kaukauna ⊘
www.kaukaunacheese.com
4/11/2007 ⊙ See *Bel Brands U.S.A.*

Kellogg's
www.kelloggs.com
5/7/2007 ⊙ (800) 962-1413

Kettle Brand
www.kettlefoods.com
3/7/2007 ⊙ (503) 364-0399
Company Notes: All ingredients are listed on the bag. All Kettle brand Potato Chips are GF and as of 1/07 made in a separate facility from gluten-containing products. Check for a "best before" date of 8/07 or later to ensure no cross-contamination.

Kid Cuisine ⊘
www.kidcuisine.com
(800) 262-6316
See *ConAgra Foods.*

Kikkoman ⊘
www.kikkoman.com
3/21/2007 ⊙ (262) 275-6181
Company Notes: No GF list is available, as many sauces contain ingredients like modified food starches and natural flavorings, for example, that may contain gluten.

King Oscar
www.kingoscar.no
5/7/2007

Kingsford
3/16/2007 ⊙ See *Argo.*

Kitchen Basics
www.kitchenbasics.net
4/9/2007 ⊙ (440) 838-1344

Kitchen Bouquet Browning & Seasoning Sauce ⊘
www.thecloroxcompany.com
4/25/2007 ⊙ Company Notes: Always read ingredient labels.

Kitchen Table Bakers
www.kitchentablebakers.com
4/9/2007 ⊙ (800) 486-4582

KitKat ⊘
3/20/2007 ⊙ See *Hershey Company, The.*

Klondike ⊘
www.icecreamusa.com
5/3/2007 ⊙ (920) 499-5151
See *Unilever.*

Knorr ⊘
www.knorr.com
3/20/2007 ⊙ (800) 457-7082
Company Notes: Most Knorr products are not GF. Ingredients like HVP, TVP and flavorings are likely to contain gluten. Always read the label's ingredient list.

Knott's Berry Farms ⊘
(877) 528-0745
See *ConAgra Foods.*

Knouse Foods
www.knouse.com
4/20/2007 ⊙ (717) 677-8181
Triumph Notes: Knouse brands include Apple Leaf, Apple Time, Lincoln, Lucky Leaf, Musselman's and Speas Farm.

Knox Gelatine ⊘
3/19/2007 ⊙ See *Kraft.*

Knudsen ⊘
3/19/2007 ⊙ See *Kraft.*

Kool Aid ⊘
3/19/2007 ⊙ See *Kraft.*

Kountry Fresh (Winn-Dixie)
4/25/2007 ⊙ See *Winn-Dixie.*

Kozy Shack
www.kozyshack.com
3/14/2007

Krackel ⊘
3/20/2007 ⊙ See *Hershey Company, The.*

Kraft ⊘
www.kraftfoods.com
3/19/2007 ⊙ (800) 323-0768
Company Notes: All Kraft and Nabisco products list gluten-containing ingredients on the ingredient statement using "commonly known terms" like Wheat, Rye, Barley and Oats. For ingredients containing gluten, such as natural flavor, the grain source will be declared in parentheses after the ingredient. For more information, visit their website for a "Gluten Fact Sheet."

Kroger ⊘
www.kroger.com
5/9/2007 ⊙ (800) 632-6900
Company Notes: While they have an "extensive" GF list, though not comprehensive, they do not provide it to the public. Since they have many suppliers that change periodically, they do not want an outdated GF list to become circulated. Call them with a UPC code for the most up-to-date information.

La Dulceria Thalia ⊘
3/20/2007 ⊙ See *Hershey Company, The.*

La Preferida ⊘
www.lapreferida.com
3/2/2007 ⊙ (800) 621-5422
Company Notes: No GF list is available at this time but will be available at a later date, after they have had time to review each ingredient statement in collaboration with their suppliers. Meanwhile, call with questions.

La Tortilla Factory
www.latortillafactory.com
4/16/2007 ⊙ (800) 446-1516
Company Notes: Their plant is certified by the GFCO.

La Tourangelle
www.latourangelle.com
4/11/2007 ⊙ (510) 970-9960

LaChoy ♨
www.lachoy.com
(800) 252-0672

Laffy Taffy
5/5/2007 ⊙ See *Nestlé Chocolate and Confections.*

Land O' Lakes ⊘
www.landolakes.com
3/15/2007 ⊙ (800) 328-9680
Company Notes: They note that the FDA and USDA have not defined what GF is and that "natural dairy products" like "natural" cheese and butter are GF to the best of their knowledge. They think the best source of information is the ingredient list.

Lapas
5/2/2007 ⊙ See *Spruce Foods.*

Lärabar
www.larabar.com
3/5/2007 ⊙ (720) 945-1155
Company Notes: All bars are GF and have undergone "gliadin testing." The packaging bears the CSA approved GF seal. All bars are manufactured in a GF certified facility.

Las Palmas
4/19/2007 ⊙ See *B&G Foods.*

Lasagna Chips ✕
www.lasagnachips.com
4/10/2007 ⊙ (718) 498-2300

Laughing Cow ⊘
www.thelaughingcow.com
4/11/2007 ⊙ See *Bel Brands U.S.A.*

Laura Lynn (Ingle's)
5/8/2007 ⊙ See *Ingles Markets.*

Lawry's ⊘
www.lawrys.com
3/6/2007 ⊙ (800) 952-9797
Company Notes: As product formulations may change, they do not maintain a GF list. Always read the ingredient list. Ingredients that may contain gluten are always listed on the label. If you are unsure if a product is GF, they suggest that you not use the product.

Lay's
4/12/2007 ⊙ See *Frito Lay.*

Lay's Stax
4/12/2007 ⊙ Company Notes: Lay's Stax are made on GF lines. ⊙ See *Frito Lay.*

Lea & Perrins
www.leaperrins.com
3/21/2007 ⊙ (800) 987-4674
See *Heinz.*

Lean Cuisine ⊘
www.leancuisine.com
5/3/2007 ⊙ (800) 993-8625
See *Nestlé.*

Lehigh Valley Dairy Farms ⊘
3/15/2007 ⊙ See *Dean Foods.*

Let's Do…
4/10/2007 ⊙ See *Edward & Sons.*

Let's Do…Organic
4/10/2007 ⊙ See *Edward & Sons.*

Libby's (Fruits & Vegetables) ⊘
4/19/2007 ⊙ See *Seneca Foods.*

Libby's (Canned Meats) ⊘
(800) 727-5777
See *ConAgra Foods.*

Libby's Pumpkin ⊘
www.verybestbaking.com
5/3/2007 ⊙ (800) 854-0374
See *Nestlé.*

Life Cereal ✕
www.lifecereal.com
3/12/2007 ⊙ (800) 234-6281
See *Quaker Oats Company, The.*

Lifesavers
3/16/2007 ⊙ See *Wrigley.*

LifeStream
4/9/2007 ⊙ See *Nature's Path.*

Light n' Lively ⊘
3/19/2007 ⊙ See *Kraft.*

Lightlife
www.lightlife.com
5/13/2007 ⊙ (800) 769-3279

Lik-M-Aid Fun Dip
5/5/2007 ⊙ See *Nestlé Chocolate and Confections.*

Lincoln
4/20/2007 ⊙ See *Knouse Foods.*

Lincoln Snacks
www.lincolnsnacks.com
3/19/2007 ⊙ (877) 547-6225
Company Notes: Always check the allergy information listed on all products, as some products are manufactured on the same lines as wheat products.

Lindt ✕
www.lindt.com
5/14/2007 ⊙ (877) 695-4638
Company Notes: They will not certify that any items are GF at this time.

Lipton ⊘
www.lipton.com
5/3/2007 ⊙ (877) 995-4490
See *Unilever.*

Lipton Sides ⊘
www.liptonfavorites.com
5/3/2007 ⊙ (800) 457-7082
See *Unilever.*

Litehouse
www.litehousefoods.com
3/2/2007 ⊙ (800) 669-3169

Little Bear ⊘
www.littlebearfoods.com
4/11/2007 ⊙ (800) 434-4246
Company Notes: No GF list is available. The best way to check for gluten is to read the label. If gluten is an ingredient, it will be listed separately. It will not be listed under "natural flavors" or "spices."

Little Sizzlers
3/2/2007 ⊙ See *Hormel Foods.*

Living Harvest
www.livingharvest.com
4/9/2007 ⊙ (888) 690-3958

Lloyd's
3/2/2007 ⊙ See *Hormel Foods.*

Log Cabin
3/19/2007 ⊙ See *Pinnacle Foods Corp.*

Lorenzi
5/2/2007 ⊙ See *Spruce Foods.*

Lorna Doone ⊘
3/19/2007 ⊙ See *Kraft.*

Lotus Foods
www.lotusfoods.com
4/9/2007 ⊙ (510) 525-3137

Louis Rich ⊘
3/19/2007 ⊙ See *Kraft.*

Louis Trauth
3/15/2007 ⊙ See *Dean Foods.*

Louisiana Gold Pepper Sauce
4/9/2007 ⊙ See *Bruce Foods.*

Louisiana Hot Sauce
4/9/2007 ⊙ See *Bruce Foods.*

Lucerne (Safeway)
5/9/2007 ⊙ See *Safeway.*

Luck's ⊘
(800) 211-0600
See *ConAgra Foods.*

Lucky Charms ⊘
3/19/2007 ⊙ See *General Mills.*

Lucky Leaf
4/20/2007 ⊙ See *Knouse Foods.*

Luna Bar ✕
www.lunabar.com
3/20/2007 ⊙ (800) 586-2227
See *Clif Bar.*

Lunchables ⊘
3/19/2007 ⊙ See *Kraft.*

Lundberg Family Farms
www.lundberg.com
4/9/2007 ⊙ (530) 882-4551

Lydia's Organics
www.lydiasorganics.com
5/2/2007 ⊙ (415) 258-9678
Company Notes: They have a dedicated GF facility.

M&M'S
www.m-ms.com
3/27/2007 ⊙ See *MasterFoods USA.*

Maggi Seasonings ⊘
www.maggi-usa.com
5/3/2007 ⊙ (800) 258-6727
See *Nestlé.*

Maggio
www.maggiocheese.com
3/15/2007 ⊙ See *Crowley Foods.*

Mahatma ⊘
www.mahatmarice.com
3/5/2007 ⊙ (800) 226-9522
Triumph Notes: The "allergy" list they provided listed only wheat gluten-free items, but made no mention of rye, barley or oats.

Mallomars ⊘
3/19/2007 ⊙ See *Kraft.*

Malt-O-Meal
www.malt-o-meal.com
3/5/2007 ⊙ (800) 743-3029
Company Notes: Always read the label's ingredient statement in case of changes.

MaMa Rosa's ⊘
(800) 262-7200
See *ConAgra Foods.*

Mamba
3/26/2007 ⊙ See *Storck.*

Manischewitz
www.manischewitz.com
5/8/2007 ⊙ (201) 553-1100

Manny's
3/2/2007 ⊙ See *Hormel Foods.*

Manor House (Safeway)
5/9/2007 ⊙ See *Safeway.*

Manwich ⊘
See *ConAgra Foods.*

MaraNatha Natural & Organic Nut Butters
www.MaraNathaNutButters.com
4/6/2007 ⊙ (510) 346-3860

Marie Callender's ⊘
(800) 595-7010
See *ConAgra Foods.*

Marrakesh Express ⊘
3/2/2007 ⊙ See *Hormel Foods.*

Marshmallow Peeps
www.marshmallowpeeps.com
3/5/2007 ⊚ (888) 645-3453
See *Just Born.*

Marshmallow Twirls ⊘
3/19/2007 ⊚ See *Kraft.*

Martinelli's
www.martinellis.com
4/9/2007 ⊚ (800) 662-1868

Marukan
www.marukan-usa.com
3/16/2007 ⊚ (562) 229-1000
Company Notes: All listed products are "wheat gluten free at a level of 10 parts per million." ⊚
Triumph Notes: Contact company directly for documentation regarding testing. The attached GF documentation referenced only wheat gluten, but not wheat, rye, barley or oats.

Mary Janes
3/6/2007 ⊚ See *Necco.*

Mary's Gone Crackers
www.marysgonecrackers.com
5/15/2007 ⊚ (888) 258-1250

Marzetti ⊘
www.marzetti.com
3/7/2007 ⊚ (614) 846-2232
Company Notes: If gluten or a gluten-containing ingredient is used in a formula, it will be declared on the ingredient list. But no products are certified as GF, nor is any claim made to that effect. For modified food starch, waxy maize starches or cornstarch are generally used, though on rare occasions, potato, rice or tapioca starch may be used.

Masala Maza
www.masalamaza.com
3/2/2007 ⊚ (503) 226-3094

MasterFoods USA
www.masterfoods.com
3/27/2007 ⊚ (800) 627-7852
Company Notes: Always read the label's ingredient list.

Masuya
www.masuyanaturally.com
4/9/2007

Maui Style
4/12/2007 ⊚ See *Frito Lay.*

Mauna Loa ⊘
3/20/2007 ⊚ See *Hershey Company, The.*

Maxwell House ⊘
www.maxwellhouse.com
3/19/2007 ⊚ See *Kraft.*

Mayfield Dairy ⊘
3/15/2007 ⊚ See *Dean Foods.*

Mazola
www.mazola.com
3/16/2007 ⊚ (866) 462-9652

McArthur Dairy ⊘
3/15/2007 ⊚ See *Dean Foods.*

McCain Foods ⊘
www.mccain.com
5/7/2007 ⊚ (506) 392-5541
Company Notes: No GF list is available. Always read ingredient statements. They label in compliance with the FDA allergen labeling regulation, and they have "policies and procedures" in place to reduce the possibility of cross-contamination in their frozen potato products line. Production facilities use the "Hazard Analysis and Critical Control Point" program and "Corporate Quality Assurance Procedures." Manufacturing procedures may change, so contact them for the most up to date information.

McCann's ⊘
www.mccanns.ie
4/10/2007 ⊚ (973) 338-0300
Company Notes: They cannot guarantee their oats are GF. They note that all their oat products are processed in a dedicated mill that handles only oatmeal. However, the possibility of cross contamination exists between the farm and mill, though they "reckon" there to be less than 0.05%

of non-oat grains. They urge consumers to "use their own judgment."

McCormick ⊘
www.mccormick.com
3/5/2007 ⊚ (800) 632-5847
Company Notes: As product formulations may change, they do not maintain a GF list. Instead, always read the ingredient list for accurate and current information. If a product does not have an ingredient list, it is a pure herb or spice and is GF. The alcohol in all extracts is GF. No product can be guaranteed to be 100% GF, but they note that they follow "good manufacturing processes" and train employees on the importance of accurate labeling and equipment wash downs to prevent cross-contamination.

McNess
www.mcness.com
4/26/2007 ⊚ (800) 999-4052
Triumph Notes: The list for McNess was dated 1/3/05.

Mead Johnson
www.meadjohnson.com
3/14/2007 ⊚ (800) 222-9123
Company Notes: They "always" recommend discussing concerns with your child's doctor.

Meadow Brook Dairy ⊘
3/15/2007 ⊚ See *Dean Foods.*

Meadow Gold ⊘
3/15/2007 ⊚ See *Dean Foods.*

Mediterranean Organic
www.mediterraneanorganic.com
4/11/2007

Melitta
www.melitta.com
4/11/2007 ⊚ (888) 635-4482

Merkts ⊘
www.merkts.com
4/11/2007 ⊚ See *Bel Brands U.S.A.*

MetRx ⊘
www.metrx.com
4/10/2007 ⊚ (800) 556-3879
Company Notes: No GF list is available. Call with specific product names and numbers, and they will research information for customers.

Mexene Chili
4/9/2007 ⊚ See *Bruce Foods.*

Meyenberg
www.meyenberg.com
4/10/2007 ⊚ (800) 891-4628

Mi Viejita
www.miviejitausa.com
3/5/2007 ⊚ (630) 303-9848

MiCasa (Stop & Shop)
5/8/2007 ⊚ See *Stop & Shop.*

Michael Season's
www.seasonssnacks.com
4/20/2007 ⊚ (630) 628-0211
Company Notes: Items marked with cross-contamination warning do not have gluten containing ingredients, but gluten is present in the manufacturing facility and on the same manufacturing line.

Michele's
www.michelefoods.com
5/8/2007 ⊚ (708) 862-5310

Midwest Country Fare (Hy-Vee)
5/8/2007 ⊚ See *Hy-Vee.*

Mighty Leaf Tea
www.mightyleaf.com
4/9/2007 ⊚ (877) 698-5323
Company Notes: The blends are GF, but may be processed in a facility that also processes gluten-containing products.

Mike and Ike
www.mikeandike.com
3/5/2007 ⊚ See *Just Born.*

Milk Duds ⊘
3/20/2007 ⊚ See *Hershey Company, The.*

Milkfuls
3/26/2007 ⊚ See *Storck.*

Milky Way ⊘
www.milkywaybar.com
3/27/2007 ⊛ See *MasterFoods USA.*

Millstone Coffee Company
www.millstone.com
3/16/2007 ⊛ See *Procter & Gamble.*

Minute ⊘
3/19/2007 ⊛ See *Kraft.*

Minute Maid
www.minutemaid.com
4/21/2007 ⊛ See *Coca-Cola Company, The.*

Miracle Whip ⊘
3/19/2007 ⊛ See *Kraft.*

Mirinda
4/19/2007 ⊛ See *Pepsi.*

Miso-Cup
4/10/2007 ⊛ See *Edward & Sons.*

Miss Vickie's
4/12/2007 ⊛ See *Frito Lay.*

Mission Foods ⊘
www.missionmenus.com
3/19/2007 ⊛ Company Notes: The corn products are GF.

Mizkan
www.mizkan.com
3/9/2007 ⊛ (800) 323-4358

Model Dairy ⊘
3/15/2007 ⊛ See *Dean Foods.*

Mom's
4/9/2007 ⊛ See *Fischer & Wieser.*

Mondo Fruit Squeezers ⊘
4/20/2007 ⊛ See *Jel Sert.*

Montebello
5/2/2007 ⊛ See *Spruce Foods.*

Moore's Marinades
www.candmfoods.com
5/2/2007 ⊛ (800) 879-8624
Company Notes: The manufacturing facility is GF.

Moosewood ✗
4/19/2007 ⊛ See *Fair Field Farm Kitchens.*

More than Tofu
www.sunergiasoyfoods.com
4/9/2007 ⊛ (800) 693-5134

Mori-Nu
www.morinu.com
3/16/2007 ⊛ (310) 787-0200

MorningStar Farms
www.seeveggiesdifferently.com
5/4/2007 ⊛ (800) 962-1413

Morton Salt
www.mortonsalt.com
3/6/2007 ⊛ Company Notes: There "should be no risk of cross-contamination." All products Morton produces should not contain gluten.

Mother's Natural Foods ✗
www.mothersnatural.com
3/12/2007 ⊛ (800) 333-8027
See *Quaker Oats Company, The.*

Mott's
www.motts.com
3/15/2007 ⊛ (800) 426-4891
See *Cadbury Schweppes.*

Mounds ⊘
3/20/2007 ⊛ See *Hershey Company, The.*

Mountain Dew
www.mountaindew.com
4/19/2007 ⊛ See *Pepsi.*

Mountain Madness Granola ✗
www.mountainmadnessnaturals.com
4/9/2007 ⊛ Company Notes: Products are wheat-free, but not GF.

Move Over Butter ⊘
(800) 988-7808
See *ConAgra Foods.*

Mr. & Mrs. T Mixers
3/12/2007 ⊛ See *Cadbury Schweppes (Beverages).*

Mr. Goodbar ⊘
3/20/2007 ⊛ See *Hershey Company, The.*

Mr. Krispers ⊘
www.mrkrispers.com
3/14/2007 ⊛ (888) 574-7737
See *TH Foods.*

Mrs. Butterworth's ⊘
3/19/2007 ⊛ See *Pinnacle Foods Corp.*

Mrs. Dash
www.mrsdash.com
3/9/2007 ⊛ Company Notes: Mrs. Dash marinades do not contain wheat but are produced on non-GF lines. They cannot guarantee trace amounts of gluten are not present.

Mrs. Paul's ⊘
3/19/2007 ⊛ See *Pinnacle Foods Corp.*

Mrs. Richardson's Toppings
3/22/2007 ⊛ See *Baldwin Richardson Foods Co.*

Mt. Olive Pickle Company
www.mtolivepickles.com
4/12/2007 ⊛ (800) 672-5041
Company Notes: Ensure that items on the GF list have a "Best if Used By Date" of 7/08 or later.

Mug
www.mugrootbeer.com
4/19/2007 ⊛ See *Pepsi.*

Muir Glen ⊘
www.muirglen.com
3/19/2007 ⊛ (800) 624-4123
See *General Mills.*

Munch Nut Bar
www.munchbar.com
3/27/2007 ⊛ See *MasterFoods USA.*

Munchos
4/12/2007 ⊛ See *Frito Lay.*

Murray's Chicken ⊘
www.murraychicken.com
5/3/2007 ⊛ (800) 770-6347

Musselman's
4/20/2007 ⊛ See *Knouse Foods.*

MVP (Wegman's)
5/8/2007 ⊛ See *Wegman's.*

My T Fine ⊘
4/20/2007 ⊛ See *Jel Sert.*

Nabisco ⊘
3/19/2007 ⊛ See *Kraft.*

Nabs ⊘
3/19/2007 ⊛ See *Kraft.*

Nakano
www.nakanovinegar.com
3/9/2007 ⊛ (800) 323-4358

Naked Juice
www.nakedjuice.com
4/16/2007 ⊛ (877) 858-4237

Namaste Foods
www.namastefoods.com
4/9/2007 ⊛ (866) 258-9493

Nan Infant Formula ⊘
www.verybestbaby.com
5/3/2007 ⊛ (800) 284-9488
See *Nestlé.*

Nance's Mustards & Condiments
3/22/2007 ⊛ See *Baldwin Richardson Foods Co.*

Nantucket Nectars
www.juiceguys.com
3/22/2007 ⊛ (888) 896-8667

Nasoya
www.nasoya.com
4/10/2007 ⊛ See *Vitasoy.*

Nate's
www.elenasfoods.com
4/9/2007 ⊛ (800) 376-5368

National Arrowroot ⊘
3/19/2007 ⊛ See *Kraft.*

Native Forest
4/10/2007 ⊛ See *Edward & Sons.*

Nature Valley ⊘
www.naturevalley.com
3/19/2007 ⊛ See *General Mills.*

Nature's Path
www.naturespath.com
4/9/2007 ⊛ (888) 808-9505
Company Notes: They make cereals

that do contain gluten, but they follow a "strict" production schedule whereby the "least allergenic" foods are made first. The entire line is cleaned after items with gluten are made. The equipment is periodically tested and inspected for gluten contamination. The Nature's Path puffed bagged cereals are not GF, as they are made in a separate factory where there is a chance of cross-contamination. People highly sensitive to gluten should consult a healthcare provider prior to consuming their products.

Nature's Promise (Stop & Shop)
5/8/2007 ◉ See *Stop & Shop.*

Navitas Naturals
www.navitasnaturals.com
4/9/2007 ◉ (888) 645-4282

Near East ✗
www.neareast.com
3/12/2007 ◉ (800) 822-7423
See *Quaker Oats Company, The.*

Necco
www.necco.com
3/6/2007 ◉ (781) 485-4500

Nerds
5/5/2007 ◉ See *Nestlé Chocolate and Confections.*

Nescafé
www.nescafe.com
5/3/2007 ◉ Company Notes: The GF list is compiled to best of their knowledge and may not be comprehensive due to new product information after the publish date. Always read ingredient statements for current information. ◉ Triumph Notes: The GF list does not mention oats and was dated last revised on 4/24/07. ◉ See *Nestlé.*

Nesquik
www.nesquik.com
5/3/2007 ◉ See *Nescafé.*

Nestea (Coca-Cola Company, The)
4/21/2007 ◉ See *Coca-Cola Company, The.*

Nestea (Nestlé)
www.nestea.com
5/3/2007 ◉ See *Nescafé.*

Nestlé ⊘
www.nestleusa.com
5/3/2007 ◉ (800) 225-2270
Company Notes: The GF list is compiled to best of their knowledge and may not be comprehensive due to new product information after the publish date. Always read ingredient statements for current information. ◉ Triumph Notes: The policy makes no mention of other sources of gluten, like rye, barley or oats. Some Nestle departments did supply GF lists and have been included in the book separately under their respective brand names or divisions.

Nestlé (Signatures) Treasures
5/5/2007 ◉ See *Nestlé Chocolate and Confections.*

Nestlé (Signatures) Turtles
5/5/2007 ◉ See *Nestlé Chocolate and Confections.*

Nestlé Chocolate and Confections
www.nestleusa.com
5/5/2007 ◉ (800) 225-2270
Company Notes: The GF list is compiled to best of their knowledge and may not be comprehensive due to new product information after the publish date. Always read ingredient statements for current information. ◉ Triumph Notes: The GF list was dated last revised 4/07. It made no mention of oats.

Nestlé Crunch ✗
www.nestlecrunch.com
5/10/2007 ◉ (800) 295-0051
Company Notes: Nestlé Crunch

is made with barley malt and also made on equipment that processes wheat.

Nestlé European Style Desserts ⊘
5/3/2007 ◉ See *Nestlé.*

Nestlé Hot Cocoa Mix
5/3/2007 ◉ See *Nescafé.*

Nestlé Ice Cream
www.nestle-icecream.com
6/20/2007 ◉ (800) 441-2525
Triumph Notes: The GF list was dated 5/15/07.

Nestlé Infant Formulas ⊘
www.verybestbaby.com
5/3/2007 ◉ (800) 284-9488
See *Nestlé.*

Nestlé Juicy Juice
www.juicyjuice.com
5/3/2007 ◉ See *Nescafé.*

Nestlé Milk Chocolate
5/5/2007 ◉ See *Nestlé Chocolate and Confections.*

Nestlé Toll House Candy Bars ⊘
5/3/2007 ◉ See *Nestlé.*

New Morning
5/15/2007 ◉ See *U.S. Mills.*

New World Pasta Company ✗
www.newworldpasta.com
3/19/2007 ◉ (800) 730-5957

Newman's Own
www.newmansown.com
5/14/2007 ◉ (781) 821-9617
Company Notes: They "feel" the products on the GF list are GF based on a "substantial quantity of technical information on the subject" that they have received. ◉ Triumph Notes: We requested this information from Newman's Own customer service which then sent a list from Shuster Laboratories, a "technical consulting organization" they retained to provide quality assurance and technical services.

Newman's Own Organics
www.newmansownorganics.com
3/17/2007 ◉ Company Notes: No gluten is added to the items on the GF list, but gluten is present in the plants where those products are made.

Newtons ⊘
3/19/2007 ◉ See *Kraft.*

Nile Spice ⊘
www.nilespice.com
5/21/2007 ◉ See *Hain Celestial.*

Nilla ⊘
3/19/2007 ◉ See *Kraft.*

Nips
5/5/2007 ◉ See *Nestlé Chocolate and Confections.*

Nishiki
4/10/2007 ◉ See *JFC International.*

No Salt Salt Substitute
4/20/2007 ◉ See *Reckitt Benckiser.*

Norbest
www.norbest.com
4/25/2007 ◉ (800) 453-5327

Norwestern
3/2/2007 ◉ Company Notes: For deli items, always ask the manager for an ingredient list. No gluten will be hidden under the term "flavoring." ◉ See *Hormel Foods.*

Not-So-Sloppy-Joe
3/2/2007 ◉ See *Hormel Foods.*

Now and Later ⊘
3/22/2007 ◉ See *Farley's & Sathers Candy Company.*

Nueva Cocina
www.nuevacocinafoods.com
4/9/2007 ◉ (800) 630-1125

Nulaid
www.nulaid.com
3/8/2007 ◉ (800) 788-8871

Nunez de Prado
5/2/2007 ◉ See *Spruce Foods.*

Nut Harvest
4/12/2007 ⊘ See *Frito Lay.*

Nutramigen Lipil
3/14/2007 ⊘ See *Mead Johnson.*

Nutter Butter ⊘
3/19/2007 ⊘ See *Kraft.*

Oak Farms Dairy ⊘
3/15/2007 ⊘ See *Dean Foods.*

Oberto Natural Style Beef Jerky
www.oberto.com
3/8/2007 ⊘ (877) 453-7591

Ocean Spray
www.oceanspray.com
3/5/2007 ⊘ (800) 662-3263
Company Notes: The GF list is based on information from ingredient suppliers. Those with a "particularly acute sensitivity" to gluten should consult their physician.

Odwalla
www.odwalla.com
4/9/2007 ⊘ (800) 639-2552
Company Notes: The bars are not GF, as they contain oats.

Oh Henry!
5/5/2007 ⊘ See *Nestlé Chocolate and Confections.*

O'Keely's
4/12/2007 ⊘ See *Frito Lay.*

Old Chatham Sheepherding Company
www.blacksheepcheese.com
4/9/2007 ⊘ (800) 743-3760

Old El Paso ⊘
www.oldelpaso.com
3/19/2007 ⊘ (800) 446-1898
See *General Mills.*

Old English ⊘
3/19/2007 ⊘ See *Kraft.*

Old Smokehouse
3/2/2007 ⊘ See *Hormel Foods.*

Old Wisconsin
www.oldwisconsin.com
5/4/2007 ⊘ (877) 451-7988

Olde Cape Cod
3/15/2007 ⊘ See *Cains.*

On-Cor ✗
www.on-cor.com
3/6/2007

Oogie's ✗
www.oogiesnacks.com
4/9/2007 ⊘ (303) 445-2107

Oompas
5/3/2007 ⊘ See *Nestlé.*

Open Pit ⊘
3/19/2007 ⊘ See *Pinnacle Foods Corp.*

Orangina
3/12/2007 ⊘ See *Cadbury Schweppes (Beverages).*

Orbit
3/16/2007 ⊘ See *Wrigley.*

Oregon Chai
www.oregonchai.com
3/6/2007 ⊘ (888) 874-2424

Oregon Fruit Products
www.oregonfruit.com
5/3/2007 ⊘ (800) 394-9333

Ore-Ida
www.oreida.com
3/21/2007 ⊘ (800) 892-2401
See *Heinz.*

Oreo ⊘
3/19/2007 ⊘ See *Kraft.*

Organic Classics ✗
4/19/2007 ⊘ See *Fair Field Farm Kitchens.*

Organic Food Bar ⊘
www.organicfoodbar.com
4/10/2007 ⊘ (800) 246-4685
Company Notes: Organic Food Bars tested for gluten results show less than 3 ppm of gluten.

Organic So Delicious
4/9/2007 ⊘ See *Turtle Mountain.*

Organicville
www.organicvillefoods.com
4/9/2007

OrgraN
www.orgran.com
4/20/2007

Original Ceylon Tea Company, The
www.ceylon-tea.com
4/9/2007 ⊘ (877) 333-9901

Ortega ⊘
www.ortega.com
4/19/2007 ⊘ Company Notes: They have been following a "strict labeling policy" and have "insisted" that suppliers notify them if gluten is in any of their ingredients and not declared on their labeling. Ortega believes its products are "fully labeled for any presence of gluten or gluten containing ingredients."

Orville Redenbacher's ⊘
www.orville.com
(800) 243-0303
See *ConAgra Foods.*

Oscar Mayer ⊘
3/19/2007 ⊘ See *Kraft.*

Otter Pops ⊘
4/20/2007 ⊘ See *Jel Sert.*

Oven Fry ⊘
3/19/2007 ⊘ See *Kraft.*

Owl's Nest ⊘
www.owlsnestcheese.com
4/11/2007 ⊘ See *Bel Brands U.S.A.*

Pace
www.pacefoods.com
4/10/2007 ⊘ See *Campbell's.*

PAM ⊘
www.pam4you.com
(800) 726-4968
See *ConAgra Foods.*

Pamela's Products
www.pamelasproducts.com
5/15/2007 ⊘ (707) 462-6605

Pangburn's ⊘
5/3/2007 ⊘ (888) 311-3734
See *Russell Stover.*

Parkay
www.parkay.com
5/14/2007 ⊘ (800) 988-7808

Pasta Roni ✗
www.ricearoni.com
3/12/2007 ⊘ (800) 421-2444
See *Quaker Oats Company, The.*

Patak's ⊘
3/2/2007 ⊘ See *Hormel Foods.*

Patio ⊘
(800) 469-5202
See *ConAgra Foods.*

PayDay ⊘
3/20/2007 ⊘ See *Hershey Company, The.*

PB Crisps ⊘
3/19/2007 ⊘ See *Kraft.*

PBM Products
www.pbmproducts.com
4/13/2007 ⊘ (800) 485-9918

Peanut Chews
www.peanutchews.com
3/5/2007 ⊘ See *Just Born.*

Pecan Passion ⊘
3/19/2007 ⊘ See *Kraft.*

Pecanz ⊘
3/19/2007 ⊘ See *Kraft.*

Pedialyte
www.pedialyte.com
3/22/2007 ⊘ See *Abbott's Ross Products Division.*

PediaSure
www.pediasure.com
3/22/2007 ⊘ See *Abbott's Ross Products Division.*

Peeps
www.marshmallowpeeps.com
3/5/2007 ⊘ (888) 645-3453
See *Just Born.*

Peloponnese
3/2/2007 ⊘ See *Hormel Foods.*

Pemmican ⊘
www.pemmican.com
3/19/2007 ⊘ (800) 320-1155
Company Notes: Always read ingredient statements on

labels. Formulae may change. Contact them with questions about specific ingredients.

Penn Maid
www.pennmaid.com
3/15/2007 ⊚ (800) 247-6269

Penrose ⊘
(800) 382-4994
See *ConAgra Foods.*

Pepsi
www.pepsiusa.com
4/19/2007 ⊚ (800) 433-2652
Company Notes: All soft drinks produced by North America's Pepsi-Cola Company are GF.

Perdue
www.perdue.com
3/19/2007 ⊚ (800) 473-7383
Company Notes: "All fresh, minimally processed chicken and turkey whole birds and parts" are GF. The GF list is routinely updated.

Perky's
www.perkysnaturalfoods.com
5/15/2007 ⊚ (888) 473-7597

Peter Pan ⊘
(800) 222-7370
See *ConAgra Foods.*

Pez Candy
www.pez.com
5/13/2007 ⊚ (800) 653-3134
Company Notes: Pez is GF and also does not contain any allergens defined by CODEX. ⊚ Triumph Notes: They only list wheat, barley and oats, but not rye, as part of the CODEX allergens.

Philadelphia ⊘
3/19/2007 ⊚ See *Kraft.*

Philly Gourmet
www.philly-gourmet.com
3/16/2007

PhillySwirl
www.phillyswirl.com
5/8/2007 ⊚ (877) 379-4757

Pillsbury ⊘
www.pillsbury.com
3/19/2007 ⊚ (800) 775-4777
See *General Mills.*

Pinnacle Foods Corp.
www.pinnaclefoodscorp.com
3/19/2007 ⊚ (877) 852-7424
Company Notes: Armour, Swanson frozen foods and Open Pit barbecue sauces "generally" contain wheat-based modified food starches or other thickening agents. Always read ingredient lists as they may change. They follow "good manufacturing practices," but do not have dedicated production lines.

Pinwheels ⊘
3/19/2007 ⊚ See *Kraft.*

Pixy Stix
5/5/2007 ⊚ See *Nestlé Chocolate and Confections.*

Planters ⊘
3/19/2007 ⊚ See *Kraft.*

Planters CarbWell ⊘
3/19/2007 ⊚ See *Kraft.*

Polaner
4/19/2007 ⊚ See *B&G Foods.*

Polly-O ⊘
3/19/2007 ⊚ See *Kraft.*

POM Wonderful
www.pomwonderful.com
4/9/2007 ⊚ (310) 966-5863
Company Notes: No gluten-containing ingredients are present. Neither gluten nor gluten-containing ingredients are in contact with their manufacturing equipment. Consult your physician about your particular condition and POM products.

Pop Ice ⊘
4/20/2007 ⊚ See *Jel Sert.*

Pop Secret ⊘
www.popsecret.com
3/19/2007 ⊚ See *General Mills.*

Poppycock
3/19/2007 ⊚ See *Lincoln Snacks.*

Pops Galore
3/15/2007 ⊚ See *Tootsie Roll Industries.*

Popsicle ⊘
www.icecreamusa.com
5/3/2007 ⊚ (920) 499-5151
See *Unilever.*

Post ⊘
3/19/2007 ⊚ See *Kraft.*

Post CarbWell ⊘
3/19/2007 ⊚ See *Kraft.*

Post Honey Bunches of Oats ⊘
3/19/2007 ⊚ See *Kraft.*

Postum ⊘
3/19/2007 ⊚ See *Kraft.*

POWERade
www.us.powerade.com
4/21/2007 ⊚ See *Coca-Cola Company, The.*

Powerbar ✕
www.powerbar.com
5/10/2007 ⊚ (800) 587-6937
Company Notes: They note that all products contain oats, barley or malt. Products are manufactured on equipment that may process wheat. They recommend reading labels and consulting your physician on whether you can consume their products.

Pregestimil
3/14/2007 ⊚ See *Mead Johnson.*

Prego
www.prego.com
4/10/2007 ⊚ See *Campbell's.*

Premier Japan
4/10/2007 ⊚ See *Edward & Sons.*

Premium ⊘
3/19/2007 ⊚ See *Kraft.*

Prestige (Winn-Dixie)
4/25/2007 ⊚ See *Winn-Dixie.*

Pria ⊘
5/9/2007 ⊚ See *Powerbar.*

Price's Creameries ⊘
3/15/2007 ⊚ See *Dean Foods.*

Primo Naturale
4/9/2007 ⊚ See *Wellshire Farms.*

Primo Taglio (Safeway)
5/9/2007 ⊚ See *Safeway.*

Pringles
www.pringles.com
3/16/2007 ⊚ Company Notes: Always read the label's ingredient list. ⊚ See *Procter & Gamble.*

Procter & Gamble
www.pg.com
3/16/2007 ⊚ (800) 332-7787
Company Notes: Always read the label's ingredient list.

Progresso ⊘
www.progressofoods.com
3/19/2007 ⊚ (800) 200-9377
See *General Mills.*

Promise ⊘
www.promisehealthyheart.com
5/3/2007 ⊚ (800) 375-0291
See *Unilever.*

Propel
www.propelfitnesswater.com
4/25/2007 ⊚ See *Gatorade.*

PureFit
www.purefit.com
4/9/2007 ⊚ (866) 787-3348

Purely Decadent
4/9/2007 ⊚ See *Turtle Mountain.*

Purity Dairies ⊘
3/15/2007 ⊚ See *Dean Foods.*

Purity Foods ✕
www.purityfoods.com
3/15/2007 ⊚ (800) 997-7358

Quaker Oats Company, The ✕
www.quakeroats.com
3/12/2007 ⊚ (312) 821-1000
Company Notes: Although gluten-containing ingredients may not be present in some products, they cannot be guaranteed GF as ingredients may have come into contact with gluten-containing grains

during growing, harvesting or storage, and thus may contain trace amounts of gluten.

Queen Anne Candy ⊘
www.queenannecandy.com
5/2/2007 ⊚ (888) 821-8452
Company Notes: While items are not produced with gluten, gluten is present in their manufacturing facility.

Quisp ✗
www.quisp.com
3/12/2007 ⊚ See *Quaker Oats Company, The.*

R.W. Garcia
www.rwgarcia.com
4/9/2007 ⊚ (408) 287-4616

Ragu ⊘
www.eat.com
5/3/2007 ⊚ (800) 328-7248
See *Unilever.*

Rain-Blo ⊘
3/22/2007 ⊚ See *Farley's & Sathers Candy Company.*

Raisinets
5/5/2007 ⊚ See *Nestlé Chocolate and Confections.*

Ranch Style ⊘
(800) 799-7300
See *ConAgra Foods.*

Range Brand
3/2/2007 ⊚ See *Hormel Foods.*

RC
3/12/2007 ⊚ See *Cadbury Schweppes (Beverages).*

Read ⊘
4/19/2007 ⊚ See *Seneca Foods.*

Ready Crisp ⊘
(800) 998-1006
See *ConAgra Foods.*

Really Nuts ⊘
3/20/2007 ⊚ See *Hershey Company, The.*

Reckitt Benckiser
4/20/2007 ⊚ (800) 888-0192
Company Notes: Always read ingredient statements, as formulae may change. Suppliers

are also subject to change, so information accurate today may become obsolete.

Red Bull
www.redbullusa.com
3/22/2007

Red Gold
www.redgold.com
4/10/2007 ⊚ (877) 748-9798
Company Notes: Tomato products made by Red Gold do not contain gluten. The sweeteners and alcohol used are corn derived. The aforementioned information does not apply to the Red Gold Bean products. Show their disclaimer to your doctor for advice on the consumption of their products.

Red Label
3/2/2007 ⊚ See *Hormel Foods.*

Red Rose
www.redrosetea.com
4/10/2007 ⊚ (877) 248-2477

Red Star Yeast
www.redstaryeast.com
3/19/2007 ⊚ (877) 677-7000
See *Bakipan.*

Reddi-wip ⊘
www.reddi-wip.com
(800) 745-4514
See *ConAgra Foods.*

Redpack
4/10/2007 ⊚ See *Red Gold.*

Redwood Hill Farm & Creamery
www.redwoodhill.com
4/9/2007 ⊚ (707) 823-8250

Reed's
www.reedsgingerbrew.com
4/9/2007 ⊚ (800) 997-3337

Reese's ⊘
3/20/2007 ⊚ See *Hershey Company, The.*

Regina
4/19/2007 ⊚ See *B&G Foods.*

Reiter Dairy ⊘
3/15/2007 ⊚ See *Dean Foods.*

Republic of Tea, The
www.republicoftea.com
5/7/2007 ⊚ (800) 298-4832
Company Notes: It's certified by the GFCO and is free from cross-contamination.

Revolution Tea
www.revolutiontea.com
5/7/2007 ⊚ (888) 321-4738

Rice
3/15/2007 ⊚ See *Galaxy Nutritional Foods.*

Rice Dream ⊘
www.tastethedream.com
5/21/2007 ⊚ See *Hain Celestial.*

Rice Expressions
www.riceexpressions.com
4/13/2007

Rice-A-Roni ✗
www.ricearoni.com
3/12/2007 ⊚ (800) 421-2444
See *Quaker Oats Company, The.*

RiceSelect
www.riceselect.com
4/9/2007 ⊚ (800) 232-7423

Ricos
www.ricos.com
3/23/2007 ⊚ (210) 253-2241

Riesen
3/26/2007 ⊚ See *Storck.*

Ritz ⊘
3/19/2007 ⊚ See *Kraft.*

Ro*tel ⊘
www.ro-tel.com
(800) 544-5680
See *ConAgra Foods.*

Robert Rothschild Farm
www.gourmetfoodrecipes.com
3/16/2007 ⊚ (800) 356-8933

Robinson Dairy ⊘
3/15/2007 ⊚ See *Dean Foods.*

Rodelle
www.rodellevanilla.com
4/10/2007 ⊚ (970) 482-8845

Rolo ⊘
3/20/2007 ⊚ See *Hershey Company, The.*

Ronzoni ✗
www.ronzoni.com
3/19/2007 ⊚ See *New World Pasta Company.*

Rosarita ⊘
(800) 365-8300
See *ConAgra Foods.*

Rosetto ⊘
www.rosetto.com
5/21/2007 ⊚ See *Hain Celestial.*

Ross Products
3/22/2007 ⊚ See *Abbott's Ross Products Division.*

Royal ⊘
4/20/2007 ⊚ See *Jel Sert.*

Royal Lunch ⊘
3/19/2007 ⊚ See *Kraft.*

Ruffles
4/12/2007 ⊚ See *Frito Lay.*

Rumford
5/13/2007 ⊚ See *Clabber Girl.*

Runts
5/5/2007 ⊚ See *Nestlé Chocolate and Confections.*

Russell Stover ⊘
www.russellstover.com
5/3/2007 ⊚ (800) 777-4028
Company Notes: Many item are GF. Read labels. GF items are produced in the same facility as gluten-containing items, though the lines are sanitized between batches.

Rustler's
4/12/2007 ⊚ See *Frito Lay.*

Ryvita ✗
www.ryvita.com
4/10/2007

S & W
www.swfinefoods.com
3/22/2007 ⊚ (800) 252-7033
See *Del Monte.*

Sabrett
www.sabrett.com
4/10/2007 ◉ (201) 935-3330

Sabritas
4/12/2007 ◉ See *Frito Lay.*

Sacramento
4/10/2007 ◉ See *Red Gold.*

Sadaf ⃠
www.sadaf.com
4/16/2007 ◉ (800) 852-4050
Company Notes: No GF list is available, but contact them to find out if a specific item is GF.

SAF
www.safyeast.com
3/19/2007 ◉ (800) 445-4746
See *Bakipan.*

Safeway
www.safeway.com
5/9/2007 ◉ (877) 723-3929
Company Notes: They do not "presume to prescribe" any of their products for any particular diet. They have over 5,000 different private label products and do not have an ingredient listing for all of them. They suggest carefully reading labels. In addition to the GF list they provided, they note that frozen vegetables and fruits should be fine, except where something besides the vegetables and fruit has been added, like the frozen vegetables in sauce. All fresh meats, seafood, eggs, "fluid" milks, cottage cheese and natural cheese they write are fine. They note that chocolate milk where starch is added, and if the source of that starch is unlisted, should be avoided. The spices are not made on dedicated lines. The GF list they provided is taken from their initiative to ask suppliers for their list of GF products. The list is correct to the best of their knowledge, but they will not guarantee that changes in ingredients or vendors will not occur. Therefore, they recommend verifying ingredients with them from time to time.

◉ Triumph Notes: Where noted, items are not produced on dedicated lines and/or are produced in facilities that also produce wheat products.

Sahale Snacks ⃠
www.sahalesnacks.com
4/9/2007 ◉ (206) 624-7244
Company Notes: They are "technically" not a GF product. Figs and dates in the Soledad and Ksar blends are sometimes dusted with oat flour, though newer batches use rice flour instead. Be sure to check the ingredient list. The Sing Buri blend contains wheat. The Valdosta, Socorro and Dauphine blends are free of wheat and oat products.

Salada
www.salada.com
4/10/2007 ◉ (800) 645-1190
Company Notes: Besides the teas on their GF list, all other Salada Green Teas will have markings on the package if they have wheat, rye, barley or oats.

San Carlos (Winn-Dixie)
4/25/2007 ◉ See *Winn-Dixie.*

San-J
www.san-j.com
4/16/2007 ◉ (800) 446-5500
Company Notes: Wheat-containing products are processed in the same facility, and they have implemented sanitation methods in an effort to prevent cross-contamination. Samples of their Organic Wheat Free Tamari Soy Sauce and Organic Wheat Free Reduced Sodium Tamari Soy Sauce are periodically tested for the presence of gluten by an "outside" laboratory. Tests for San-J's Organic Wheat Free Tamari for gluten fall within the threshold limit for gluten free foods according to the Codex Alimentarius Commission. The alcohol used in these products is corn derived.

Sanka ⃠
3/19/2007 ◉ See *Kraft.*

Santa Barbara Salsa
www.sbsalsa.com
4/9/2007 ◉ (800) 748-5523

Santitas
4/12/2007 ◉ See *Frito Lay.*

Sara Lee ⃠
www.saralee.com
4/23/2007 ◉ (800) 261-4754
Company Notes: All ingredients are listed on the package. Always read ingredient labels, and if the product contains any gluten, it will be listed.

Sargento ⃠
www.sargentocheese.com
3/19/2007 ◉ (800) 243-3737
Company Notes: Most Sargento "natural cheeses should be acceptable" on a GF diet. The exception is Sargento Blue Cheese. The anti-caking agents microcrystalline cellulose, calcium carbonate and potato starch are not derived from wheat, rye, barley or oats. The vinegar in the Sargento Ricotta Cheese is triple distilled. Consult a physician with any questions about how their products may affect you.

Sathers ⃠
3/22/2007 ◉ See *Farley's & Sathers Candy Company.*

Sauceworks ⃠
3/19/2007 ◉ See *Kraft.*

Scharffen Berger
www.scharffenberger.com
4/9/2007 ◉ (510) 981-4050
Company Notes: There is no gluten in their chocolate. No cereal grains are present in the manufacturing facility. However, the Cocoa Powder and Sweetened Cocoa Powder are processed in another facility that also handles wheat, opening up the possibility of cross-contamination.

Schepps Dairy ⃠
3/15/2007 ◉ See *Dean Foods.*

Schreiber Foods ⃠
www.schreiberfoods.com
4/23/2007 ◉ (800) 344-0333
Company Notes: No products are guaranteed to be GF because formulae may change and while they do not intentionally add gluten to products, they do not screen for "incidental" amounts of gluten.

Schweppes
3/12/2007 ◉ See *Cadbury Schweppes (Beverages).*

Seattle's Best Coffee ⃠
3/19/2007 ◉ See *Kraft.*

Seeds of Change ⃠
www.seedsofchange.com
3/22/2007 ◉ (888) 762-4240
Company Notes: They follow "Good Manufacturing Processes" and "HACCP" to prevent cross-contamination of allergens, like wheat. ◉ Triumph Notes: No GF list was provided. The list they provided had items without wheat gluten.

Select Brand (Safeway)
5/9/2007 ◉ See *Safeway.*

Seneca Foods ⃠
www.senecafoods.com
4/19/2007 ◉ (800) 872-1110
Company Notes: No GF list is available, as formulae may change. Gluten sources will be "correctly identified" in plain language on the label's ingredient list. They have an allergen policy, encompassing gluten, for both labeling and manufacturing. A plant must "incorporate the necessary controls of cleaning, scheduling, indemnification and manufacturing" to prevent cross-contamination.

Sensible Foods
www.sensiblefoods.com
4/9/2007 ◉ (888) 222-0170

Sesmark ✗
www.sesmark.com
4/10/2007 ◉ (201) 843-8900
Company Notes: Though all production lines are "thoroughly

cleaned and sterilized between manufacturing runs," they will not guarantee that any product is GF due to the possibility of cross-contamination. They note that the maltodextrin is from a corn source and that the natural flavor is a wheat-free soy sauce.

Seven Seas ⊘
3/19/2007 ◉ See *Kraft.*

Seven Stars Farm
www.sevenstarsfarm.com
4/9/2007 ◉ (610) 935-1949

Shake 'N Bake ⊘
3/19/2007 ◉ See *Kraft.*

Shenandoah's Pride ⊘
3/15/2007 ◉ See *Dean Foods.*

Sierra Mist
www.sierramist.com
4/19/2007 ◉ See *Pepsi.*

Siljans ✗
www.siljanscrispycup.com
4/9/2007 ◉ (403) 275-0135

Silk
www.silksoymilk.com
3/22/2007 ◉ (888) 820-9283
Company Notes: They note the FDA does not have GF guidelines for labeling, but the Silk line is GF to the best of their knowledge.

Silver Spring ⊘
www.silverspringfoods.com
3/21/2007 ◉ (800) 826-7322
Company Notes: They cannot state that the ingredients are 100% GF. The vinegar is distilled from corn.

Similac
www.similac.com
3/22/2007 ◉ See *Abbott's Ross Products Division.*

Simple Food
www.simplefood.com
4/9/2007 ◉ (978) 388-1444

Simply Enjoy (Stop & Shop)
5/8/2007 ◉ See *Stop & Shop.*

Simply Lemonade
4/21/2007 ◉ See *Coca-Cola Company, The.*

Simply Limeade
4/21/2007 ◉ See *Coca-Cola Company, The.*

Simply Organic ⊘
4/9/2007 ◉ See *Frontier Natural Products Co-op.*

Simply Potatoes
www.simplypotatoes.com
3/21/2007 ◉ (866) 533-7783

Skippy ⊘
www.peanutbutter.com
3/22/2007 ◉ (866) 475-4779
Company Notes: No GF list is provided as product formulations may change. Always read the label's ingredient listing. Any ingredient that may contain gluten will always be listed on the label.

Skittles
www.skittles.com
3/27/2007 ◉ See *MasterFoods USA.*

Skondra's (Hy-Vee)
5/8/2007 ◉ See *Hy-Vee.*

Skybar
3/6/2007 ◉ See *Necco.*

Skyr.is
www.skyr.is
4/18/2007

Slim Jim ⊘
www.slimjim.com
(800) 242-6200
See *ConAgra Foods.*

Slim-Fast
www.slim-fast.com
3/22/2007 ◉ (800) 754-6327
Company Notes: They write that Slim-Fast Easy to Digest Shakes are GF and that their supplier guarantees that all its ingredients are GF. They add that there may be other Slim-Fast shakes and snack bars that do not contain gluten sources, but that those are not guaranteed to be GF.

Smartfood
4/12/2007 ◉ See *Frito Lay.*

Smartwater
5/2/2007 ◉ See *Glacéau.*

Smucker's ⊘
www.smuckers.com
4/5/2007 ◉ (888) 550-9555
Triumph Notes: Call them for the most current information.

Snack Barz ⊘
3/20/2007 ◉ See *Hershey Company, The.*

Snacksters ⊘
3/20/2007 ◉ See *Hershey Company, The.*

SnackWell's ⊘
3/19/2007 ◉ See *Kraft.*

SnackWell's CarbWell ⊘
3/19/2007 ◉ See *Kraft.*

Snapple
www.snapple.com
3/16/2007 ◉ (800) 762-7753
See *Cadbury Schweppes (Beverages).*

Snickers ⊘
www.snickers.com
4/9/2007 ◉ (800) 627-7852
See *MasterFoods USA.*

Sno-Caps
5/5/2007 ◉ See *Nestlé Chocolate and Confections.*

Snyder's of Hanover
www.snydersofhanover.com
3/21/2007 ◉ (717) 632-4477

So Delicious
4/9/2007 ◉ See *Turtle Mountain.*

Social Tea ⊘
3/19/2007 ◉ See *Kraft.*

Sorrento ⊘
www.sorrentocheese.com
5/20/2007 ◉ (800) 699-2701
Company Notes: While the grains and starches currently used in their finished products are allowable for people with gluten

intolerance, they will not make any claims that their finished products are GF.

Sour Patch Kids
www.sourpatchkids.com
5/1/2007 ◉ (800) 565-6317

South Beach Diet ⊘
3/19/2007 ◉ See *Kraft.*

Soy Dream ⊘
www.tastethedream.com
5/21/2007 ◉ See *Hain Celestial.*

Soy Feta
www.sunergiasoyfoods.com
4/9/2007 ◉ (800) 693-5134

Soyfee
www.soycoffee.com
3/20/2007

Spam
3/2/2007 ◉ See *Hormel Foods.*

Spangler Candy Company
www.spanglercandy.com
4/9/2007 ◉ (419) 636-4221

Speas Farm
4/20/2007 ◉ See *Knouse Foods.*

Spectrum ⊘
www.spectrumorganics.com
5/21/2007 ◉ See *Hain Celestial.*

Spice Hunter
www.spicehunter.com
4/12/2007 ◉ (800) 444-3061
Company Notes: None of their box and cup product are guaranteed GF, as they are made using "common" processing equipment. The equipment is cleaned between use, but all traces of gluten cannot be guaranteed to be removed. Spices and spice blends are GF, but all products are manufactured in the same building.

Spice Islands
3/16/2007 ◉ See *Durkee.*

Splenda
www.splenda.com
3/21/2007 ◉ (800) 777-5363
Company Notes: Splenda brand sweeteners do not contain gluten, and contain no ingredi-

ents or proteins derived from wheat. The maltodextrin in Splenda No Calorie Sweetener is derived from corn.

Spree
5/5/2007 ⊚ See *Nestlé Chocolate and Confections.*

Sprite
4/21/2007 ⊚ See *Coca-Cola Company, The.*

Spruce Foods
www.sprucefoods.com
5/2/2007 ⊚ (949) 498-0735

Squeez-Eez
5/1/2007 ⊚ See *Concord Foods.*

Squirt
3/12/2007 ⊚ See *Cadbury Schweppes (Beverages).*

Stacy's Snacks ⊘
www.stacyssnacks.com
4/11/2007 ⊚ (866) 478-2297
Company Notes: Stacy's Soy Thin Crisps do not contain wheat. The Pita Chips and Bagel chips contain wheat.

Stagg
3/2/2007 ⊚ See *Hormel Foods.*

Starbucks ⊘
3/19/2007 ⊚ See *Kraft.*

Starburst
www.starburst.com
3/27/2007 ⊚ See *MasterFoods USA.*

StarKist Tuna
www.starkist.com
3/22/2007 ⊚ (800) 252-1587
See *Del Monte.*

Steaz Green Tea Soda
www.steaz.com
4/9/2007 ⊚ (800) 295-1388

Stewart's Beverages
www.drinkstewarts.com
3/12/2007 ⊚ (800) 762-7753
See *Cadbury Schweppes (Beverages).*

Stokely's ⊘
4/19/2007 ⊚ See *Seneca Foods.*

Stoned Wheat Thins ⊘
3/19/2007 ⊚ See *Kraft.*

Stonyfield Farm ⊘
www.stonyfieldfarm.com
3/20/2007 ⊚ (800) 776-2697
Company Notes: YoBaby Plus Fruit and Cereal contains gluten from oats. Otherwise, while no gluten is added to their products, there may be trace amounts in flavored yogurts that contain natural flavoring. Consult a doctor if you have any questions about consuming their products.

Stop & Shop
www.stopandshop.com
5/8/2007 ⊚ (877) 846-9949
Company Notes: Their Consumer Affairs department and Corporate Brands team work with suppliers to verify the GF status of items, and such information is provided to the best of their knowledge. Always read ingredient statements, which can change at any time. They cannot be held responsible for customer reactions to a product. ⊚ Triumph Notes: The list was marked updated 1/1/07.

Storck
www.storck.us
3/26/2007 ⊚ (800) 621-7772
Company Notes: Products cannot be said to be "completely" GF because there may be some gluten on the line of a "co-supplier" that may have used gluten for another manufacturer. Purchase only products you know for sure are GF. Items listed meet the standard of the German association for Celiac disease with a gluten content of less than 200 ppm, which is also the international guideline based on the Codex Alimentarius.

Stouffer's ⊘
www.stouffers.com
5/2/2007 ⊚ (800) 225-1180
See *Nestlé.*

Stove Top ⊘
3/19/2007 ⊚ See *Kraft.*

Streit's
www.streitsmatzos.com
4/16/2007 ⊚ (212) 475-7000
Company Notes: The macaroons are made in a GF factory.

Stretch Island Fruit Company
www.stretchislandfruit.com
4/10/2007

Sugar Babies
3/15/2007 ⊚ See *Tootsie Roll Industries.*

Sugar Daddy Pops
3/15/2007 ⊚ See *Tootsie Roll Industries.*

Sugar Mama Caramels
3/15/2007 ⊚ See *Tootsie Roll Industries.*

Sun Soy ⊘
3/15/2007 ⊚ See *Dean Foods.*

Sunbird
5/3/2007 ⊚ See *Williams Foods.*

Sundrop
3/12/2007 ⊚ See *Cadbury Schweppes (Beverages).*

Sunkist (Cadbury Schweppes/Soda)
www.sunkist.com
3/12/2007 ⊚ (800) 696-5891
See *Cadbury Schweppes (Beverages).*

Sun-Maid ⊘
www.sunmaid.com
4/9/2007 ⊚ (559) 896-8000
Company Notes: Sun-Maid Natural Sun-Dried Raisins and Zante Currants do not contain any additives or preservatives and are packed in a GF facility, except as noted. Products packed at plants that also produce wheat-containing products are labeled as follows: "Packed in a facility that also packs..."

SunRidge Farms ⊘
www.sunridgefarms.com
3/15/2007 ⊚ (831) 786-7000
Company Notes: No items can be guaranteed to be GF due to the possible presence of

gluten-containing dust during the manufacturing process. They follow "strict guidelines" for cleaning equipment in between runs and adhere to labeling laws. Always read the ingredient list.

Sunrise Valley (Stop & Shop)
5/8/2007 ⊚ See *Stop & Shop.*

Super Blow Pops
3/15/2007 ⊚ See *Tootsie Roll Industries.*

Super Bubble ⊘
3/22/2007 ⊚ See *Farley's & Sathers Candy Company.*

Sure-Jell ⊘
3/19/2007 ⊚ See *Kraft.*

Swanson (Frozen Foods) ⊘
www.swansonmeals.com
3/19/2007 ⊚ See *Pinnacle Foods Corp.*

Swanson Broth & Canned Poultry
www.swansonbroth.com
4/10/2007 ⊚ (800) 442-7684
See *Campbell's.*

Sweet & Salty Granola Bars ⊘
3/20/2007 ⊚ See *Hershey Company, The.*

Sweet 'N Low
www.sweetnlow.com
4/25/2007

Sweet Nothings
4/9/2007 ⊚ See *Turtle Mountain.*

Sweetarts
5/5/2007 ⊚ See *Nestlé Chocolate and Confections.*

Sweethearts
3/6/2007 ⊚ See *Necco.*

Swiss Dairy ⊘
3/15/2007 ⊚ See *Dean Foods.*

Swiss Miss ⃠
www.swissmiss.com
(800) 457-6649
See *ConAgra Foods*.

T.G. Lee Dairy ⃠
3/15/2007 ⊚ See *Dean Foods*.

Tabasco
www.tabasco.com
3/19/2007 ⊚ (888) 468-3274
Company Notes: Vinegar and
sauces have been tested
for residual gluten by two
independent laboratories, the
Food Allergy Research and
Resource Program at the University of Nebraska-Lincoln
and Oregon Food Products
Laboratory. No detectable
amounts of gluten were found
by either laboratory in any
Tabasco brand pepper sauces
or Tabasco brand soy sauce.
According to the definitions
set by the Codex Alimentarius
Commission, Tabasco brand
products are GF. ⊚ Triumph Notes:
The statement provided was
dated revised 8/10/04.

Tabatchnick Fine Foods
www.tabatchnick.com
4/11/2007 ⊚ (732) 247-6668

Taco Bell ⃠
3/19/2007 ⊚ See *Kraft*.

Take 5 ⃠
3/20/2007 ⊚ See *Hershey Company, The*.

Tamarind Tree
www.tamtree.com
4/9/2007 ⊚ (707) 254-3700

Tampico
www.tampico.com
3/15/2007 ⊚ (877) 826-7426

Tang ⃠
3/19/2007 ⊚ See *Kraft*.

Target ⃠
www.target.com
5/14/2007 ⊚ (866) 423-2135
Company Notes: No GF list is
available, but call with specific
individual product inquiries.

Tassimo ⃠
www.tassimo.com
3/19/2007 ⊚ (877) 834-7271
See *Kraft*.

Taste of China, A ⃠
3/19/2007 ⊚ See *Taste of Thai, A*.

Taste of India, A
3/19/2007 ⊚ See *Taste of Thai, A*.

Taste of Thai, A
www.andreprost.com
3/19/2007 ⊚ (800) 243-0897

**Taster's Choice Instant
Coffee (Nescafé)**
www.verybestcoffee.com
5/3/2007 ⊚ See *Nescafé*.

Tazo ⃠
3/19/2007 ⊚ See *Kraft*.

Teance
www.teance.com
4/9/2007 ⊚ (510) 524-1696

Teas' Tea
www.itoen.com
4/10/2007 ⊚ (888) 832-7832
Company Notes: No materials with
wheat, rye, barley or oats are
used in Teas' Tea products.

Teddy Grahams ⃠
3/19/2007 ⊚ See *Kraft*.

Teenee Beanee
3/5/2007 ⊚ See *Just Born*.

Tempo
5/1/2007 ⊚ See *Concord Foods*.

Terra Chips ⃠
www.terrachips.com
5/21/2007 ⊚ See *Hain Celestial*.

Terrapin Ridge
www.mcness.com
4/26/2007 ⊚ (800) 999-4052
Triumph Notes: The GF list was
dated 6/2/04.

Terry's ⃠
3/19/2007 ⊚ See *Kraft*.

Tetley ⃠
www.tetleyusa.com
3/19/2007 ⊚ (800) 728-0084
Company Notes: Always read the
ingredient list. All tea bags

contain only tea leaves. The
caramel coloring used in the
iced tea mix is GF. The decaf-
feination method is GF.

Teuscher
www.teuscherfifthavenue.com
4/11/2007 ⊚ (800) 554-0924

Texas Pete
www.texaspete.com
4/9/2007 ⊚ (888) 875-3111

TGI Friday's Salsa
3/21/2007 ⊚ See *Heinz*.

TH Foods ⃠
www.thfoods.com
3/14/2007 ⊚ (815) 636-9500
Company Notes: They note that
the FDA has not defined what
GF is and so do not "call" any
of their products GF. They
note that wheat-containing
products may be produced on
the same line as those with
no wheat ingredients, though
they do use "good cleanup
procedures." Tests of Crunchmaster and other products
have gluten amounts ranging
from undetectable to 100 ppm.

Thai Kitchen
www.thaikitchen.com
5/13/2007 ⊚ (800) 967-8424

Thrifty Maid
4/25/2007 ⊚ See *Winn-Dixie*.

Tillamook
www.tillamookcheese.com
3/15/2007 ⊚ (503) 815-1300
Company Notes: "Most "ice cream
flavors are GF, but those that
list ingredients like cookie
dough, cake, pie, etc. will
contain gluten.

Timpone's Organic
4/9/2007 ⊚ See *Fischer &
Wieser*.

Tinkyada Rice Pasta
www.tinkyada.com
4/13/2007 ⊚ (416) 609-0016

Toblerone ⃠
3/19/2007 ⊚ See *Kraft*.

Toffifay
3/26/2007 ⊚ See *Storck*.

Tofurky ⃠
www.tofurky.com
4/9/2007 ⊚ (800) 508-8100

TofuTown ⃠
www.tofutown.net
3/15/2007 ⊚ See *Dean Foods*.

Tom Sawyer
www.glutenfreeflour.com
5/15/2007 ⊚ (877) 372-8800
Company Notes: The flour is
prepared in a dedicated GF
environment and tested for
gluten by a laboratory. Test results exceed "all code requirements."

Tombstone ⃠
3/19/2007 ⊚ See *Kraft*.

Tone's
3/16/2007 ⊚ See *Durkee*.

**Tone's, Durkee & Spice
Islands**
3/16/2007 ⊚ Triumph Notes: This is
three different companies with
the same parent company.
Each company is also listed
separately in the directory. ⊚
See *Durkee*.

Tootsie Pops
3/15/2007 ⊚ See *Tootsie Roll
Industries*.

Tootsie Roll Industries
www.tootsie.com
3/15/2007 ⊚ (773) 838-3400
Company Notes: They do not
use wheat, barley, rye, oats,
triticale, or spelt, including the
dusting on conveyor belts.

Tootsie Rolls
3/15/2007 ⊚ See *Tootsie Roll
Industries*.

Torrefazione Italia ⃠
3/19/2007 ⊚ See *Kraft*.

Tostitos
www.tostitos.com
4/12/2007 ⊚ See *Frito Lay*.

Totino's/Jeno's ⃠
3/19/2007 ⊚ See *General Mills*.

Tradiciones
5/3/2007 ☉ See *Williams Foods.*

Traditional Medicinals
www.traditionalmedicinals.com
3/22/2007 ☉ (800) 543-4372
Company Notes: Except as noted, the lines do not contain wheat, rye, barley or oats.

Trappey
4/19/2007 ☉ See *B&G Foods.*

Tribe Mediterranean Foods
www.tribehummus.com
5/7/2007 ☉ (800) 848-6687

Trident
www.tridentgum.com
3/19/2007 ☉ (800) 874-0013

Triscuit ⊘
3/19/2007 ☉ See *Kraft.*

Trix ⊘
3/19/2007 ☉ See *General Mills.*

Trolli ⊘
3/22/2007 ☉ See *Farley's & Sathers Candy Company.*

Tropical Dots
3/15/2007 ☉ See *Tootsie Roll Industries.*

Tropical Stormz Pops
3/15/2007 ☉ See *Tootsie Roll Industries.*

Tropicana Juices
www.tropicana.com
4/20/2007 ☉ (800) 237-7799
Company Notes: 100% juice products are GF, but any other products cannot be guaranteed GF. The percentage of juice information is located above the Nutrition Facts Panel on the package.

Tropicana Twister Soda
4/19/2007 ☉ See *Pepsi.*

Tumaro's ✕
www.tumaros.com
4/9/2007 ☉ (323) 464-6317

Tuna Helper ⊘
www.bettycrocker.com
3/19/2007 ☉ (800) 446-1898
See *General Mills.*

Turkey Hill
www.turkeyhill.com
3/15/2007 ☉ (800) 693-2479
Company Notes: All extracts are GF. Corn and tapioca modified food starches are used. If an item contains wheat, it will be listed on the label in a "CONTAINS:…" statement. Wheat is the only gluten-containing ingredient that they use. Ice creams containing cake and cookies will contain gluten.

Turtle Island Foods
www.tofurky.com
4/9/2007 ☉ (800) 508-8100

Turtle Mountain
www.purelydecadent.com
4/9/2007 ☉ (866) 388-7853
Company Notes: Turtle Mountain's Quality Assurance department sample tests finished products for gluten, requiring results of < 20ppm. ☉ Triumph Notes: Visit the company website for more information on their "Allergen Program," including more information on ingredient suppliers, production scheduling, equipment cleaning procedures and more.

Tuscan ⊘
3/15/2007 ☉ See *Dean Foods.*

Tuttorosso
4/10/2007 ☉ See *Red Gold.*

Twix ✕
www.twix.com
3/27/2007 ☉ See *MasterFoods USA.*

Twizzlers ⊘
3/20/2007 ☉ See *Hershey Company, The.*

Tyson ⊘
www.tyson.com
3/29/2007 ☉ Company Notes: No GF list is available. Wheat is one of the eight major al-

lergens, and if present, will be listed as follows: "CONTAINS: WHEAT." If rye, barley or oats are ingredients, they will be listed under "INGREDIENTS."

U.S. Mills
www.usmillsinc.com
5/15/2007 ☉ (781) 444-0440

Uncle Ben's
www.unclebens.com
3/22/2007 ☉ (800) 548-6253
See *MasterFoods USA.*

Underwood
4/19/2007 ☉ See *B&G Foods.*

Uneeda ⊘
3/19/2007 ☉ See *Kraft.*

Unilever ⊘
www.unilever.com
5/3/2007 ☉ (800) 338-8831
Company Notes: No GF list is provided as product formulations may change, as well as other factors. Always read the label's ingredient listing.

Utz
www.utzsnacks.com
4/9/2007 ☉ (800) 367-7629

V8
www.v8juice.com
4/10/2007 ☉ See *Campbell's.*

Valley Fresh ⊘
3/2/2007 ☉ See *Hormel Foods.*

Value Brand
3/2/2007 ☉ See *Hormel Foods.*

Van Camp's ⊘
(800) 826-2267
See *ConAgra Foods.*

Van de Kamp's ⊘
3/19/2007 ☉ See *Pinnacle Foods Corp.*

Van's International Foods
www.vanswaffles.com
4/11/2007 ☉ (323) 585-5581
Company Notes: All their wheat-free waffles are also GF.

Vegan
3/15/2007 ☉ See *Galaxy Nutritional Foods.*

Vegan Gourmet
5/3/2007 ☉ See *Follow Your Heart.*

Vegenaise
5/3/2007 ☉ See *Follow Your Heart.*

Vegetable Thins ⊘
3/19/2007 ☉ See *Kraft.*

Veggie
3/15/2007 ☉ See *Galaxy Nutritional Foods.*

Veggie Patch ✕
www.veggiepatch.com
4/9/2007 ☉ (888) 698-3444

Veggy
3/15/2007 ☉ See *Galaxy Nutritional Foods.*

Velocity Fitness Water (Wegman's)
5/8/2007 ☉ See *Wegman's.*

Velveeta ⊘
3/19/2007 ☉ See *Kraft.*

Vermont Butter & Cheese Company
www.vtbutterandcheeseco.com
4/25/2007 ☉ (800) 884-6287

Vermont Maid
4/19/2007 ☉ See *B&G Foods.*

Vernors
3/12/2007 ☉ See *Cadbury Schweppes (Beverages).*

Veryfine ⊘
3/19/2007 ☉ See *Kraft.*

Villa Flor
5/2/2007 ☉ See *Spruce Foods.*

Virgil's
4/9/2007 ☉ See *Reed's.*

Vitaminwater
5/2/2007 ☉ See *Glacéau.*

Vitasoy
www.vitasoy-usa.com
4/10/2007 ☉ (800) 848-2769

VitaSpelt ✕
3/15/2007 ☉ See *Purity Foods.*

Viva ⊘
3/15/2007 ◉ See *Dean Foods.*

Vlasic
www.vlasic.com
3/19/2007 ◉ See *Pinnacle Foods Corp.*

Wagners
5/3/2007 ◉ See *Williams Foods.*

Walkers Shortbread
www.walkersshortbread.com
4/9/2007 ◉ (800) 521-0141

Wallaby Yogurt Company
www.wallabyyogurt.com
3/20/2007 ◉ (707) 553-1233
Company Notes: The plain yogurt is GF, as the only ingredient is milk. However, while no gluten is added to flavored yogurts, they write that there may be trace amounts that come from extracting the natural flavors with grain alcohol.

Wal-Mart ⊘
www.walmart.com
5/15/2007 ◉ (800) 925-6278
Company Notes: They do not have a GF list, but their Great Value store brand products will be labeled with a GF statement. If there is a possibility of cross-contamination, an item will not be labeled GF.

Walnut Acres ⊘
www.walnutacres.com
4/12/2007 ◉ (800) 434-4246
Company Notes: No GF list is available. The best way to check for gluten is to read the label. If gluten is an ingredient, it will be listed separately. It will not be listed under "natural flavors" or "spices."

Wasa ✕
www.us.wasa.com
4/9/2007

Wedge (Wegman's)
5/8/2007 ◉ See *Wegman's.*

Wegman's
www.wegmans.com
5/8/2007 ◉ (800) 934-6267

Company Notes: They work with suppliers to "investigate and verify" what items are GF, and such information is compiled to the best of their knowledge. If a supplier cannot guarantee items to be GF, it may not appear on their GF list, though it may appear to be GF. GF status on the list is based on "the product as packaged." "You will need to verify the gluten status of any additional ingredients used in preparation." The list is updated regularly. ◉ Triumph Notes: The GF list was dated 5/7/07.

Welch's
www.welchs.com
3/16/2007 ◉ (800) 340-6870
Company Notes: If individuals have any questions concerning "dietary decisions," they should consult their physician.

Welch's (Soda)
3/12/2007 ◉ See *Cadbury Schweppes (Beverages).*

Wellshire Farms
www.wellshirefarms.com
4/9/2007 ◉ (877) 467-2331

Wellshire Kids
4/9/2007 ◉ See *Wellshire Farms.*

Werther's
3/26/2007 ◉ See *Storck.*

Wesson ⊘
(800) 582-7809
See *ConAgra Foods.*

Westbrae Natural ⊘
www.westbrae.com
5/21/2007 ◉ See *Hain Celestial.*

Western Family Foods ⊘
www.westernfamily.com
3/15/2007 ◉ Company Notes: The list is not comprehensive and is based on supplier replies for different marketing areas. Always read labels. ◉ Triumph Notes: Contact the company directly for a GF list for your area.

WestSoy ⊘
www.westsoy.biz
5/21/2007 ◉ See *Hain Celestial.*

Whatchamacallit ⊘
3/20/2007 ◉ See *Hershey Company, The.*

Wheat Thins ⊘
3/19/2007 ◉ See *Kraft.*

Wheaties ⊘
3/19/2007 ◉ See *General Mills.*

Wheatsworth ⊘
3/19/2007 ◉ See *Kraft.*

WhiteWave ⊘
www.whitewave.com
3/5/2007 ◉ (303) 635-4000
Company Notes: They note that the FDA has not provided GF labeling guidelines and that gluten is not a big 8 allergen, and that "to the best of [their] knowledge" their products are GF.

Whitman's ⊘
5/3/2007 ◉ (888) 311-3723
See *Russell Stover.*

Whole Foods ⊘
www.wholefoodsmarket.com
4/22/2007 ◉ (512) 542-0656
Company Notes: GF information for private label items can be found for individual stores at http://www.wholefoodsmarket.com/specialdiets/index.html.

Wholesome Sweeteners
www.wholesomesweeteners.com
4/12/2007 ◉ (800) 680-1896
Company Notes: The products on the GF list are processed and packed in a GF environment. The powdered sugar contains an unmodified organic cornstarch. The sugar and sweeteners distributed by Wholesome Sweeteners are manufactured under various labels. ◉ Triumph Notes: The statement was dated 1/07.

Wholesome Valley Organic
3/15/2007 ◉ See *Galaxy Nutritional Foods.*

WholeSoy & Co.
www.wholesoyco.com
4/25/2007 ◉ (877) 569-6376

Whoppers ⊘
3/20/2007 ◉ See *Hershey Company, The.*

Wild Ride Beef Jerky
www.wildridejerky.com
3/15/2007 ◉ (303) 444-2846

Wild Thornberry's ⊘
3/19/2007 ◉ See *Kraft.*

WildBerry Dots
3/15/2007 ◉ See *Tootsie Roll Industries.*

Williams Foods
www.williamsfoods.com
5/3/2007 ◉ (800) 255-6736
Company Notes: The same equipment is used for GF and gluten-containing products, though "Good Cleaning Practices" are performed between products.

Winn-Dixie
www.winn-dixie.com
4/25/2007 ◉ (866) 946-6349
Company Notes: The GF list is not intended as medical advice, and should only be used as a guide. Always read ingredient statements as there is no guarantee they will not change (making it possible that even the foods on the GF list could contain gluten if formulations change). ◉ Triumph Notes: The list was dated 4/27/06.

Winterfresh
3/16/2007 ◉ See *Wrigley.*

Wise ⚓
www.wisesnacks.com
(888) 759-4401

Wish Bone ⊘
www.wish-bone.com
3/16/2007 ◉ (800) 343-9024
Company Notes: No GF list is pro-

vided as product formulations may change, as well as other factors. Always read the label's ingredient listing. If that is not enough to determine whether an item is GF or if you are uncomfortable about any ingredient, they recommend not using them.

Wispride ⊘
www.wispride.com
4/11/2007 ⊙ See *Bel Brands U.S.A.*

Wizard's, The
4/10/2007 ⊙ See *Edward & Sons.*

Wolf Brand ⊘
www.wolfbrandchili.com
(800) 414-9653
See *ConAgra Foods.*

Wolfgang Puck's
www.wolfgangpucksoup.com
3/16/2007 ⊙ (800) 282-8070
Company Notes: Always read ingredient lists, as ingredients may change.

Wonka
www.wonka.com
5/3/2007 ⊙ See *Nestlé.*

Woody's ⊘
3/19/2007 ⊙ See *Kraft.*

World Harbors ⊘
www.worldharbors.com
5/9/2007 ⊙ (800) 355-6221
Company Notes: When tested, World Harbors, Acadia and Angostura brand sauces, including those with soy sauce made with wheat, have below .0078% gluten, which is the lowest detectable level. If gluten is present in the product, it is below a detectable testing level. World Harbors Sauces that contain soy sauce are Bar-B, Cheriyaki, Hot Teriyaki, Jerk, Mandarin Sesame, Sweet 'n Sour, Sweet 'n Tangy, and Teriyaki. Acadia sauces that contain soy sauce are Raspberry Jerk, Sweet 'n

Sour, and Teriyaki. Angostura sauces that contain soy sauce are Soy, Lite Soy, and Teriyaki.

Wranglers ⊘
3/2/2007 ⊙ See *Hormel Foods.*

Wright's
4/19/2007 ⊙ See *B&G Foods.*

Wrigley
www.wrigley.com
3/16/2007 ⊙ (800) 974-4539
Company Notes: "No packaging material directly next to our product" has gluten. If starches are on the label surrounding the stick of gum, they are made from corn or potatoes.

Wyler's ⊘
4/20/2007 ⊙ See *Jel Sert.*

Wyman's
www.wymans.com
4/9/2007 ⊙ (800) 341-1758

Yogi Tea
www.yogitea.com
4/9/2007 ⊙ (800) 964-4832

Yoo-hoo
www.drinkyoo-hoo.com
3/16/2007 ⊙ (800) 966-4669
See *Cadbury Schweppes (Beverages).*

Yoplait ⊘
www.yoplait.com
3/19/2007 ⊙ (800) 967-5248
See *General Mills.*

York ⊘
3/20/2007 ⊙ See *Hershey Company, The.*

Yuban ⊘
3/19/2007 ⊙ See *Kraft.*

Yves Veggie Cuisine ⊘
www.yvesveggie.com
5/21/2007 ⊙ See *Hain Celestial.*

Zagnut ⊘
3/20/2007 ⊙ See *Hershey Company, The.*

ZenSoy
www.zensoy.com
3/20/2007

Zero ⊘
3/20/2007 ⊙ See *Hershey Company, The.*

Zico
www.zico.com
3/15/2007 ⊙ (866) 729-9426

Zip-A-Dee-Mini Pops
3/15/2007 ⊙ See *Tootsie Roll Industries.*

Zoe's ✕
www.zoefoods.com
3/15/2007 ⊙ (781) 453-9000
Company Notes: While the granolas and bars are wheat-free, they do contain oats. Zoe's O's contain wheat.

ZonePerfect
www.zoneperfect.com
3/16/2007 ⊙ Company Notes: Always read the ingredient list. Although no gluten-containing ingredients are added to items on the GF list, they are made in a facility that also manufactures gluten-containing ingredients for other products. ⊙ See *Abbott's Ross Products Division.*

Zours
www.zours.com
3/5/2007 ⊙ (888) 645-3453
See *Just Born.*

Zwieback ⊘
3/19/2007 ⊙ See *Kraft.*